Language Planning

ℓℯ

**Chandler & Sharp Publications in Anthropology
and Related Fields**

General Editors: L. L. Langness and Robert B. Edgerton

Language Planning

An Introduction

CAROL M. EASTMAN

UNIVERSITY OF WASHINGTON

CHANDLER & SHARP PUBLISHERS, INC.
San Francisco

Library of Congress Cataloging in Publication Data

Eastman, Carol M., 1941–
  Language planning, an introduction.

  (Chandler & Sharp publications in anthropology and
related fields)
  Bibliography: p. 255–269.
  Includes index.
  1. Language planning. 2. Linguistics. 3. Sociolinguistics. I. Title. II. Series.
P40.5.L35E2 1983   401′.9   83-1991
ISBN 0-88316-552-X

International Standard Book Number: 0-88316-552-X
Library of Congress Catalog Card Number: 83-1991
Printed in the United States of America.

Book design by Joe Roter.
Cover design and art by Jackie Gallagher.
Edited by Rudite J. Emir.
Composition by Marin Typesetters.

Contents

Preface

Language planning is a branch of sociolinguistics. It is a developing field that sees language as a social resource. As such, language requires planned action if it is to be used to its full potential. Language planning is done through the cooperative efforts of political, educational, economic, and linguistic authorities (Jernudd and Das Gupta 1971).

Traditional ethnographies, as descriptions of societies, dismiss language, looking instead at other "systems" such as those of kinship, religion, economics, and politics. Traditional studies in the broader fields of anthropology, economics, political science, education, and even linguistics also leave out the function of language as an important factor in the practical application of ideas in each field. However, the educator needs to understand how to plan language with regard to programs in bilingual education and literacy; the political scientist needs to understand how decisions involving the choice of national and official languages are made; the sociologist needs to see how language influences social structure; the economist needs to understand the role of pidgins and trade languages (*lingua francas*) in influencing the exchange of commodities; the anthropologist needs to know how to standardize languages, develop practical writing and spelling systems, and record oral traditions; the linguist needs to know how to plan language change; the second-language teacher needs to know how to plan a curriculum so that the desired learning takes place.

This book is an introduction to the field of language planning from an interdisciplinary perspective. It is intended to acquaint people from a number of fields with ways in which language planning can be useful to them. Medical, law, and business students might find many of the ideas of interest as well, since in these fields language use for special

ix

purposes is especially significant. Lawyer/client, patient/doctor, and sales-person/customer relations are particularly sensitive to the social aspects of language that affect communication and that can be affected by proper attention to language-planning ideas.

Languages have distinct functions within any sociopolitical entity. Planning affects which language fulfills which function. For example, language plans put national and official languages into effect, encourage or discourage certain trade languages, or determine the role of mother tongues versus second languages. In the pages to follow a number of examples will be provided to illustrate the range of possible language situations that can be planned. Undoubtedly the examples shown will bring others to your mind. The orthography problems for Hebrew are echoed in many other parts of the world. The choice of Swahili as the national or official language in East Africa, the attempt to establish Irish in a diglossic situation with English in Ireland, the problem of choosing a national language in a multilingual situation such as India's are all situations with parallels all over the world. The commonality of the problems that require a sensible planning approach is largely what makes language planning an exciting area of applied sociolinguistics.

This book seeks to demonstrate that the language-planning aspect of the SOCIOLOGY OF LANGUAGE is an area in which a great deal can be learned about the interaction of social and linguistic behavior and the consequences each type of behavior has for the other. The idea of language as a plannable societal resource developed as an area of sociolinguistic research in the 1960s. Up to the present time only collections of articles and scholarly papers exist, but there is no general introduction to the field despite a growing recognition by planning agencies (governmental, educational, economic, and others) that both language planning and language planners are required. Perhaps this work will inspire students interested in the social use of language in general to consider language planning as a potential area of specialization—as an application of knowledge of language and culture to social ends in a rational and productive way.

I would like to thank my students at the University of Washington, particularly Elizabeth Edwards and Thomas Reese, for their comments on an earlier draft of this book. I am grateful to the University of Nairobi, Department of African Languages and Linguistics, for my visiting year there, which afforded me the time to write this book. I also appreciate the help of my colleagues in Nairobi. Martin Mould listened incessantly. Both he and Richard Hayward put up with the noise of my eternal typing. John Jacobsen gracefully stayed out of it. A cowardice of curs kept me at it.

Seattle, Washington   Carol M. Eastman
Summer, 1982

Language Planning

Chapter One
LANGUAGE PLANNING

1.0   INTRODUCTION

Humans use language for specific purposes, goals, and intentions. They use it in particular contexts to accomplish particular ends. When we speak of language use this way, it is helpful to think of language as a system of communication. This communicative system has both an internal structure and an external manifestation in speech. The distinction between the use of a language (its speech aspect) and its grammatical system (its structural aspect) was first made by a Swiss linguist named Ferdinand deSaussure (1857–1913), who used the French word LANGUE to refer to a language's internal structure and the French word PAROLE to refer to its use by speakers and listeners. People who conceive of language as a system of communication in this way are generally referred to as structuralists.

In recent years, the structuralist approach to language has begun to look beyond the study of a language's structure and the manifestation of that structure in speech to include an analysis of how *both* language structure and language use function in the real world. The real-world context of linguistic communication is the speech community. The term SPEECH COMMUNITY refers to the unit of analysis of a language in its context; that is, the speech community is the unit of analysis of language in a culture or in society. A speech community is a set of individuals who share the knowledge of what is the appropriate conduct and interpretation of speech. These individuals also share the understanding of at least one language so that they may communicate with each other.

The study of LANGUAGE PLANNING focuses on the decision-making that goes into determining what language use is appropriate in particular speech communities. Language planning is concerned with how language can be conducted and interpreted successfully in a speech community, given the language goals of that community. The study of language planning looks at the choices available to a speech community and at possible recommendations of language policy for adoption by that community. For example, the United States is a nation that may be considered in some respects to be a speech community. Americans purportedly share a knowledge of a form of English and its appropriate use. This English is different from what is used in England (as a nation and a speech community). Recent and past immigration to the United States has brought a number of speakers of other languages to certain areas of the country. This influx has had an impact on the official language policy of the United States. At the beginning of this century, English was the one language chosen for the nation as a whole, although other interesting language "policies" preceded the final choice; for instance, "during the American Revolution, a movement was launched to replace English with Hebrew as the official language of the new nation" (Wallace, Wallechinsky, and Wallace 1982:16). Since English smacked of the monarchy and Hebrew was seen as "the mother of all languages, the key to scriptures and the cornerstone of a liberal education" (16), Hebrew seemed the preferable choice. Many "rebel" towns still bear names from the Bible from this historical period (for example, Salem and Bethlehem). "Though the idea never caught on, Hebrew remained a required course at many major American universities well into the 19th century" (16).

In the United States, speakers of languages other than English were all supposed to be in the "melting pot" together and emerge speaking English. The result, not surprisingly, was that American English has some of the flavor of the various ingredients melted together in it.

Today, as a result of the Bilingual Education Act of the late 1960s, it is possible for students to be educated in their mother tongues or first languages other than English while they are simultaneously learning English. This development is a reflection of an official shift in educational language policy—from the melting-pot idea and a monolingual language policy to a limited multilingual policy. In communities where bilingual education exists (that is, where non-native English speakers enter school), we see some members who have knowledge of another language (for example, Spanish) *and* who are also acquiring English, and we also see people who know English only. In response to the recent influx of immigrants the United States government has declared it acceptable to use a language other than English, whereas previously it had always declared the opposite. In other words, it is now becoming appropriate to use non-English languages in the United States—as long as the users also learn English.

A number of people oppose the policy of other-than-English in United States communities. They feel that such linguistic fragmentation will lead to political and social problems. The interplay of linguistic, political, and social issues is the stuff of which language planning is made.

The study of language planning centers on the *conscious* use of language in speech communities. Consequently, the interesting study of unconscious aspects of individual speech and language structure is beyond the scope of our concern. These concerns are issues of psycholinguistics, whereas language planning is a branch of sociolinguistics.

Language planning has to do with the way people's ideas about language are coordinated. For example, will Americans eventually accept the idea that linguistic diversity is all right? Language planning involves the gathering of data for making decisions about which language or languages are best in certain situations. It also has to do with developing the technical tools for choosing among alternative decisions (Rubin and Jernudd 1971:xiv).

Language planning is necessarily future-oriented. We plan language to enhance communication with and between nations to encourage feelings of national unity and group cooperation. Governments are learning that they may go to social scientists and educators to receive help in formulating, implementing, and, occasionally, evaluating language policy.

The name of Joshua A. Fishman appears in connection with practically all aspects of the study of language planning. We will see this to be the case throughout our introduction to the field. Fishman is considered the founder of the sociology of language, the area of sociolinguistics that includes language planning and is devoted to examining the interaction of language use and social behavior. This interaction includes the attitudes people have about language and the way people behave toward language and toward language users (1969:45). In speaking of his own career and how he became interested in applied sociolinguistics and in what has now developed into the field of language planning, Fishman, providing a glimpse of himself as well as of his profession, tells us:

It started with a childhood as a member of a family and of a struggling speech community to which few things mattered as much as keeping the Yiddish language alive, and well, enriching it, ennobling it, liberating it of the linguistic and social impediments set up against it by conscious and unconscious enemies and opponents, at home and abroad. It started, even more germanely for academic work, with parents and teachers who encouraged me to intellectualize and extrapolate *from* the daily pains and pleasures of the all-engrossing struggle for creative Yiddish-English societal bilingualism *to* more generally relevant theoretical questions and answers. Starting from such origins it is no longer any wonder that "small languages" everywhere are my particular passion and that

4 *Language Planning*

their stable functional complimentarity with "wider languages" (yes, even with the very widest) is my particular joy. Neither the doubts of advisors as to whether "any such field" existed, nor the concern of friends as to whether one could really "make one's way" under such a flag, ever succeeded in making me doubt that I and the sociology of language were created for each other (Fishman 1972b:357).

In the pages to follow, the focus of our concern will be: What goes into language planning in order to arrive at sensible policies with respect to language? We will take a look at what the field—as it has developed so far—consists of and where the study appears to be going.

1.1 LANGUAGE PLANNING AS APPLIED SOCIOLINGUISTICS

The systematic sociolinguistic study of language planning begins with the study of how writing systems are created and spelling systems revised, and extends to the study of how to assist government or other official efforts to manipulate language (Fishman 1971a:365). SOCIOLINGUISTICS, in general, may be defined as the study of the patterned covariation of language and society. However, some people, such as Fishman, who work in the area of language planning prefer to use the phrase "sociology of language" to refer to that aspect of sociolinguistics which refers to their work. The sociology of language studies the ways in which language behavior and social behavior are related. Other sociolinguistic studies may focus more on specific language variables that reflect social structure than on their interrelationship.

The study of language planning as a branch of sociolinguistics involves a number of concepts that need to be kept in mind from the outset. It is a good idea to understand that language as an object of planning is language in use—generally spoken language. It is used in a speech community, that is, a place where rules for how language is used and interpreted are shared by community members (Hymes 1972:52). It is also important to understand that language plans are deliberately made by authorities (usually governmental or educational) with particular aims in mind. Language planners, then, who work at the behest of such authorities have to recognize that they have ethical and moral as well as linguistic obligations when they make recommendations about what can or should be done about language. It is also important in language planning to know what relationship writing has to speaking, what it means to standardize a language, what a practical orthography is, what occurs in language learning, and so forth. In deciding and planning for writing and speaking languages in social and political contexts, it cannot be overstated that extra-code factors are as important as the languages themselves (Fishman 1971a:355). What do the people who are affected by language choices, policies, and plans consider to be acceptable? If the speech community in question does not accept the purposes, goals, and recommendations of language use established by politicians and educators on the advice of sociolinguists, no matter how sensible the plan seems, it cannot be successful.

We will see that a major aspect of language planning is the evaluation of a plan's guiding policy after the plan has been put into effect so that changes can be made where necessary. Unfortunately, evaluation is the vaguest and least researched area of the planning process so far and the one to which most attention needs to be paid in the future. Revision of an orthography may be necessary after a particular writing system has been in practice for a long time. Vocabulary may need to be updated from time to time. Standard languages may need to be extended so that they can be used over wider areas than previously, or in other spheres such as at higher levels of education. It may become necessary after a particular type of plan is in effect to make some changes in a language for ease in printing. A policy might need to be altered with respect to the position it has on borrowing from other dialects, particularly if the political climate is changing.

When we want to make decisions about the effect of language use on society, we may say that we hope to apply, or find applications for, the results of research in the sociology of language. All societies use language as a medium (and some also use it as a symbol) of interaction. The observable manifestations of how language is used for social interaction are of interest in language planning (Fishman 1968e). The language planner applies what is known about the relationship of language and social behavior to the job of planning. Planners are applied sociolinguists who choose languages for certain situations and try to ascertain that those languages work in the given situations.

1.10   How Language Choices Are Made

The choice of language by a state or nation is most often tied to elements of nationalism. Languages are allocated either officially or unofficially in terms of the functions they serve in the state or nation where they are used. Language functions or situations can be classified into ten categories that exist in multilingual settings. These ten types of language situations, classified by type of language, were first set forth more than thirty years ago in a UNESCO report on the use of vernacular languages in education. The ten options of language choice are:

1. INDIGENOUS LANGUAGE—the language of the original inhabitants of an area

2. LINGUA FRANCA—a language used habitually by people who have different first languages so they can communicate for certain specific purposes

3. MOTHER TONGUE—the language one acquires as a child

4. NATIONAL LANGUAGE—the language of a political, social, and cultural entity

5. OFFICIAL LANGUAGE—a language used to do government business

6. PIDGIN—a language (formed by mixing languages) used regularly by people of different language backgrounds

7. REGIONAL LANGUAGE—a common language used by people of different language backgrounds who live in a particular area

8. SECOND LANGUAGE—a language acquired in addition to one's first language

9. VERNACULAR LANGUAGE—the first language of a group socially or politically dominated by a group with a different language

10. WORLD LANGUAGE—a language used over wide areas of the world (a "language of wider communication," or LWC)(UNESCO 1951: 689–90)

Official language policies are often based on decisions about what languages are to be designated as national, official, and world languages. In contrast, the other language situations arise informally or naturally. Both pidgins and lingua francas arise for practical ends. Second languages are acquired for a number of reasons both practical and aesthetic. Vernaculars are often imposed. In Kenya, for example, the noted, though controversial, author Ngugi wa Thiong'o is urging that the label "national language" be applied to the languages usually called "vernaculars" in order to maintain the idea that ethnic groups in Kenya are all equal as political, social, and cultural entities and are not dominated by any one group with a different language. This opinion is complicated by an implicit language policy in Kenya which has established Swahili as the national language. In addition, both Swahili and English are official languages, while efforts are being made to see that primary education is provided all children in their first languages.

This Kenyan example is just one illustration of the type of complexity involved in the allocation of languages within a political entity and indicates the need for language planning as a guide to policy formation. No societies exist without a language policy, although many policies exist implicitly and in the absence of planning. A study of the purpose of language use—an analysis of what would make language sense in a political context—would be of substantial benefit to policy-makers. However, the time has not yet come for most officials to see applied linguistics as an area in which policy consultation is a must. As governments now seek counsel from economic and social advisors, they would be well advised also to seek linguistic consultation in the form of language planning to support their implicit and explicit language policies. The language planner has a responsibility to offer advice to policy-makers, yet the planner's task is made particularly difficult because those who actually carry out plans, that is, legislators, government agencies, language academy personnel, language specialists in private industry, and so forth, have not yet begun to turn, to any great extent, to language-planning research to guide them (Fishman 1974a:15).

The two major components of a language plan are (1) the policy to be followed, and (2) the choice of language or languages to which the policy relates. A third component of planning is the evaluation of both policy (in all its aspects) and choice, which will be our concern in later chapters. We will now focus on the components of language policy and the factors involved in the choice of the language(s) being planned.

1.100 Language Planning: Policy

Language policies are formulated, codified, elaborated, and implemented. The FORMULATION of language policy is a process of deliberation and decision-making. A number of social, economic, and political factors of policy formulation and their consequences appear in the available literature, but little research has been done to date on the actual process of policy formulation. The main political deliberative factor in language policy formation is the goal of the body (for example, the nation) formulating the policy. So far, much of the research on political factors of policy formulation has taken place in Africa. In East Africa, studies have looked at the formulation of language policy in Tanzania as it is tied to the development of a Swahili political culture (Abdulaziz 1971). In Kenya, the government is seeking assistance from educational and religious organizations regarding the formulation of a policy to foster the development of a Kenyan national culture without tribal, colonial, or religious links.

The CODIFICATION of language policy, which occurs after policy formulation has taken place, refers to the technical preparation of the decided-upon policy. But codification involves more than the mechanics of putting a policy into effect; it also means paying attention to the feelings, attitudes, values, loyalties, preferences, and practices of both the policy-makers and the recipients of the policy. When a language policy is codified, the planner should remember that people in modern speech communities want their language "to be more than neat and trim and handy" (Fishman 1974a:23). They want it to be a reflection of who they are: who they have been as well as who they will be. This point cannot be overemphasized.

Language Planning

By ELABORATION of a language policy is meant the extension of the decided-upon language(s) or writing system(s) to all spheres of activity in which its use is envisioned. An orthography has to be detailed enough and adaptable enough to accommodate new words and borrowings; a writing system has to fit available techniques of printing, handwriting, and graphics. The particular language that has been decided upon and codified has to be kept flexible so as to retain its integrity as well as continue the goals of the policy. Not only does the language that the policy refers to have to be adaptable technologically, but it also has to be capable of internal modernization by allowing for the expression of new ideas in words. The elaboration aspect of language policy is generally handled by a language academy or language-planning agency.

Elaboration, unlike formulation and codification, goes on the whole time that a policy is in effect. The process of policy elaboration, like that of policy formulation, is one on which very little research has been done and is thus an area where many interesting questions remain unanswered. Very little is known about who accepts and who rejects newly proposed technical words. We don't know which words people perceive to be new or how they determine which are foreign and which native. We don't know what people consider the sources of lexically modern vocabulary. We don't know how a codified policy designed to be uniform may actually vary when it is put in effect in different contexts (Fishman 1974a:24).

The IMPLEMENTATION of language policy is the procedure used to bring about the change in language that allows the policy objectives to be realized. Implementation has to do with how a plan is put into operation to achieve a stated goal. An organization needs to be set up so that the policy can be successfully implemented. The structure of implementing bodies needs to be spelled out in detail.

Elaboration and implementation of policy can be illustrated by some examples. In elaboration, language academies can play a key role. LAN-GUAGE ACADEMIES are language-planning agencies that make decisions about the direction of language policies and the form their elaboration takes in a particular context. For example, three Arab academies—Syrian, Egyptian, and Iraqi—have addressed policies involving the elaboration of classical Arabic. Each has as its main objective "the preservation and renovation of classical Arabic as an effective and unified language for all Arabic-speaking people" (Altoma 1974:302). Each has tried to suppress the internal development of colloquialisms in Arabic and has tried to prevent loanwords from intruding from the outside. But none of them has effectively elaborated such a policy while retaining a language effective enough to meet the needs of modern life. In each case the academy has had to approve changes in spelling, grammar, and vocabulary (302).

A number of language academies also exist in Latin America and are modeled after the Royal Spanish Academy, which goes all the way back to 1713. Today the Spanish Academy is an organization representative of Spain's literary left. It has authority in matters of language policy because it has the "protection of the state. . . . It can guide the linguistic activity of the country after the manner of a supreme tribunal" (Guitarte and Quintero 1974:317). It is modeled after the French Academy with the purpose of giving dignity to a national form of communication and expression. Language academies typically sanction their own "official" dictionary, orthography, and grammar; this is the case with both the Spanish and French academies.

Associate academies were set up in Latin America modeled after the Spanish academy in Spain. The academies brought together the important literary people of the country and all those involved in language matters. Academy membership in all Spanish academies was based on literary merit (Guitarte and Quintero 1974:324). Between 1870 and 1890, associate Spanish academies were set up in Colombia, Mexico, Chile, and Guatemala. Once the founders of these academies passed on, some disintegration of the organizations took place, but the influence of the Royal Spanish Academy in Spain was so great that additional new academies developed in Chile (1914), Peru (1918), Ecuador (c. 1913), El Salvador (c. 1923), Guatemala (c. 1930), and Venezuela (c. 1930). Also, in the 1920s, associate academies were founded for the first time in Bolivia, Costa Rica, Cuba, Panama, the Dominican Republic, and Paraguay. Honduras developed a Spanish Academy in 1948 and Puerto Rico in 1952 (325). Today, the Latin American associate Spanish academies and the Royal Spanish Academy are linked together in an Association of the Academies of the Spanish Language with a Permanent Commission that implements the decisions of the entire association.

The Commission coordinates and channels the activities of the academies, takes charge of seeing that the agreements arrived at by the academies in their congresses are carried out, serves as a consultative body to the Spanish Academy, and keeps watch over the development of the life of the language (Guitarte and Quintero 1974:329).

Language policies are elaborated by an academy (or an association of academies as in the Spanish case) through the writings of its members: they actively practice the general linguistic norms of the policy. Academy members are charged with infusing the language and the policy with prestige so that they would be highly valued.

The Association of the Academies of the Spanish Language is now updating its grammar to include the ideas of some Latin American as well as Spanish writers. The Association's dictionary is now being revised to include Latin American regional lexicons and also Philippine usage (Guitarte and Quintero 1974). Policy elaboration in the Spanish associated academies is characterized by stressing the linguistic unity of all nations of Spanish influence. In order to accomplish this elaboration, the separate language academies of Spain, Latin America, and now the Philippines have to cooperate in establishing joint linguistic programs.

It is safe to say that there are no instances of the establishing of a language policy without the guidance of at least an implicit form of planning agency or academy. In the United States, where most Americans believe that no official English language policy exists, a norm is constantly being elaborated through a very effective academy in the form of newspaper, radio, and television reporting. In American English language policy, truly the media is the message! Recent broad-based American language policy (mentioned in Section 1.0) may be seen in the current policy of bilingual primary education, in government funding for bilingual-bicultural programs and textbooks, and in the appearance of voting materials in Spanish and Chinese in addition to English. In this case, the government, rather than the media, has the academy role of policy elaboration. However, the media do play a major role as well, as evidenced by the advent of Spanish-language broadcasting on radio and television and the presence of Spanish-language newspapers in large cities.

An example of how a language policy may be implemented is the effort to restore Irish in Ireland. The policy aimed to preserve and achieve both English proficiency and separate Irish identity through the continuing development of the Irish language. A body called the Consultative Council for the Irish Language was set up to guide the policy of language restoration. The Council recognized that many institutions would be required for implementing an overall plan to restore Irish and to develop it in a bilingual context. It was considered essential to intensify people's desire to be bilingual. In order to achieve this intensification, the domains in which each language was to be used needed to be studied. Then the policy-makers could determine which areas of use were most favorable to which language. In domains where existing attidues were already favorable to Irish, Irish use could be extended; in areas where attitudes toward Irish were negative, English would be best encouraged. According to the Consultative Council, the studies established that the Irish language needs to be associated with progress and economic development if it is to be useful in new economic situations and that it should be used as a medium that will equip people for successful functioning as adults (Fishman, ed., 1974:530).

The implementation of the policy to restore Irish is based on an extension of the sociolinguistic concept of DIGLOSSIA: distinct domains of language are associated by social convention with each language. Diglossia refers to the practice by some speakers of using "two or more varieties of the same language... under different conditions" (Ferguson 1959:325). In the above-mentioned example, where English is, in effect, the sole medium of communication but English-Irish bilingualism is the goal, a diglossic approach to language-policy implementation mainly involves the enlightened selection of separate domains for each language. In Ireland, the selected domains for the Irish language included the home, the church, arenas of national heritage, primary education, work, and the like while English remained the language of higher education and commerce.

Achievement of a policy goal relies on the degree of success in intensifying people's motivation for going along with the plan and in clarifying their attitudes about the plan (Fishman, ed. 1974:529). The Irish Consultative Council noted that an Irish language policy, as any language policy about to be implemented, has to be set up within the existing framework of public administration.

Further, to implement a language policy, existing government machinery, in turn, needs to adapt itself to language-policy needs (Fishman, ed. 1974:533). No language policy can successfully be implemented without the support of the authoritative body. *All* departments of the authoritative body (usually a government) must be involved, even if only one department or affiliated agency has primary responsibility. The head of the body with primary policy responsibility *must* be a person of power and influence and must have a predominant interest in language policy.

All language policy, like that for Irish restoration, needs to be "associated with the whole spectrum of national life and not merely with selective or 'high culture' activities" (Fishman, ed., 1974:534). The areas of the country where the language in question is already in general use should receive special treatment and development. These areas should be assigned to the same authority of the government to which the language policy is assigned. For example, the implementation of the policy to restore Irish in Ireland placed the main government functions of language restoration and the development of the area already using Irish in a single ministry, the Ministry for the Irish Language (*Roinn na Gaelige*). An Irish Language Board was set up to extend to other areas the use of Irish as a medium of general communication. Irish was to be extended by (1) applying language research, (2) setting up language-learning facilities, and (3) advocating the use of the language in public and private sectors. The Ministry, as policy authority, periodically examines the proposals of the Board and works with Board members to formulate policy, which would then be accepted by the Minister and endorsed by the government. The Irish Language Board was set up for a period not to exceed five years; its structure and powers are open to review throughout that period.

Just recently, along the same lines, the British county of Cornwall has begun to implement a plan to revive the Cornish language, which had almost faded away entirely in the late eighteenth century. Cornish, a language related to Breton, the Celtic language of Brittany in Northern France, had long given way to English. However, amid local enthusiasm a number of county schools are now giving Cornish lessons and some parents have begun to teach the language to their children. A Cornish Language Society and a Cornish Language Board have been set up. The goals of Cornish revival are more modest than those for the restoration of Irish, the hope being that Cornish can become another subject for the General Certificate of Education (both Ordinary and Advanced levels). The secretary of the Cornish Language Society (the policy-implementing body) does not visualize that Cornish will become the official language of the county, but he does stress its important role in preserving the culture and individuality of Cornwall.

Thus, the policy aspect of language planning has so far been shown to relate to:

1. FORMULATION of the policy by setting its goals

2. CODIFICATION of the policy by setting out strategies for the practical achievement of the goals

3. ELABORATION of the policy by seeing that the language(s) involved may be extended into the arenas specified by the policy goals

4. IMPLEMENTATION of the policy by providing the authoritative backbone to achieve the goals and the motivation for the use of the language of the policy by the people affected

1.101   Language Planning: Choice

Before a language policy can be formulated, codified, elaborated, and implemented, and before a language plan can be said to be, the policy-makers need to *choose* the language(s) that the policy and plan refer to. Perhaps the most clearcut situation in which to look at language choice as an aspect of language planning is in the area of deciding what should be NATIONAL LANGUAGES and what should be LANGUAGES OF WIDER COMMUNICATION (LWCs) in developing nations. Fishman has claimed that language choices are made with respect to the presence or absence of six features underlying three distinct categories of choice.

Language choices are of Type A, B, or C. Type A choices are made by "a-modal" nations characterized by one type of feature configuration; Type B by "uni-modal" nations with another configuration, and Type C by "multi-modal" nations.

Table 1. Types of Language Choice
(modified from Fishman 1969a:192)

Features	a-modal nations (Type A)	uni-modal nations (Type B)	multi-modal nations (Type C)
1. Is there a Great Tradition?*	no	yes	many
2. Reason for selection of national language	for political integration	for nationalism	for compromise
3. Reason LWC is used	as a national symbol	for the transition	as a unifying force
4. LP activity to be done	standardization	diglossia	modernization
5. Is bilingualism a goal?	no	yes, but situational	yes
6. Is biculturalism a goal?	no	yes, but situational	yes

*The term *Great Tradition* refers to a literary tradition of long standing thought to be great by the people who have it, and considered a part of their cultural heritage.

A-modal nations make language choices in order to politically integrate a linguistically complex area wherein primarily oral rather than written traditions exist. Many developing or Third World nations are of this type and frequently choose an LWC as an official language and as a national language. At the same time, in Type A nations language standardization is being carried out so people can learn to read and write their first language as well as the LWC. The choice of English in the Western Cameroon (in West Africa) and of French in Eastern Cameroon are examples.

Type B nations are called uni-modal and are characterized by an indigenous language with a literary tradition, plus an LWC that often exists as a result of colonial policy. Newly educated people tend to be educated in the LWC, while the indigenous language with the literary tradition is favored for purposes of nationalism. An example of such a uni-modal nation would be Tanzania, where Swahili has a long literary tradition and is being made modernistically functional as a national language to replace the LWC, English.

Type C nations are multi-modal and have a number of languages with literary traditions. Under these conditions, a compromise is needed to choose one of these languages as a national language. Whichever is chosen will then also have to be modernized to function in a national context. In multi-modal nations, people are encouraged to know both their own and the national language. That is, in multi-modal nations bilingualism is desired. An example of a multi-modal Type C nation is India, which has many competing indigenous languages with literary traditions but which also has an indigenous language as a national language (Hindi).

In a-modal nations, the LWC is encouraged as the dominant language. In uni-modal nations, the national language is stressed, but situational bilingualism is tolerated. Uni-modal nations have one dominant indigenous language. Multi-modal nations have many dominant indigenous languages. A-modal nations have none. An understanding of these types of language-planning contexts helps the language planner make reasonable language-policy recommendations. By understanding the language situation in a nation, the planner would know, for example, that Swahili is a sensible candidate for a possible national language in Tanzania, that India presents a situation of competing languages, and that in the Cameroons no indigenous language is ready to carry out nationalism functions (Fishman 1969a:192).

In the area of language choice, the term DEVELOPING LANGUAGE is used to refer to languages undergoing large and rapid changes in social function. In a-modal nations, developing languages are those local tongues that are selected out in favor of an LWC; in uni-modal situations, developing languages are those languages modernized for use along with another or several others; and in multi-modal situations, developing languages are those meant to be maximally planned for common use. Developing languages are most affected by a language plan, for they are the languages that are changed. Where LWCs are chosen, language development does not occur. In countries where indigenous languages are chosen for national purposes, such processes as modernization and standardization constitute language "development."

Nationism and *nationalism* are also important factors influencing language choice. NATIONISM refers to the degree of effective operation of a political entity and is best served by political integration. The more nationistic a political entity is, the more integrated it is. Practically and linguistically, nationism is best served by an LWC (Fishman 1969a:193).

NATIONALISM, on the other hand, is more concerned with "ethnic authenticity" than operational efficiency and is best served by developing an indigenous language with an ethnic-based patriotic force and by continuing a great tradition, as in a Type B situation.

Whether language choice has a primarily nationalistic or nationistic basis, or even if it is based on *both* types of considerations, the choice needs to be backed up by the engineering of consent to the choice (Fishman 1968d:10). When acceptance of a choice is at issue in language planning, we have entered into the *policy* aspect of planning activity (discussed above), which, along with *choice*, constitutes the main components of language planning.

Most available research to date has indicated that language choice must be a decision based on an amalgamation of social, cultural, and psychological factors. Generally, when several major languages are competing for final choice for a particular policy, it is best not to impose one language. Imposition will create more problems than it will solve. However, if there are many competing languages but minimal political challenges, imposition could succeed (Das Gupta 1968:23).

Japan provides a very clear example of an a-modal nation that was able to modernize using a language of its own instead of an LWC. Japan had a relatively homogeneous population in terms of race, language, and culture despite its lack of an indigenous Great Tradition in literature. In the case of Japan, we have an unusual instance of a language without an indigenous body of revered literature as part of its cultural heritage. Yet the language has been able to function as a national language with a politically integrative role. The Tokyo dialect was standardized and made the national language (Passim 1968:450). Japan is unique as a Type A nation in that it had an "open-ended relationship with Chinese, drawing upon it for new concepts and vocabulary," even though it had no Great Tradition of its own (450). A Japanese-type development may be possible for other countries if they have escaped colonialism or if they have an adequate linguistic basis for the growth of a modern language. In countries that experienced a long period of colonial domination or that have either no usable literate language or no single language with an unambiguous claim to priority, the situation is quite different. India, the Philippines, and most of Africa are cases in point.

The situation of Hindi as a national language for India, a multi-modal nation, is a good example of a Type C language choice. India has dozens of ethnic groups. Fourteen major languages and hundreds of minor languages and dialects are spoken. English became the common language of the educated classes during the colonial period and filtered down to the semi-educated, since it was the language of administration as well as of education. The choice of Hindi as India's national language ran into opposition from many people who thought their languages were superior to Hindi. The Bengali and Marathi speakers argued that their languages had more highly developed literatures. The speakers of the southern Dravidian languages argued that Hindi was hard for them to learn since it is unrelated to their languages; they had a native language at home and had to learn the national language as well. Many also felt that they needed to know English as an international language in order to get along in the world. For some speakers from dialect areas in the South, it would be necessary to know four languages—three of them unrelated to each other—just in order to operate! These people would need the native dialect, the standard language of a region, Hindi, and English (Passim 1968:451–52).

In the example of the restoration of Irish discussed above, the factors that influence language choice in a uni-modal situation were shown. In Ireland, Irish is the language being developed, while English remains as a result of colonial policy.

Language choice, of course, has to be made prior to the formulation, codification, implementation, and elaboration of language policy. Since language choice entails the need to implement a literacy program in a multilingual nation (usually of the multi-modal variety), particular problems arise. A number of questions need to be asked when decisions are being made regarding what language or languages are to be used for literacy:

1. Is literacy desired in the first language alone?

2. Is literacy desired in the language of a larger regional group if that language is neither a first language nor the national language?

3. Is literacy desired in the language of a person's domicile regardless of region of birth?

4. Is literacy desired in both the first language *and* a second language (most often the official national language)?

5. Is literacy desired in the official national language alone? (Bowers 1960).

If these questions are answered when literacy is being planned, language-planners can more easily make language choices.

1.11 How Writing Systems Are Created

Language planning is a form of applied sociolinguistics used in determining what and how languages are to be used in political and social contexts and also used in determining how languages are to be represented. Writing systems necessarily reflect only one dialect or variety of a language. This dialect is usually known as the standard. A standard language is a particular dialect chosen by authorities to be STANDARDIZED; that is, it is selected as the language for reading and writing. An orthography (spelling system) is developed for it, and conventions are set up for how it is to be written. Writing conventions refer to rules for punctuation, capitalization, word division, and so forth. Also, principles are often devised regarding procedures for borrowing from other languages and for the creation of new words in the standard. When a language is standardized, it usually represents a particular language of a certain group of native speakers; for example, standard Swahili represents the *KiUnguja* dialect as spoken by native speakers of Swahili living on the island of Zanzibar in the 1930s. As time goes by, the standardized (written language) version is perpetuated and disseminated among all speakers of the language as a tool of literacy, and it is also taught to people studying the language as a second language. Eventually the standard no longer even represents the dialect on which it is based, since it will have changed through time. This situation is true in the case of Swahili, for there are no longer any people who natively speak the exact version of the language that has been standardized.

DESCRIPTIVE LINGUISTS specialize in analyzing and describing languages that have never been previously written down. They first do a phonetic transcription of the speech of native speakers as they hear it, using the International Phonetic Alphabet (IPA), and then they try to find out what the important, or EMIC, distinctions are in the language they are describing. Emic distinctions are those that make a difference to native speakers. After the linguist's total analysis of the language at the phonemic (sound), morphemic (word), and syntactic (word order) levels, it is possible to develop a PRACTICAL ORTHOGRAPHY for a language. Such a writing system uses symbols that represent distinct sound and meaning units that the language's native speakers recognize as being "real" in their language.

Writing systems need to be kept distinct from spoken codes and from phonetic transcriptions of actual perceived speech, because these codes and transcriptions contain both what the native speaker perceives as important and also extras that hinder rather than help communication. In English we write *through, bough, tough,* and *cough* to represent the sounds [ðru], [bau] [təf], and [kɔf], respectively. Writing systems are visual systems with peculiar regularities that often reflect their histories. It is more important for a writing system to be accepted and used than for it to be phonetically true.

Acceptability, then, is perhaps the most crucial factor in the creation of writing systems. The goal of creating such a system is that it be used. Let us now turn to some factors relating to the application of language planning to writing systems.

1.110 Application of Language Planning to Writing Systems

Perhaps the most critical feature in the creation of writing systems is that attention be paid to EXTRA-CODE aspects, those aspects of writing beyond the system itself. Extra-code aspects refer to what people want and don't want from writing conventions. The complexity of the process of adopting an alphabet and using it has yet to be fully analyzed. However, we do know in general that it is crucial to look systematically outside the linguistic system itself in order to locate the reasons for acceptance or rejection of programs of linguistic change (Fishman 1971a:358). The study of how best to achieve a writing system's acceptance should be done in the context of general acceptance of other forms of planned language change. Planners of writing systems need to examine the functioning of the society for which the writing system is being devised. The linguist-cum-planner also needs to observe how writing systems, by bringing literacy, change societies. Further, planners need to be mindful of the fact that the acceptance and use of a writing system has implications for an associated loyalty and identity. It is no accident that some coastal Swahili people in Tanzania and Kenya have a sense of Arabic ethnicity, since Swahili literacy in the Arabic script came centuries before romanization!

When a writing system is being selected and a policy set up to promulgate it, planners first need to ask if the system is accurate, economical, and consistent. Next, it is wise to see if the system is similar to the orthographies of related languages—*if* the people have said that they want their system to be like others. Conversely, *if* the people have said that they want a writing system markedly different from that used for related languages, the planners need to determine if the system being selected is distinctive enough.

In Bamako (Mali) in 1966, at a meeting to discuss the use of first languages for literacy, it was recommended that newly devised writing systems should be similar to writing systems for unrelated yet important languages for the learners. It was also recommended that non-European diacritics* and special letters should be avoided as much as possible so that printing and publishing could be economically accomplished (Passim 1968:356). The idea behind having new orthographies similar to orthographies in unrelated languages is that people can then transfer first-language literacy to literacy in a second unrelated language such as an LWC.

Today, in the case of many languages acquiring a writing system for the first time, the people who will use the language and the writing system are already literate in another language. For example, a practical orthography developed for the North American Indian language Haida is based on English orthography, because for most Haida speakers today English is the primary language and the language of literacy. It has been claimed that the Tlingit neighbors of the Haida "insist" that their own Tlingit orthography "follow the rather chaotic orthographic patterns of English wherever possible in order to conform to the demand of the broader society" (Sjoberg 1966:217)!

Technology, too, needs to be considered in the adoption and acceptance of writing systems. If special letters and diacritics are required, they may

---

*Diacritics are marks on letters such as a cedilla under the *c*, *ç*, or a tilde over the *n* in Spanish, *ñ*; both of these diacritical marks are used in European languages.

raise the cost of printing and affect the availability of printing and typing equipment. Such costs are already inflated in newly literate societies because of the limited number of consumers (Sjoberg 1966:357). Still, future advances in technology could conceivably lessen the cost of special letters and diacritics and make separate letters and symbols more practical than has hitherto been the case. An example of such advances may be seen in the recent development of IBM Selectric typewriter typing elements (balls) with special symbols for particular purposes. Thus, it is possible to devise writing systems that are sensitive to ethnic and cultural differences *if* the people desiring such systems will accept and use them. If we now have typing elements for linguistics, mathematics, Arabic, Japanese, and so forth, it is possible to devise new ones for new scripts as well.

Until now, cases of literate communities desiring such specialized writing systems are less fully documented than those of communities adopting systems within the mold of a larger LWC. Interestingly, the phenomenon might be due to a reluctance on the part of linguists, as Fishman sees it, "to recognize the frequent desire of nonliterate peoples to be themselves . . . rather than merely to be imitative copies of *ourselves*" (Passim 1968:357)!

1.111 Types of Writing Systems

Various types of SCRIPTS are used in writing systems throughout the world. When it is decided to devise a writing system for a language, the choice of script necessarily precedes the development of a policy with respect to that script. The most familiar script to English speakers is, of course, the ROMAN (or Latin) SCRIPT, which is the basis of most of the symbols in the International Phonetic Alphabet (IPA) as well and hence is used most often by linguists to develop practical orthographies for unwritten languages. Even if the choice is made that the roman script is to be used to create a particular writing system, further policy is required in deciding how to adapt the roman script to the language. In most of Africa south of the Sahara, the writing systems developed have used the roman script. In addition, the way the script has been used has been influenced by the way it was used in the area's colonial language. By looking at the writing system for standard Swahili, we can see the influence of English. By looking at the writing system for Vietnamese, we can see the influence of French romanized writing. The name of the capital of the Central African Republic, *Bangui* [baɲi], shows the use of the French *ngu* for the equivalent *ng* in English orthography. Interestingly, in Swahili, the same phonetic word is rendered orthographically as *bangi* (although the word differs in meaning—in Swahili, [baŋgi] means "marijuana").

In South Africa, where the early settlers who created writing systems were from Dutch, German, and British backgrounds and the script used was roman, we see another interesting phenomenon in contrast to what happened with romanization in British East Africa. In South Africa, in Bantu languages such as Zulu and Xhosa, whole sentences were written as single words (a CONJUNCTIVE ORTHOGRAPHY was adopted), whereas in East African Bantu languages such as Swahili, the elements of the sentence were more broken up (a DISJUNCTIVE ORTHOGRAPHY was accepted). Linguists working in East and South Africa engaged in quite peppery debates about whether disjunctive or conjunctive orthography ought to be used. Standard Swahili is still disjunctive, whereas Xhosa and Zulu, although still in the process of standardization, appear to favor a conjunctive script. The case of Xhosa and Zulu is also interesting since the two languages are so closely related that they could share exactly the same writing system with very minor differences were it not for the desire of the two populations to keep the two somehow distinct.

In areas with long literary traditions using a nonroman writing system— such as Arabia, China, India, the Soviet Union, or Thailand—the roman script is not the usual choice. Swahili, which now uses the roman script primarily, has a long literary tradition of being written in the ARABIC SCRIPT as well. Swahili scribes as far back as the thirteenth century were writing poetry and songs using an Arabic system of writing. Unfortunately, since the Arabic script uses symbols representing Arabic sounds only and since Arabic has three vowels while Swahili has five, it is difficult today to decipher much of the old Swahili poetry, since every scribe would use his own system of symbols to make up the vowel difference. Given the coexistence of an oral tradition alongside Swahili written poetry, certain epics and wedding songs can be deciphered with the help of people who remember them. In fact, in Coastal Kenya today, perhaps as an outgrowth of the economic prosperity of the Arab world, Swahili people are experiencing somewhat of an ethnic revival in their "Arabic roots," including a renewed interest in the language and writing of their early literature.

Planners involved in choosing writing systems and devising policies with regard to creation (formulation, codification), extension (elaboration), and use (implementation) need to pay attention to whether the facts of the language, as well as the acceptance of the system being proposed, are best served by the use of an alphabet or a syllabary. A SYLLABARY is a writing system wherein symbols are used to represent syllables. A syllabary is practical for a language with a simple syllable structure. In a syllabary, a combination of symbols representing a group of syllables conveys a spoken word. Languages that lend themselves to syllabaries include those whose syllables are composed of a vowel alone (V) or a consonant plus a vowel (CV), as contrasted with languages that make use of clusters of vowel and consonant sounds. Thus, syllabaries do not suit languages such as English, which allows clusters of up to three consonants, as in *scrambled*, plus combinations of most of its consonants and also clusters with vowels.

Syllabaries evolved from early writing systems that used pictures to represent speech. Such systems are known as LOGOGRAPHIC systems.

Syllabaries arose from logographic systems according to the REBUS PRINCIPLE. Suppose, in English, you wanted to represent the word *belief* in pictures, that is, write it logographically. You could draw a bee and a leaf and ask someone to read the pictures out loud in order to get *belief.* Eventually, such pictures become stylized and abstract, developing into a set of symbols that no longer have a concrete pictorial reference. You would use the abstracted "leaf" symbol in words such as *relief,* and the "bee" symbol in words like *frisbee, beware,* and so forth. In this way, syllabary symbols developed from logographic symbols. Logographic systems (*logograph* = "speech picture" or "word picture") represent a transition stage between pure ideographic writing (*ideograph* = "idea picture") composed of symbols representing ideas and a pure phonetic system with symbols representing sounds.

English has too many combinations of consonants and vowels for people to learn separate symbols for all possible syllables. When a language allows for multiple-consonant clusters at the beginning and at the end of a single syllable, as English does, a syllabary cannot be used to reflect these sound combinations. A syllabary generally contains only symbols for simple open syllables of a consonant-plus-vowel type. That is, a syllabary has symbols only for syllables that end in vowels, not for those that are closed by a consonant or consonant cluster. It would be easy to use a syllabary to write a two-syllable English word such as *la-zy,* since it consists of simple open syllables; however, the monosyllabic word *strength* would have to be written something like *se-te-re-ne-ge-the.* The resulting representation of sounds would be far from satisfactory: A one-syllable English word would require six syllabary symbols, and the result would radically misrepresent the way the word is pronounced. For a script to be completely syllabic, it would have to contain the number of consonants of the language multiplied by the number of vowels, thus requiring a much greater number of symbols than needed in alphabetic writing (Diringer (1968:12). Still, as our example shows, closed syllables could not be represented.

Language planners who choose and develop a writing system need to consider the purpose the system is to serve in order for it to be successfully proposed and acceptably put into effect. Despite the apparent simplicity, adaptability, and suitability of alphabetic systems for writing in general, the purpose for which a writing system is intended may make a syllabary more practical or useful—even if more cumbersome. It is also possible that in languages with a small number of possible syllable types a syllabary could be superior to an alphabet because of the textual economy it affords and because it can be learned more quickly (Don Graham Stuart in Berry 1968:736). In any event, the type of alphabet or syllabary being chosen needs to be considered in the light of psychological and sociological factors related to the intended purpose of the writing.

The creation of writing systems where none traditionally existed is necessarily a result of new cultural contacts. Often writing systems are an outgrowth of external political and economic domination. It is hard to imagine the development of a writing system in total objectivity without emotional pressures. When we accept a writing system, we accept some form of loyalty to and association with a related cultural group. The imposition of the Latin, Arabic, Cyrillic, or Chinese writing system did not necessarily reflect desired social changes or enthusiastically undertaken cognitive and emotional reorganization. These accepted and extended systems, where they have been taken up, have had immediate implications for the distribution and direction of new skills and ranks related both to literacy and to the associated philosophy or ideology of the culture which introduced the writing system (Fishman 1971:358). The Arabic alphabet is frequently associated with Islam and, after Latin, is the most generally used alphabet in the world today. It has been adopted for such divergent languages as Slavic and Spanish in Europe; Swahili, Hausa, and Malagasy in Africa; and Persian, Turkish, Malay, Afghan, and Hindustani in Asia (Diringer 1948:215).

Interestingly, missionaries in North America often devised syllabaries rather than alphabets in order to translate the Bible. In addition to religiously inspired choices of particular writing systems, there is the syllabary invented by the Cherokee Indian Sequoya in 1821 for the Cherokee language. Sequoya chose a syllabary form of script in order to differentiate it from the alphabet used for English.

Alphabets are the most common choice for new writing systems for languages in the modern world, and generally *new* alphabets are devised rather than old ones adapted. New alphabets have three purposes: (1) to write languages never before written, (2) to provide an auxiliary system for a standard script (for example, to romanize Hebrew, Japanese, or Swahili), and (3) to remedy inadequate systems (for example, to effect spelling reform or eliminate costly diacritics) (Berry 1968:737).

1.112 Revision of Orthographies

Once a particular form of writing system is chosen for a particular purpose—be it an alphabetic system, syllabary, ideographic system, or a combination—policy needs to be set up with regard to the manner of its use. In the case of alphabets, the letters are used in a system of conventionalized spelling or orthography. It is possible to alter spelling and orthographic conventions even to the extent of replacing one writing system by another. Often, after an orthography has been developed and is in use, drastic reform is suggested affecting the whole writing system. In such cases, the need for reform most likely arose in the context of "revolutionary structural processes" (Fishman 1971a:360); that is, reform was directly associated with the goals of a new social order. Spelling and orthography reform in the absence of any social, cultural, or political turnover is not likely to succeed. Fishman (363) sees four possible types of co-occurrence relationships between social conditions and attempts at orthographic reform. There are successful and unsuccessful orthographic revisions with or without revolutionary social change. These may be represented on a matrix along with specific examples; for example:

Table 2. Orthographic Revision

	+ *Social Change*	− *Social Change*
+ *Success*	USSR	Romanian
− *Success*	Yiddish	Chinese

The Romanian example refers to the successful shift in 1863 from Cyrillic alphabet to the Latin script, a shift that took place without any accompanying political change. The unsuccessful Yiddish case refers to Soviet attempts to "rationalize" Yiddish orthography after successfully revising Soviet orthography. The Chinese example refers to attempts to phoneticize Northern Mandarin. The Chinese example is interesting because *now*—since the new regime came into power and Pinyin was adopted—phoneticization is being accepted. Prior to social change (during the reign of Mao), efforts at orthographic revision in the absence of social change failed, true to Fishman's model.

Planners can use certain principles in deciding if an orthography, whether or not socially acceptable, is *scientifically* acceptable. The orthography may be evaluated on linguistic grounds. Does it economically, consistently, and unambiguously represent the grammar of the language? On pedagogical grounds one can determine if the orthography helps people learn to read and write. On psychological grounds, one can decide if the system allows people to feel that they are really reading and writing. Finally, one should establish if the system is suited to writing, typing, printing, reading, and viewing, that is, for representing speech as needed.

As with any aspect of language subject to planning, in establishing an orthography both linguistic and extralingual factors need to be considered. These factors include people's social attitudes toward their language, the status of the language of the writing system, the relation of the written language to neighboring languages, and the need to heed dialectal differences within the language (Berry 1968:740–41). When an orthography is being adapted for a language and it is being taken from an existing script (for example the roman script), additions and omissions need to be sensibly handled. Of greatest importance is the clarity and distinctiveness of the differential features of the symbols. Letters need to look sufficiently different so they can be discriminated in reading and writing.

Spelling Reform was attempted in Israel in 1968. It was an example of proposing orthographic revision for practical ends in the absence of revolutionary social change. Hebrew had had two spelling systems, with cumbersome ways to indicate vowels in both. There were also problems in making a transition from one spelling system (from vocalized pointed texts) to another (to nonvocalized or full-spelling texts). All proposals for reform sought (1) to represent vowels so that they could be printed within a line (more economical than pointed texts marked by interlinear diacritics), or (2) to introduce additional letters for vowels. Some reform proposals also suggested adopting the roman script.

The Academy for the Hebrew Language (established in 1953 as a language-planning agency) was urged by the Movement for an Unambiguous Hebrew Spelling, an independent entity, to stop reaffirming its position that the two orthographies be maintained. The Movement suggested that if the Academy could not come up with a proposal for reform, the government should convene a body of experts to do the job (Rabin 1971:116). Eventually the positions of the Movement and the Academy were reconciled to the extent that the Academy released a set of proposed rules of unambiguous spelling seen as "at least a partial solution" (117). The Movement wanted further reforms in developing one full spelling system, whereas the Academy's directive was that *both* spelling systems be used, but according to established unambiguous spelling rules.

Since 1968, there has been much controversy about the advantages of one unambiguous system as opposed to the maintenance of coexisting systems. For example, some people feel that pointed spelling impedes the process of learning to read. Others feel that for those who know the system based on grammar learning the pointed system is confusing. As of now, little empirical verification exists for such arguments. To assess the usefulness of the two systems as well as of the unambiguous spelling rules, substantial research is necessary.

For spelling reform to succeed, it cannot be introduced gradually but requires an immediate willingness to change habits. For this reason reform plus social change appears to be the best guarantee of success. Orthographic revision also requires an outlay of money to pay for technological adjustment to the change, to pay writers, reprint schoolbooks, and, where reform is far-reaching, to reprint large numbers of books in common use. The people who are most affected by orthographic revision, however, are not the "technical experts indifferent to linguistic niceties" but the educators, writers, journalists, proofreaders, and printing-room supervisors. Ironically, these are the people "most closely tied up with the working of the previous spelling system and probably emotionally attached to it through the long process of having gotten skilled in handling it" (Rabin 1971:118)!

In the case of the 1968 attempt at reform in Hebrew spelling, it became clear that no one then knew (nor knows up to now) how the reform was to be put into practice. Successful implementation is one of the major unknowns in the area of orthographic revision and an open area of research. Even when an orthography is more or less standard for a particular language, decisions are required as to whether the form of words and phrases is to be disjunctive (each "word" is written separately) or conjunctive (the "words" are written together). Among the Bantu languages of Africa, as mentioned earlier, languages in the South tended to adopt conjunctive orthographies, while in East Africa disjunction was the choice. Consequently, languages like Swahili and Zulu look quite different despite the fact that they are genetically related and both use the roman script.

The recent spelling reform in China has now been in practice for a few years and can soon be evaluated in terms of the success of its implementation. The reform in China leading to the introduction of the *Pinyin script* (and the subsequent change in transliteration of the capital city's name from Peking to Beijing) has been long in coming. The Script Reform Committee that led to the introduction of Pinyin was first set up in 1951 by the Chinese (People's) Government to simplify the traditional script and also to draft a new, phonetic script and make recommendations for its use (Halliday 1960, in Berry 1968:749). In 1956, an alphabet based on *Latinxua Sinwenz* (one of three phonetic scripts of Chinese origin), using only letters of the roman alphabet, was adopted by the committee. Although it was thought then that the advantages of the alphabetic script would ensure its adoption in place of characters, it appears that only now is this in fact becoming the case. *Pinyin*, the name of the reformed script, is also the name of a journal that published long debates about the reform in progress, including many opposition opinions.

1.2 SUMMARY

In this chapter we talked about languages, as systems of human communication, deliberately manipulated for social and political goals, in light of the different forms of decision-making that go into choosing them and making policy about them in social and political contexts. LANGUAGE PLANNING is the activity performed by people who make language choices and policies. Language plans are carried out by means of policies that are formulated, codified, elaborated, and implemented once the target language or languages are chosen.

We saw how writing systems and orthographies as well as languages are chosen. We discussed what should be included in policies designed to establish writing, spelling, and entire linguistic systems. We looked at how each phase of a particular language policy is developed and considered the factors of language choice in both a political context (in terms of national interests) and in an applied context (in terms of political and social needs) surrounding literacy aims. Language policy and language choice are the major aspects that ensure the acceptability, practicality, and workability of a language plan. In the next chapter our attention turns to actual language planning and its political and social aspects, in particular.

Chapter Two

THE POLITICAL AND SOCIAL ASPECTS OF LANGUAGE PLANNING

2.0 Introduction

Language planning may be seen as an approach to the study of change in language and language use in order to make predictions about how to bring about change (Rubin 1973:v). Implicit in language planning is the idea of language as a changeable societal resource requiring planned action through the cooperative efforts of political, educational, economic, and linguistic authorities (Jernudd and Das Gupta 1971:196–97). If we can understand how language changes naturally, we can find out how to bring about desired language changes on purpose. The well-known language-planning scholar Einar Haugen defines language planning (LP) as "the evaluation of linguistic change" (1966:52). Another scholar, Jiři Neustupný, sees language planning to be just one type of a broader category of activities he calls language treatment, encompassing all forms of attention people pay to language problems. Language planning, in contrast to language treatment, refers to the development, implementation, and evaluation of particular approaches to specific language problems (Rubin 1971:vii). Language planning is a process that is best seen by looking at actual situations throughout the world involving problems with particular languages.

Language planning as language change is generally considered to be DELIBERATE language change (Rubin and Jernudd 1971:xvi). As such, language planning is usually not concerned with the changes in particular languages through history, nor is it directly concerned with the nature of linguistic features marking dialect differences. Instead, LP is concerned with how to put language changes into effect in order to reach specific goals.

In an early definition of LP, Haugen saw it as "the activity of preparing a normative orthography, grammar, and dictionary for the guidance of speakers in a nonhomogeneous speech community" 1959:8). This definition is actually an example of the type of plan that might be implemented as an approach to a particular problem, such as setting up a standard language. As an approach to language change, LP is concerned with accomplishment of the actual changes in grammar or speech, or both, that planning agencies suggest. LP looks at language in context and attempts to devise ways to facilitate change as a means to solving specific problems. If an especially prestigious group in a multilingual speech community speaks a language that has no writing system, the plan for implementation (within Haugen's definition) would be to see that the entire community has access to that language *if* the political, educational, economic, and linguistic authorities deem such a plan desirable.

Another LP scholar, Moshe Nahir (1977), suggested that language planning be seen as having five distinct functions based on the activities in which language-planning agencies engage. In Nahir's scheme, it is possible to break down the sociolinguistic tasks of LP according to the objectives of the different types of plans. The five objectives of LP are:

1. LANGUAGE PURIFICATION—prescription of "correct" usage and the preservation of the language's "purity"

2. LANGUAGE REVIVAL—restoration of an old language to its previous status or the revival of a dead language

3. LANGUAGE REFORM—facilitation of the use of a language through, for example, simplification of its vocabulary or spelling system

4. LANGUAGE STANDARDIZATION—ensuring that one language or dialect in a region is accepted as the major language of that region for general use

5. LEXICAL MODERNIZATION—bridging the gap between a language's lexicon and new terminology arising from modern technology

In the discussion of language academies in Chapter One, lexical modernization (Objective 5) was seen to be one of the major functions of such bodies—a part of their task of general policy elaboration. Each of the five language-planning objectives has at various times served as a goal of specific planning agencies in the world. Language purification has been attempted with French, revival with Cornish and Irish, reform with Chinese, standardization with Swahili, and lexical modernization with Egyptian, Arabic, Danish, Hebrew, and many other languages. Chapter Seven provides examples of plans geared to accomplish each of these objectives. According to Nahir, LP agencies may engage in various of these activities from time to time and "shift from one function class to another, abandon functions, or adopt new ones, when a change in needs, circumstances, or ideology in a society or speech community takes place" (1977:120).

The history of particular languages can be looked at in stages dominated by the prevalence of the various LP functions at different times. An agency may pursue more than one function or objective at a given time, and at another time it may give priority to one function over the other(s). The French Academy started out by pursuing purification and also carried out some standardization activities. Today, hundreds of years later, lexical modernization is taking place with Academy sanction.

Language planning is the activity of manipulating language as a social resource in order to reach objectives set out by planning agencies which, in general, are an area's governmental, educational, economic, and linguistic authorities. The study of language planning is the study of organized efforts to find solutions to societal language problems and, thus, is necessarily dependent not only on linguistic concerns but also on the concerns of social science "in order to move from theory to informed practice" (Fishman 1974:1750).

2.1 INTERDISCIPLINARY NATURE OF LANGUAGE PLANNING

Within the broad sphere of anthropology and sociology, in a world where "only certain contemporary languages, in fact, have been developed as languages of all science and technology" and where "it is a serious proposition to suggest that Japanese [as an a-modal nation] may be the last language to 'make it' as an independent language of science and technology," the question of what can or should be done with regard to a given language in relation to its speakers and their context is a real and vital one (Hymes 1974:1451). As Hymes has stated it,

> Despite the potential equality of all languages, many of those responsible for the development of their countries cannot afford the luxury of confusing potentiality with actual equality. We confront a world in which specialization of function among surviving languages will be a paramount reality (1451).

The interdisciplinary nature of language planning is largely a result of the fact that planning occurs in a vast sociocultural milieu. The way in which language is the object of people's attention, reflection, and emotion (that is, how it is used in society) is referred to by some linguists as "language cultivation." When overtly carried out by official bodies, language cultivation is actually the same as language planning. That is, the system devised by the people in power for language cultivation is equivalent to the formulation of language policy.

In its strictest sense, however, language cultivation refers to the manifestation of language attitudes, be they positive or negative.

Language cultivation manifests itself in varied sociohistorical situations. For example, if a peasant wants to use an urban idiom and he learns and intentionally imitates it, it is a phenomenon of language cultivation, more precisely characterized as one of language pedagogy. If, however, this person ridicules another peasant's pronunciation, be it out of local patriotism (everything that is our own is better) or for social reasons (his way of speech represents a symbol of social inferiority to him), both phenomena belong to the domain of language cultivation (Johnson 1978:34).

Once language becomes an object of attention and people develop opinions about it, it is not only a means of communication but also a social or societal resource. It becomes an entity with component parts that may be subjected to planning. It can be manipulated to have certain effects on the society in which it is used and in which people express their ideas about it.

Language attitudes arise when a culture expands. (We can talk of a culture "expanding" when one social group comes in contact with a second group possessing a different language. Each group then develops ideas about the other group's language vis-à-vis its own.) When such language cultivation begins to appear, we start to see "systematic interventions by society in language development" (Johnson 1978:35). Desired attitudes, emotions, and actual usage of language are brought about through the development of language policies in relationship to the concerns of the social sciences (political science, sociology, economics, and anthropology). Language is also cultivated by linguists working with government bodies to develop, for example, specialized dictionaries. Linguists may also study language planning processes toward theoretical ends—to see how prior cultivation or planning, or both, have affected language change, how policy has affected meaning in language, and how language can be planned once it is recognized that language planning involves more than the realization of a language in speech. People's attachments to language have to be considered in the planning process (some linguists are even trying to find out how language can be "unplanned" or "liberated").

Language may also be cultivated by leaders in the fields of education, law, medicine, the arts, and civic affairs, for they are all specialists with regard to particular facets of culture and see language as useful to the perpetuation of the values they associate with their specific spheres of influence. In Section 2.10, we will look at language planning as an aspect of social science in general. Then we will look at language planning as it figures in political science and sociology in particular.

2.10 Language Planning and Social Science

Whereas the *general* subject matter of the sociology of language "reaches far beyond interest in case studies and very far beyond cataloging and classifying the instances of language conflict and language planning reported in chronicles, old and new" (Fishman 1974:1630), language planning as a *specific* aspect of the sociology of language deals precisely with such topics. Language planning looks precisely at how people behave with regard to language and what attitudes are expressed toward uses of various languages. It is this aspect of sociolinguistics which comes to the attention of political leaders and educators all over the world. It is perhaps the only aspect of linguistics we see frequently making headlines in the newspapers (1629)! Media attention has focused on many instances of public participation in various aspects of language planning: the opposition of French-Canadians in Quebec to the continued use of English in government and education; the protest of Belgian Flemings against the lack of Dutch-language equality in Brussels; the anti-English demonstrations of Welsh nationalists who rubbed out English highway signs in Wales; the search by Irish revivalists for government support of language restoration; the current controversy over English/Spanish bilingual education in the United States; and the protests by Jews throughout the world against Soviet "extermination of Yiddish writers and the forced closing of Yiddish schools, theaters, and publications" (Fishman 1974:1629–30).

Elsewhere in the world, with limited media attention, languages such as Swahili, Filipino, Indonesian, Malay, and many of the languages of India "are all being consciously expanded in vocabulary and standardized in spelling and grammar so that they can increasingly function as the exclusive language of government and of higher culture and technology" (Fishman 1974:1630). While these languages are seeking entry into the modern world, still others—in areas where there is a dominant language of government and technology—are seeking a role connected to the national or ethnic origin of smaller groups within the polity. Because Hebrew was successfully revived, other communities such as the Catalans, the Provençals, the Frisians, the Bretons, and now the people of Cornwall as well are striving "to save *their* ethnic mother tongues (or their traditional cultural tongues) from oblivion" (1630). Modernization and preservation efforts are seemingly happening everywhere, to provide all people with access to the modern world through technologically sophisticated languages and also to lend a sense of identity through encouraged use of their first languages (mother tongues). New and revised writing systems are being accepted, and at times rejected, in many parts of the world by communities that hitherto had little interest in literacy at all. This activity is a by-product of all the other language activities going on with respect to emergent rights to one's first language and to a language of world government, trade, and communication (Fishman 1974).

All of these examples of organized and conscious manipulative behavior toward languages and their users show the interdisciplinary breadth of LP. The close association of LP with political science and sociology, in particular, should be clear. What language (or languages) is used to do the business of government is extremely important in the study of government and politics; what language (or languages) is used by people in a community as a reflection of their status and class structure provides important clues to the sociologist in determining the class and status structure in a community.

So far, language-related attitudes have not been well understood. Planners also know very little as yet about the possible relationship between language attitudes and language use. Nevertheless, language planning is an overt attempt to make use of what we do know about attitudes, feelings, and beliefs about language. Much, if not most, LP activity (for example, formulation of a plan, codification and purification of a language, implementation of a revived language) constitutes either LANGUAGE MAINTENANCE or LANGUAGE SHIFT. In other words, LP activity largely involves a recommendation that the present language situation either be changed (shifted) or continued (maintained). Language shifts have occurred "where huge populations adopted a new language or variety into their repertoires, whether or not at the same time they also gave up a language or variety that they had previously used" (Fishman 1974:1701). The results of language shift can be seen in English-dominant North America and Spanish-dominant South America. Language maintenance, on the other hand, occurs where shift does not. Maintenance or shift can take place in those contexts where the degree of change (or stability) in language-use patterns relates to psychological, cultural, or social processes. Where more than one speech variety is used, language planning needs to assess the sociocultural and psychological factors associated with the use of each variety before a certain form of maintenance or shift is recommended (1703). Had language planning existed in previous centuries, the degree of English dominance in North America and Spanish dominance in South America might not be so pronounced, and we might know a great deal more about the languages and cultures of the aboriginal Americans than we now do or ever will.

Planners need to find out the possible relationships between language planning and actual language use. What does it mean, for example, if a country has a designated national language that nobody speaks? What happens if the language of education is a language the students don't respect? Behaviors toward language that center on attitudes about language fall into the area of language planning and sociology, for considerations of attitude are more social than political. LP and sociology in concert look at "the features of language that are considered attractive or unattractive, proper or improper, distinctive or commonplace" (Fishman 1974:1728). However, behaviors toward language that center on *implementing* attitudes, feelings, and beliefs are a different matter. These are the concern of LP and political science. Once we know that a group sees a certain language as valuable to it, LP and politics can use that language in planning national or state unity, for example.

Language planning insofar as it deals with attitudinal and affective behaviors toward language (such as language loyalty or antipathy) is in the domain of sociology. Language planning is linked to political science insofar as it deals with "overt behavioral implementation (control or regulation of habitual language use via reinforcement, planning, prohibition, etc.)" (Fishman 1974:1734).

Language-planning research looks at linguistic diversity in a social and political context. It makes recommendations about the putting into effect and development of language policies in those contexts. This type of sociolinguistic research has relevance in many parts of the world, including those areas mentioned above as foci of intense media coverage.

The linguistic diversity represented by the ten likely language situations that prevail in multilingual communities (as conceived of by the UNESCO report and discussed in Chapter One) often include the juxtaposition of a language of wider communication and a language representing a person's ethnic identity, one's mother tongue. Language planning is an effort to recognize not only our loyalty to our native language but also the need of the community to have a uniform and efficient means of communication. Thus, all langauge planning has to be sensitive to the complex cultural diversity of the community in which planning takes place.

2.11 Language Planning and Politics

By far the most common form of authority involved in developing language policy is the government. In fact, without government sanction, a language policy stands little chance of success unless it is a policy internal to a small group for a specific purpose. An example of the latter is the case of an ethnic group wishing to express its solidarity by means of its language in order to accomplish specific aims such as the achievement of political, social, or financial recognition in the eyes of a larger authoritative group. Governments see language planning as a way to foster attachment to and involvement in the national system. Herbert C. Kelman, a scholar of LP and politics, has expressed the idea that language may be considered to be a "uniquely powerful instrument in unifying a diverse population and in involving individuals and subgroups in the national system" (1971:21).

We will be looking at LP in the context of multilingual societies in which the goal of planning is to accomplish political cohesion. In so doing, we will pay particular attention to the ways language influences people's image of themselves relative to the political system under which they live. In Kelman's view, people may be either sentimentally or instrumentally attached to a nation or state, and language is one of the factors determining the particular form of attachment.

2.110 Sentimental and Instrumental Attachment to the Nation-State

People are SENTIMENTALLY ATTACHED to a national system when they see it as representing themselves; they are INSTRUMENTALLY ATTACHED to a national system when they see it as a vehicle for achieving their "own ends and the ends of members of other systems" (Kelman 1971:24–25). A shared language has the potential to unify a national population because it can strengthen *both* sentimental and instrumental attachments to a national system and because it can be used to reinforce both attachment processes (30–31). The idea of attachment in general is an important one in the study of the formation of both ethnic groups and nations. Some scholars contrast instrumental attachment, not with sentimental attachment, but with PRIMORDIAL ATTACHMENT:

> The primordialist argues that every person carries with him through life "attachments" derived from place of birth, kinship relationships, religion, language, and social practices that are "natural" for him, "spiritual" in character, and that provide a basis for an easy "affinity" with other peoples from the same background (Brass 1979:1).

People who have a primordial attachment to a state feel that it represents more than themselves, that it symbolizes their heritage as well. One could say that primordial attachment is a strong form of sentimental attachment. At either a sentimental or primordial level, a national language would act as a major symbolic means of forming such an attachment by bridging immediate loyalties (the need to be one nation or state) with transcendent ones (the need for a unique linguistic and cultural heritage).

In contrast to a national language, which rests on immediate loyalties, a first language ties an individual to earlier days and different loyalties. A child's mother tongue exposes the child to the traditional wisdom of his or her people—their songs, tales, and other cultural riches. The language in which a child and mother communicate with each other and with the immediate environment serves to link the child by right and necessity with a "wider group most of whose members are distant in time and place" (Kelman 1971:31). National languages need to satisfy these primordial/sentimental needs of unity and spiritual affinity. People need to develop feelings about their national language much as they do about their mother tongue; that is, they need to be sentimentally or primordially attached to it. At the instrumental level, that is, where it is useful for specific ends, a national language allows political, economic, and social institutions to be developed that serve the entire population. Where no common national language exists, sentimental and instrumental attachments may differ and conflict can arise. Whenever language conflict erupts in a multilingual society, one group with a sentimental attachment to a language will lack access to a dominant other language and will experience discrimination at the instrumental level "because its language is not given due recognition" (Kelman 1971:35). The group feels that it is excluded from complete participation in the national system and that its access to socioeconomic mobility is cut off. French-Canadians in Quebec certainly experience this exclusion outside their own province. Spanish speakers in the United States are likewise having difficulty developing any form of attachment to an American national system through language. Both groups express anger at the fact that they are perceived as linguistically handicapped when it comes to sharing in national funds, jobs, education, and the like.

Thus, most linguistic conflicts are rooted in grievances that relate to instrumental rather than sentimental (or primordial) attachment. People become upset when they cannot get what everyone else can because they lack the ability to use the language that is the key that opens the door to the good life. The instrumentally based conflict may be intensified, however, by what Kelman (1971) calls SENTIMENTAL ELABORATIONS. "Since language is so closely tied to group identity, language-based discrimination against the group is perceived as a threat to its very existence as a recognizable entity and as an attack on its sacred objects and symbols" (36). Scholars seem to feel that language planning within a political system ought to be geared to realizing policies based on considerations such as the establishing of communication patterns that help people gain access to social and economic goals. Policies should address questions of how people from different language backgrounds could have equal access to the national system.

For the political scientists, then, language planning is an area where language is seen to function as an aspect of a people's attachment to a nation or a state. We will now look at how different language situations may be considered within national systems and will review the major types of language situations in the world in order to see how they figure in language planning.

2.111 *National Languages*

As seen in Chapter One, when language choice is discussed as a decision to be made prior to policy formation and planning activity, the choice of national languages is based upon considerations of NATIONISM, NA-TIONALISM, or a combination of both. Given Kelman's sentimental (primordial) versus instrumental types of attachment to a state, we can add this dimension to the nationism/nationalism distinction. Considerations of nationism involve instrumental attachments—an emphasis on how well and to what extent the language is useful in seeing to it that the political entity "works." Considerations of nationalism, on the other hand, involve sentimental attachments—an emphasis on how well the language aids the ethnic or national authentification of the political entity.

The term NATIONAL LANGUAGE "indicates that a given language serves the entire territory of a nation rather than just some regional or ethnic subdivision"; it also "indicates that a language functions as a national symbol" (Garvin 1973:71). Thus a national language is meant to be both national and nationalist *and* to foster instrumental and sentimental (primordial) attachments to the nation.

From a planning viewpoint, a particularly difficult problem in choosing a national language arises when a decision needs to be made between adopting a language of wider communication (LWC) and selecting one of the existing languages of the country. A nation may be composed of a number of different linguistic groups whose languages, like the groups themselves, have various functions. The LP scholar Heinz Kloss provides a useful discussion of the relationship between linguistic groups and nations that allows us to see the role of language planning in deciding what language(s) might best be used where. Kloss sees four variables as determining the relationship of language to nation:

1. the type of nation

2. the status of specific languages in the nation

3. the juridical (official, legal) status of the linguistic groups in the nation

4. the relative numerical strength of the nation's different linguistic groups

Considering these factors, Kloss distinguishes nations as ENDOGLOSSIC when the national official language(s) is indigenous, EXOGLOSSIC when it is imported. A nation is entirely exoglossic when none of its indigenous languages is used for national government purposes. A nation is partly exoglossic when one or more indigenous languages are designated national or official, or both (1968:71). Linguistic groups in a nation are categorized not only with regard to their legal, specialized roles and relative numbers of speakers in the nation but also with regard to where they may be located on a STANDARDIZATION CONTINUUM. The continuum, suggested by Kloss, ranges from MATURE use of a group's language (that is, use in science, technology and higher education) to PRELITERATE use (1968:78). From the perspective of standardization, a group's language may be seen as:

mature	small-group	archaic	young	alphabetized	preliterate

SMALL-GROUP languages are those associated with fewer than 200,000 people. ARCHAIC languages are those which are used for "great poetry and deep-searching religious and philosophical treatises"; however, they "may as yet be unfit for the teaching of modern biology and modern physics" (78). YOUNG languages are those generally used only in primary education. ALPHABETIZED languages are those that have been recently put into writing, such as American Indian languages with new practical orthographies.

The juridical (official, legal) status of a group's language refers to its recognized situational role in the business and daily life of the nation. Kloss sees juridical status to be a variable that might best be seen, like degree of standardization, on a continuum.

official	regional	promotional	vernacular	proscribed

At one end of a JURIDICAL-STATUS CONTINUUM are OFFICIAL languages—those used as languages for the business of government. Next on the official-status continuum come languages which are REGIONAL. These are used by people of different language backgrounds who live in a particular place where communication among the groups is required. Moving further along the continuum, we encounter PROMOTIONAL languages, which have neither official nor regional status but are, nonetheless, sanctioned by governmental, municipal, and other public authorities. A VERNACULAR language has no real legal status yet it does have recognition as the mother tongue of a group politically dominated by another group with a different language. At the opposite end of the juridical-status continuum are PROSCRIBED languages—the antithesis of official languages. A language with proscribed status is one whose "speakers are not permitted to use it in their communal life, in their religious congregations, or in their secular clubs, nor may they do any printing in it, let alone to cultivate it in schools. Even its use among members of . . . families may be restricted to the four walls of their homes, it conceivably being dangerous to use it in the streets or over the telephone" (79).

By considering whether a nation is endo- or exoglossic, by evaluating the situational status and standardization status of its various languages, and by considering the size of the nation's various linguistic groups, Kloss feels that it is possible to come up with sensible, reasonable, and workable language plans. Within the categories of the juridical-status continuum are subsumed most of the ten language-choice situations which occur in multilingual societies. The situations of choice involving indigenous languages and mother tongues are classifiable as endoglossic while world languages are exoglossic. Thus the planner may consider language choice to be closely linked to language status.

The language situations where pidgins, lingua francas, and second languages (again see Chapter One) occur are also important in the context of politics and language planning. But in these situations economic factors as well as political factors enter in. These forms of language choice have to do more specifically with the political aspects of language planning and multilingualism than with nationalism and national languages. Yet, when language planners are choosing the language(s) best suited for particular plans, it helps to pay attention to the relationship the nation's language groups have to the nation with regard to Kloss' four variables and his status continua. It also helps in multilingual contexts to consider how the language choices made will affect both nationalism and nationism—even if the likely effect will not be primary.

2.112   National Multilingualism

It is thought in language-planning circles that linguistic diversity, that is, multilingualism, "has always set the stage for the development of lingua francas" (Samarin 1972:660). The term LINGUA FRANCA (which literally means "French language") arose as the name for the language that the Crusaders ("thrown together for a common cause") used to communicate with each other and "with the non-French speaking peoples who had learned it." Today, lingua francas are used to communicate across linguistic barriers.

A PIDGIN is a hybrid language that resembles a lingua franca in development and structure; it necessarily "traces its lineage to at least one natural language" (Samarin 1972:662). A pidgin arises in a language-contact situation and is a simplified language form that is no one's native language. In contrast, a lingua franca may be a natural language that has native speakers, but differs from the full form of the language by being less complex grammatically to facilitate communication across linguistic barriers. Swahili is such a lingua franca. Lingua francas may also be artificially created languages designed to ease communication across linguistic barriers. Esperanto and Loglan are examples of this type.

However, most often lingua francas are pidgins. In East Africa, KiNubi, for example, is a pidgin form of Southern Sudanese Arabic which was brought to Kenya by mercenary soldiers from the Southern Sudan by Lord Lugard during the last century (Hayward 1979). These mercenaries eventually formed the backbone of the King's African Rifles, the East African territorial army. The descendants of these mercenaries speak KiNubi today as a native or first language (mother tongue). They live in Nairobi and other large towns in Kenya and in Uganda. KiNubi has Arabic vocabulary for the most part, but with a simplified sound system and no prefixes or suffixes. Instead of using such affixes, it strings sentence elements together by means of independent particles (much like up-country "settler"-type Swahili) and it has a strict SVO (subject-verb-object) word order (see Owens 1977). Because the mercenaries assembled by Lord Lugard came from various tribes in the Southern Sudan, the KiNubi pidgin arose so they could talk to each other; hence its use as a lingua franca. Today, in urban areas of East Africa, the Nubians comprise a subculture with KiNubi as a native language. Once there are native speakers of a pidgin, the language—by definition—is no longer a pidgin but a CREOLE.

All lingua francas, as a result of use, necessarily change. As they do so, they begin to pidginize. The reinterpretation of a lingua franca through pidginization affects its grammatical structure by simplifying it, as we have just seen with the KiNubi example. As a language becomes a hybrid or pidgin, a common feature is the loss of affixes that show how parts of sentences interrelate.

Another example of the process of pidginization may be seen with Ngbandi (a tone language spoken in the Central African Republic), which regularly makes use of combinations of pronouns and verbs to mark tense and aspect. Nouns in Ngbandi may be derived from verbs by means of differences in tone. Ngbandi, however, has a contact language which evolved from it, known as Sango. As a hybrid, Sango still has significant tone, as does Ngbandi, but tone in Sango does not distinguish words or mark tense and aspect differences. In the process of the pidginization of a language, grammatical and vocabulary simplification always takes place; changes in tone have only recently been investigated. William Samarin, a linguist working with both Ngbandi and Sango, believes that if Sango were not "a lingua franca used almost exclusively by Africans, who already speak tone languages, the distinctive function of tone might be altogether lost" (1972:668). It is interesting to note, however, the phenomenon of English in the West Indies; it seems to be picking up tone as its pidgin form evolves into a full-fledged form from a creole. Children in Jamaica today speak a native language that is an English-based creole with expressive intonation.

It is quite possible that the language planner faced with the task of "welding a heterogeneous multilingual political state into a unified and harmonious nation" might see pidgins and lingua francas to be viable planning options. Clearly more research is needed in the area of social and linguistic aspects of language hybridization if those aspects are to be considered by the language planner.

In most multilingual societies, language planners need to modernize the language their plan centers on—even if it is a current living language. If a local language is being chosen to be developed as a national, official, and mature standard language, modernization is a necessary associated task.

> It is difficult enough for Arabic, which had to step from the Middle Ages into the twentieth century. How much more difficult it is for an undeveloped lingua franca such as Swahili (Samarin 1972:669).

In certain geographical areas planners may discover that a lingua franca (or pidgin) is the vehicle of sentimental and instrumental attachment to a nation and thus makes a good choice as a national language. Suffering from a cultural "blindness to the real facts... people in the more prestigious strata have been known to deny the very existence of a pidgin language (like Jamaican Creole) or to claim that 'everybody knows' the official language (like French in the Central African Republic)" (Samarin 1972:669. Once hybrid languages are creolized and become natural languages, they are then more and more likely to figure in planning activity in a national context.

A good example of a recognized creole is Krio, the national language of Sierra Leone in West Africa. The very name Krio is the word in the language for "creole," which in fact the language, now a first language of many, is. In addition, Krio is still also used in Sierra Leone as a lingua franca. That is, people who don't speak Krio natively use it to communicate with people from other linguistic backgrounds, but in this application a simplified version of the language is used. Krio in West Africa as both a mother tongue and lingua franca is becoming situationally much like Swahili in East Africa, with one version spoken by native speakers and another used as a hybrid throughout the country. It makes sense to look at creolized languages (creoles) like other natural languages in terms of their endo- or exoglossic characteristics and people's sentiments about them. Their positions on the standardization and status continua are also revealing to the language planner considering using them in a language policy.

2.113   Diglossia and Triglossia

Not only does language planning have to be aware of multilingualism as a breeding ground for lingua francas, but it must also be sensitive to the role of each of the languages in particular states and how planning may be applied to each of them. The terms *multilingualism* and *bilingualism* need to be distinguished from the terms *diglossia* and *triglossia*. However, the distinction is not always easy to maintain. The most well-known definition of BILINGUALISM is that attributed to the linguist Uriel Weinreich, who called it the practice of alternately using two or more languages (1953:1). Yet—to expand on his definition—when more than two languages are used alternately, we have a MULTILINGUAL rather than a bilingual situation. That is, multilingualism and bilingualism *can* be the same thing; but when more than two languages are used by individuals, they are multilinguals.

DIGLOSSIA, on the other hand, refers to the use of different varieties of the same language (be they social or geographical). The term TRIGLOSSIA has been proposed to refer to the situation in Tanzania, where three different languages have distinct roles in a single society. Although the literature on diglossia (and by extrapolation on triglossia) intended the term to refer to *different varieties of a single language,* in actual application the term has also referred to different languages used for different roles and with different prestige values.

When we talked about implementing the language policy to restore Irish (in Chapter One), we talked about diglossia as the concept on which the policy implementation there was based. We defined diglossia in that discussion as the practice by some speakers of using "two or more varieties of the same language under different conditions" (Ferguson 1959:325). Whereas the Irish being restored and the English in use in Ireland do not constitute varieties of the same language, the concept of diglossia still does provide a useful policy basis in the Irish national context. Both the restored Irish and the English in use are forms of speech that may be seen as functionally interrelated. The situation in Ireland provides an example of "a special kind of functional relationship" between two varieties of speech alike in some ways yet still constituting different linguistic systems (Stewart 1968:541). The linguistic system used in formal situations is the H(high) variety—English; while the one used for informal purposes can be seen as the L(low) variety—restored Irish.

Similarly, in Tanzania—where triglossia characterized the language situation—each of the three language systems had distinct but interrelated functions: English was used in government, Swahili in primary education, and the vernaculars in religion.

Abdulaziz suggested the term *triglossia* to cover situations where "three languages with both varying and overlapping roles interact" (1972:129). Each language has a different functional allocation. In the Tanzanian case, when Abdulaziz examined the situation, there were two developing diglossic situations. One diglossic situation existed in the case of a person speaking Swahili and also using his or her vernacular language: the Swahili and the mother tongue thus had mutually exclusive uses. The other developing diglossic situation existed in a person's use of Swahili and English. Triglossia, then, refers to a language situation in which three languages have some well-defined yet complementary functions in certain contexts. Typically (as in the Tanzanian case), triglossia is present where vernaculars are used for intragroup communication; a standard lingua franca (such as Swahili) is used in education, the media, and government, but is still not well enough developed for modern urban use; and a world language (a language of wider communication such as English) is used for modern technological applications. In Chapter Four we will see that the functional allocation of different languages and language varieties within speech communities has been a primary concern of LP research throughout the 1970s.

The functional and interrelated use of forms of speech in a society (that is, diglossia or triglossia) exists along with the knowledge and use of more than one language by individual members of the society (that is, bilingualism or multilingualism). How multilinguals perceive each of their many languages in terms of status and prestige should be a focus of investigation by planners dealing with language in a political (national) context.

2.114   The Politics of Language Planning in Multilingual Contexts

Again East Africa provides a good example of how the interdisciplinary nature of language planning has a political-science component. The three countries of East Africa (Kenya, Tanzania, and Uganda) have developed along quite different political lines. The language policies that have arisen in each country (both implicit and explicit) require markedly different plans in response to the different political contexts.

The contrasting linguistic situations in Kenya, Tanzania, and Uganda may be traced to pre-independence times. Their current language differences are bolstered by their political ideological differences as well. What languages are used in each country, how people feel about specific languages in use, and decisions about national and official language status are matters being handled differently by the present-day language policies in the three nations. The policies are "firmly rooted in history" and are "instruments of those political and socioeconomic forces which are dominant in each of the three nations" (Scotton 1978:719).

Language policies as instruments of political forces result from language planning based on knowledge of the language situation in a state and how it may be manipulated to serve the ends of the government or body politic. We have seen that language choice (national, official, and regional languages; lingua francas; the use of functional distinctions such as diglossia and so forth) results from decisions made by authorities to accomplish national political goals (nationism, nationalism) using given language situations (first languages, bilingualism, regional languages, world languages) to serve those ends. The term *social engineering* has been suggested to refer to how language policy may be put into effect in a political setting (Scotton 1978). From a language-planning perspective, we may consider the manipulation of multilingual situations to be the defining activity geared to social engineering that aims at political integration. Such manipulation relates both to a given society (with respect to situations of choice) and to the individual (with respect to bilingualism, triglossia, and so on).

To demonstrate how language policies are social forces (and how language plans are political tools), consider again East Africa, where a situation that first appears incongruous actually turns out to make sense:

> Given its egalitarian outlook, Tanzania's expenditures to "equip" Swahili (in terms of texts, trained teachers, general prestige) are logical. In Kenya and Uganda, given the apparent intention in both countries to maintain societies in which socioeconomic mobility is restricted and power stays in the hands of an entrenched few, the choice to continue with an elitist language, English, as the official language is understandable (Scotton 1979:736).

When the politics change, the plan changes, and the policies being implemented are also altered. The world situation of language politics is such that only a relatively few languages are in a position to ever become *the* future standard of the world (for example, English, French, Russian, or Chinese). The reality or even need "for a single world language does not arise unless and until a single world government is established" (Haugen 1966a:263–64). In today's world this still appears to be a very distant possibility. In the meantime, anyone who needs to learn one of the current languages of wider communication will do so, and concurrently each designated national language has to try to make itself as rich and responsive to modern culture as possible.

> To legislate linguistic diversity out of existence is not only futile, it is culturally crippling. . . . By the natural political trends of the world, we have moved from local tribes to regional unions to nation states, and, along with these, from the natural diversification of language to a pruning and grafting which has given us the relatively small number of standard languages now existing in the world. When the time is ripe, we will move beyond the nation, into world government, and with it we will find our way to a world language (Haugen 1966a:263–64).

The development of Swahili as a national language in Tanzania is a good example of how historical, social, and political events fostered the growth of a language from a first language to a territorial lingua franca to a national language. By tracing the development of language policy with respect to Swahili in Tanzania, we can see how the processes of language development and nation development may be parallel. People in Tanzania today have a positive attitude toward Swahili and accord it prestige, while it, in turn, provides them with a sense of national identity. Tanzanians need Swahili to get ahead in Tanzania, and they want to know it. At the same time they have a natural sentimental attachment to their first languages (mother tongues), which gives them a sense of primordial identity. All the first languages (including Swahili) represent the total heritage of the country as a source of its cultural and linguistic history. The native languages, which give the people their primordial attachment to the nation or define their legitimacy as a people, might be seen as a cultural base upon which the national language, Swahili, can be built. Clearly, Swahili as the national language is being influenced by the many other (mostly Bantu) languages in the country.

It is possible that someday Swahili could become a language of wider communication, for it follows, on the African continent, what Haugen sees as world political trends. It already qualifies in many respects as a regional language in all of East Africa. But in the context of language and political science, it is important to remember that nationalism "stresses the inherent unity of populations that have never been aware of such unity before" (Fishman 1971:3). Most problems immediately facing new nations like Tanzania have to do with reconciling primordial ethnic loyalties with those of the nation as a whole. New nations that want to unify have to reconcile the many "mother tongues" and "fatherlands" within them. They can bring about this reconciliation by developing an instrumental attachment that can be superimposed upon sentimental attachments to existent diverse ethnicities. Language planning in a developing nation needs to pay particular attention to how both intrumental attachment to the nation may be achieved and how sentimental attachment may be shifted from one's group to one's country by means of language. In the case of Tanzania, the promotion of a policy of one indigenous language is intended to foster both psychological and material attachment to its national system. Where it is not possible to plan a policy of "one nation-one language," the reconciliation of ethnic and linguistic differences will take the form of policies proposing that different languages be used in functionally different situations.

2.12 Language Planning and Sociology

Language planning and sociology interrelate when language attitudes are an issue. Certain sociological concepts used for revealing social behaviors that reflect attitudes can be applied meaningfully in language planning. Particularly useful are the notions of social class, social dialect, and ethnic or social identity. The applicability of sociology in the field of language planning generally centers on the area of study seeking to resolve CULTURE CONFLICT. Multilingualism (including bilingualism) and language-based ethnic and social differences often occur in a context of actual or potential conflict related to those differences and the feelings people have about them. In contrast, societies characterized by primordial ethnicity are relatively conflict-free. A society so characterized is one where people feel they have a right to be and that right is unchallenged. Often such societies occur in "a limited human and geographical environment uncomplicated by broad causes, loyalties, slogans, or ideologies" (Fishman 1965:179). Where primordial or sentimental attachment to one's group prevails, we find isolated societies in which religious, national, or social class behaviors are relatively nondistinct. Peasant and tribal societies are examples of societies in which primordial loyalties are emphasized more than instrumental ones. The social structure of such societies

as viewed by us "from the outside," reveals no fully differentiated roles corresponding to those of pastor, politician, union leader, etc. Instead we find a fully integrated set of beliefs, views, and behaviors, a "way of life" that is "traditional" in that it invokes timeless custom as the directive guide to all the processes, problems, and perspectives of life (Fishman 1965:179–80).

However, once societies become structurally and functionally differentiated as in the Tanzanian example of a nation being formed, the primordial nature of ethnicity is transformed. Then the question arises: How can everyone belong equally? Once social classes are differentiated and institutions are established, a consciousness of differences arises, and people use cultural factors to separate themselves as a group from others. They perceive themselves to be different ideologically and compete in terms of social mobility. Language is one of the cultural factors used by people in complex societies to identify themselves as different from others.

In contrast, in the simpler, less complex primordial world, language is not usually "something separately recognized, valued, loved, protected, cultivated, and ideologized" (Fishman 1965:180). People know that others speak different languages, and the language differences keep "us" separate from "them." The separation is desirable. But when "we" and "they" are thrown together (that is, when cultural contact takes place) in a complex society, our languages become a way to unite "us" against "them."

With increasing social organization, what was an "unconscious primordial ethnicity is transformed in the direction of conscious nationality" (Fishman 1965:181). "We" develop pride in our literature, and a consciousness of our language as "ours" develops as well. "Language . . . becomes something to love, to fight for, to live for, to die for; something to safeguard, to develop, to enrich, to bring to others who are less fortunate" (182). The cohesive nondifferentiated segments of primordial ethnicity come apart during sociocultural change. People begin to articulate religious, class, and political institutions, and language is one tool they use to do this. Language planners need to consider where on the continuum—moving from primordial ethnicity to nationality—different groups in a society are situated when they formulate plans involving particular languages. The language that is subject to planning from a sociological perspective is often a symbol of ethnicity used to evoke social identity. The language which gives a person his or her social identity is not necessarily one that the person speaks; it may be just a label the person uses to form an association with a felt ethnicity. Cases in point are Italian Americans who don't speak Italian or Navaho who don't know their language. In the words of Fishman, a person's language "evokes 'something' in addition to itself" (1977:25). Although anything can symbolize ethnicity (food, land, religion, or dress, for example), language as "the prime symbol to begin with" is commonly used "to enact, celebrate, and 'call forth' all ethnic activity" (25).

In addition to seeing how language is a factor of ethnic identity which allows groups to differentiate themselves, sociologists of language also need to see how language is used within a community ostensibly sharing a language to further differentiate people from each other. That is, language planners need to see how language is used to mark class, sex, geographical, and other intergroup differences. How do social groups in America, for example, use different forms of American English to indicate who is "in" and who is "out" of their group? That is, how do social dialects as well as ethnic languages function in complex societies? How, then, is language used differentially in multilingual communities to cut across both ethnic and social dialect boundaries?

The noted newspaper columnist William Safire (1981) addressed the issue of who is "in" and who is "out" in the American household and community at the beginning of the 1980s. In a lighthearted vein, he listed vocabulary differences that show who is "with it" and who is not. The "outs" say "porch," "stove," "socket," "coffee table," whereas the "ins" say "deck," "oven," "fixture," and "cocktail table." In the American kitchen people in the mainstream say "juicer," "coffee maker," "washer," and "tea towel." Those who don't know any better say "squeezer," "coffeepot," "washing machine," and "dishwiper." The trendy woman "on the cutting edge" wears a "gown" while her significant male other is out "jogging" in his "shorts" and "running shoes." The woman who is not avant-garde is in her "bathrobe" while her husband is out "running" in his "trunks" and "sneaker" (or worse, "tenny runners"!).

These and other observations, which tend to be amusing to speakers of either "dialect," show how language separates modern speakers into social groups. Members of either group perceive their usage as somehow more correct socially.

Insofar as these different perceptions of correctness affect group attitudes about each other, language differences are of interest to planners. If a plan has as one of its components the modernization of vocabulary, for example, the plan has to be sensitive to the characteristics of competing social groups who will use the vocabulary. Some people in 1981 read the

Bible and are "saved," while others study the scripture and are "born again," but all of them share a common language and live together in the same nation.

2.120 Ethnicity

Many scholars who believe that language influences ethnic identity implicitly accept the idea that language influences the way people see the world. Some even think it determines one's world view. Alternatively, others feel that it is culture instead which influences the way people see things and the way they talk about them. From this perspective, the role of language is to transmit culture. So, as we discuss language planning and sociology, we will focus on certain factors that need to be considered in efforts to carry out sensible language planning: language as a factor of ethnic identity, language as a marker of social class, and language as a reflection of status and mobility in a multilingual context. There is little debate about the fact that language has a role in ethnicity, though there is strong disagreement about whether it determines it, influences it, or transmits it.

If we were to take a determinist stance, we would say that language structures reality. That is, the structure of our language imposes a structure on the world. For instance, if our language has only one word for snow ("snow"), then we see snow as an undifferentiated white cold mass of stuff on the ground in the winter. Other languages may have different words for different forms of snow, depending on its consistency. People in those cultures, the idea goes, see many different things when they look at snow, whereas we see just one. If we were to say language structure imposes a structure on our world, we might be led to thing that "if different languages differentially influence the thinking of their speakers ... becoming a speaker of a different language would change the way one thinks" (Pool 1979a:3). Extending this thought, becoming a speaker of a different language would change a person's self-identity. We could change our ethnic identity by changing our language.

Taking a middle road, however, we could say that language and ethnicity are most likely linked because of the general symbolic function of language; people use it in identifying themselves as primordially different from others (Fishman, 1977:41). To survive as a distinct group, people use language to set themselves apart. But according to this view, language is not the *cause* of the group differences, as it would be in the determinist approach.

The way we use language to symbolize our view of ourselves and ascribe social identity to ourselves may be looked at as an ETHNIC SPEECH STYLE:

Indeed, Jews the world over speak with a distinct accent in their host languages, and with words and phrases peculiar to their own culture and experiences. Similarly, the Irish and Scots speak with a very distinctive accent that they would be loath to relinquish. A distinctive language, then, need not be a necessary or sufficient symbol of one's ethnicity, but some speech style distinctive to one's group might be (Giles, Bourhis, and Taylor 1977:327).

In my research on the Northwest Coast of North America, I found that it is also possible that even though a language is no longer used as a means of communication, it can still function as a factor of ethnic identity and consequently be a necessary consideration for the language planner. Such a language may not even have an ethnic speech style associated with it. In this case, language as a symbol of ethnicity may be defined as "cultural communication through use" (Eastman 1980:10). Such a culture language might consist of a "set of speech elements which reflect culturally specific items" (Eastman 1979:1). The key characteristic is the use by members of a particular ethnic group of particular words from their own heritage in the host language.

From a sociological standpoint, the language that planners need to be concerned with is "speech used in actual situations to express cultural and behavioral notions" (Eastman 1980:11). Given this conception of language, feasible language plans can be devised that would both ease the preservation of diverse ethnic groups in complex societies and facilitate the necessary interaction required for the complex societies to work as unified wholes. The idea of a "culture-loaded" vocabulary has been proposed to characterize culturally specific items for which there is usually no equivalent term in the host language, that is, in the LWC of the prevailing sociocultural entity.

> Items in such a vocabulary would be the types of lexical categories labeled in a particular culture that refer to the customs and practices that would be of ethnographic interest to someone documenting cultural differences. It contains what the ethnic group perceives in its world that the larger society either perceives differently or selects not to perceive at all (Eastman 1979:8).

For example, the Northwest Coast Haida Indians have words for the moieties (social divisions) and clans (kinship divisions) that mark their social structure (Eagle, Raven, Bear, and so on); a word for the bentwood box used traditionally to store food; and many separate words for different kinds of salmon that outsiders perceive as just salmon or even just fish! By looking at language as speech with the functions of both communication and symbolic use, we can see how the language planner, interested in factors of self- and other identity, is able to use language to alter identity or plan for its sensible social integration.

When we consider the problem of how to analyze language use among members of different ethnic groups, we should start by considering the power relationships among the different groups in a particular place (Parkin 1973). To ethnic groups, language either demarks ethnic boundaries or transcends them. Where boundaries are transcended, groups use a lingua franca, which is usually the case when socioeconomic differences have to be expressed. Boundary transcendence takes place particularly in multi-lingual settings, since in homogeneous ethnic communities or in efficiently functioning subcultures the expression of differences is not required. When a group actually uses its own language—not a lingua franca, ethnic speech style, or culturally loaded lexicon—it expresses, by implication, its world view as socially integrated, culturally homogeneous, and economically well off. When a group does not use its own language, its members are most likely not at the top of the socioeconomic hierarchy of the larger society.

2.121 *Social Dialects*

Within large, complex societies, people belong not only to ethnic groups but also to SUBCULTURES or STATUS GROUPS, or both; these interact with each other and with ethnic groups. The "ins" and "outs" noted above by Safire constitute loose status groups in the United States. Subcultures and status groups are marked off from the larger society by linguistic and cultural differences. Strictly speaking, we can say that the languages used to mark one's distinct ethnic identity, social status, and various subculture memberships are instances of social dialects. The study of social dialects is the study of how speech is used appropriately in specific contexts (see Gumperz and Hymes 1972:11–14). The description of social dialects highlights those linguistic features that indicate social class, ethnic identity, peer group, sex, profession, and so forth. Studies point out the distinguishing characteristics of a variety of social dialects: upper-class versus lower-class speech patterns in a community with a common language; Chicano English as contrasted with Detroit English; the language of plumbers; women's language as contrasted with men's; and so forth. Social-dialect studies look at how such socially related linguistic differences work in a culture to preserve social differences.

A subculture is "the symbolic system of knowledge people use to order their behavior as members of a group" (Spradley 1970:263); it interacts in all sorts of ways with the institutions of a larger culture. People who share a common form of employment in a community often form a subculture. Some examples are: prostitutes; "urban nomads"—people who have no family, travel from town to town, seldom work, and drink heavily (263); university professors; truck drivers; politicians; musicians; and so forth. The way members of each group use the language of the larger culture and the jargon (or *argot*) they develop that is peculiar to their profession (and to their life-style) set them off from the larger society.

One socially telling factor of English arises just from the two terms *argot* and *jargon*. Doctors, lawyers, and professors use "jargon," while thieves, prostitutes, and urban nomads have an "argot"! An ARGOT is a shared vocabulary set with a slang component and a lower-class connotation, whereas a JARGON connotes exclusivity.

Activity-related forms of a shared language—such as argots or jargons—make up a social dialect. Planners need to consider the relative prestige of the various social dialects in a speech community when they make recommendations for language policy. Social dialects assert ethnicity, class consciousness, professionalism, religion, age, peer-group status, privilege, and seniority. In areas where social dialects abound, planners are well advised to see how particular classes of speakers influence the language use of others. Many lexical items or ways of pronouncing vowels or consonants (the variable use of /r/ in American English, for example) that find their way into a speech community have originated within social dialects of particular subcultures. It is often thought that borrowing between dialects or languages "always takes place from higher to lower prestige groups" (Labov 1972:308). Sociolinguists refer to this as Tardes' Law, first proposed in 1913. However, this tendency does not mean that people imitate the speech of their social superiors. Instead, they are influenced linguistically by what they feel to be a prestigious language, regardless of what social class it originates in. In fact, Tardes' Law seems to work quite well as long as we realize that high-prestige groups that people seek to imitate need not be high-class groups. In fact, it is often considered fashionable to pick up slang from lower-class subcultures. Upper-class people who practice this habit do so to show that they are socially aware!

The notion of prestige figures significantly as the main variable influencing how social dialects affect the prevailing language of a speech community. Women are said to be the first to pick up and use newer forms and to use them more readily than men. Teenage argot is frequently picked up by adults. Do such adults think it prestigious to "sound young"? In order to answer this we have to see what social information is communicated by people who adopt these variations. William Labov, who has done a number of studies of how social variables influence language change, feels that the notion of prestige must be defined in terms of the people using it and the situation in which it is used; that is, the notion should be brought out of the area of speculation and made the focus of empirical investigation. It is quite clear that people pick up new vocabulary to which they attach prestige; it is less certain, however, why and even whether women do this more than men. The primary need, then, is to figure out how to identify prestige and then find an objective way to measure and explain how it affects language change.

People in groups within a larger society also use the language of that larger cultural entity in a way that reveals their social status within the larger speech community. Regardless of how individuals use language to mark their ethnicity, speakers also indicate what social class they belong to, their sex, their geographical "home" within the community, and their relationship with their peers. The fact that language variation exists where societal differentiation exists is important in the study of social organization and social change (Fishman 1974:1665). For the language planner, the language that reflects a society's organizational structure in terms of class (including sexual, locational, prestige, and peer-group aspects of class) provides indications of impending social change, which need to be taken into account in their planning. It has been found that "lower classes tend to be regionally and occupationally separated from each other to a far greater extent than do upper and middle classes" (Gumperz 1958, in Fishman 1974:1685). As a result, a society may have several lower-class language varieties based on regional, occupational, or other specializations. Thus, there tend to be many social dialects among lower classes, whereas upper- and middle-class speech has "greater uniformity and greater regional neutrality" (1685). Whereas upper- and middle-class speech tends to be relatively undifferentiated in a region, lower-class speech often reveals the status, occupation, and regional origin of the speaker. In Massachusetts, lower-class speech differs among residents of neighboring South Boston and Roxbury. Both areas also have many middle- and upper-class speakers whose speech is undistinguishable one from the other and increasingly does not even sound like characteristically New England speech.

In Indonesia, a 1967 study of linguistic differences within an elite group found that whereas the lower classes speak only their native languages, the elite know a number of varieties of Indonesian. One of the varieties used by the middle and upper classes is a regionally neutral variety with little influence from particular local varieties, which is in accord with what language-planning research leads us to expect. Non-lower-class Indonesians were found to know English and Dutch as well. Considering this situation, we can expect that the regionally neutral Indonesian language will gain in importance, reinforcing the role of the upper classes in society. It will be differentiated more from foreign languages than from non-neutral local dialects. In fact, as Joshua Fishman sees it,

> One can predict that as these elites lose their local ties and affiliations and assume Pan-Indonesian roles, establishing speech communities of their own in Djakarta and in a few other large cities, their need for local languages and for locally influenced and informal Indonesian will lessen and their stylistic variation will proceed, as it has with elites in England, France, Germany, Russia, and elsewhere in the world via contrasts with foreign tongues (1974:1685).

In all societies, the speech of males and females is socially differentiated. For the planner, marked speech differences need to be considered so as to avoid perpetuating situations of social subordination of particular groups. The English language "reflects and helps maintain women's secondary status in our society by defining her and her 'place' while men are often referred to in terms of their occupations" (Henley 1977:81). Likewise, in Japan, the Japanese system of speech levels reflects the dependency of children on parents, employees on employers, poor on rich, students on teachers. . . . the female is considered as dependent on the male for her own identity and existence, and as such inferior in the social scale of value" (Saint-Jacques 1973:93).

The way language defines women's place in American society can be seen when we read phrases such as "the Washington banker" or "a team of surgeons"—and male images flash through our minds. In contrast, women are more often referred to by relational phrases such as "the 29-year-old doctor's wife and mother of three" (Henley 1977:81).

When we plan language so as to take social differentiation into account, it is desirable in the process to alleviate the oppressed or subordinate status of various groups. It should go without saying that sensible language planning would avoid racism and sexism, for example. In addition, in some cases planners may wish to accommodate purposeful social differentiation. For example, it might be prudent planning to recognize nonstandard dialects for certain purposes, such as Black English as acceptable speech in the schools. Planners need to be aware of social dialects within larger speech communities and consider their likely influence on the goals of the plan being proposed for the whole community. They need to know what effect linguistic social differentiation can have on a society. Any social dialect imparts a sense of exclusivity to its speakers. A jargon or popular argot not only unites members of a group, but also has an accompanying element of concealment. If we can talk the language of the people in a given group, we wear "a badge of membership in the guild" (Bolinger 1975:344).

> College slang is to some extent a way of closing the doors on conventional speakers, while the educational establishment is supposedly trying to open doors a crack in the opposite direction: "There is reason to believe that this is exactly the success that education is after, for it serves to mark many people as unsuccessful and to let into the club only those who are willing to play the success games that the class in control asks them to play" (Bolinger 1975:344, quoting O'Neil 1970:2).

Language planners may want to formulate policies that encourage certain social dialects yet discourage others.

2.122 Societal Multilingualism

Some language plans require that the policy to be aimed at involves more than one language. "One nation–one language" is not always a possible nor a desirable goal, particularly from a sociological viewpoint. Planning usually takes two directions in multilingual societies:

1. It attempts to eliminate all but one language, the national language; that is, the plan is a "one nation–one language" plan.

2. It attempts to see that important languages in the area are recognized and preserved and that one or more languages are adopted for official use and for communication across internal language boundaries (Stewart 1968:532; that is, the plan is a "one nation–more than one language" plan.

   The first type of plan is implemented when the goal is to develop a "national" culture as it is in Tanzania. The second one is used when cultural pluralism as a national aspect is the goal. Latin American multilingual societies often choose the first direction, whereas African nations other than Tanzania tend to choose the second (Stewart 1968:532).
   The role of each language in a multilingual society is largely the result of the pattern of acquisition of the various languages in that society. To describe interrelationships among languages in a linguistically complex society, we have to consider the fact that languages may differ both structurally and historically. Some of the languages may not be indigenous or standardized, others may be dying out, still others may be expanding regionally, and so forth. Some may have no writing system and no published grammars, while others may have a long literary tradition. These situational social and technical factors will have a bearing on the role a particular language will play in a multilingual society. "Different configurations of such attributes will tend to fall into different categories of intrinsic social value, insofar as their use in a particular polity is concerned" (Stewart 1968:532). William A. Stewart calls the social value patterns or categories of multilingualism LANGUAGE TYPES. He claims that language type is an "important factor in determining whether or not a particular linguistic system is likely to be accepted by the members of a national society (including its language planners) as suitable for some specific role, such as for use as an official language" (1968:533).
   A language is "typed" according to four attributes that range (not surprisingly) along continua. The attributes are:

1. degree of standardization

2. degree of autonomy

3. degree of historicity and

4. degree of vitality

DEGREE OF STANDARDIZATION refers to whether a language is MONOCENTRIC (has one set of norms of "correct" usage) or POLYCENTRIC (has alternative sets of criteria for what is "correct"). The standardization attribute also has to do with whether the language is endonormative or exonormative. An ENDONORMATIVE language uses a model of correct usage derived from its own area, whereas an EXONORMATIVE one employs foreign models of correct usage.

DEGREE OF AUTONOMY refers to whether the language is related genetically to other languages of the area while still remaining sociologically distinct. If it is distinct, it is autonomous. From the point of view of autonomy, however, it is also possible for a language to be close to others in the area but be used only in certain sociolinguistic situations while not in others. In such a case the language would have little autonomy. An autonomous language is one that is sufficient for all situations in a speech community and distinct from the language of a neighboring speech community.

DEGREE OF HISTORICITY refers to whether a language is natural in origin (not made up such as Esperanto) and to whether it is associated with a national or ethnic tradition. Languages without historicity are contrived or invented, and used to cross national or ethnic boundaries. Lingua francas and pidgins as well as fabricated and artificial languages are low on the scale of historicity.

DEGREE OF VITALITY refers to whether or not a language is used by an unisolated community of native speakers. If it is, it is a vital language. If it is used by an isolated community of non-native speakers (such as the speaking of Latin by priests in the Vatican), it is not vital (Stewart 1968:534–36).

Beyond considering language types in multilingual societies, planners need to evaluate the existing language functions in those societies. The ten UNESCO situations of language choice discussed in Chapter One involve the language functions important in complex societies. The UNESCO language situations are included in ten functional categories proposed by Stewart to typify the situations in which language types occur. Stewart's functional categories have a societal, functional, and attitudinal basis rather than a political perspective, for language choice from the perspective of social roles, has not so much to do with political goals as with what people do and think. The categories he enunciates are:

1. official languages

2. provincial languages (such as regional languages)

3. languages of wider communication (LWCs), which are used within a multilingual nation to cross ethnic boundaries

4. international languages, which are LWCs used between nations

5. capital languages (the means of communication near a national capital)

6. group languages (often vernaculars)

7. educational languages (used as the media of education)

8. school-subject languages (those taken as second languages)

9. literary languages (for example, Sanskrit) and

10. religious languages (such as Islamic Arabic in Kenya) (Stewart 1968:540–41)

Multilingual situations are stable when the languages involved do not compete functionally, socially, and regionally. Language conflicts can occur when a stable relationship is "upset either by a natural historical process or by direct administrative intervention" (Stewart 1968:541). For example, in one nation two or more languages may serve a regional and group function. When one of them is placed in the context of the others (as an official or educational language, perhaps), the likelihood of conflict increases. Having Swahili as an official language in Kenya upset the balance in many noncoastal areas that already had regional languages much as the coast had Swahili. Why extend Swahili and not some other regional language? Again in Kenya, the language used in and near the capital city of Nairobi is Kikuyu, yet English (an LWC) is an official language there along with Swahili. And Swahili, which already has a group and regional function, is being promoted further as both the official language and the langauge of national unity. Until these functions sort themselves out over time, it would be difficult to enforce a policy with regard to any of these languages without risking language conflict.

2.2 Planning Change

Taking social dialects and multilingualism into consideration, political scientists and sociologists interested in language planning and involved in the planning process may try to make plans in light of likely language change. By studying the social and political factors of differential language use in complex societies, it may be possible to come up with language plans that will both assess potential change and make provisions to accommodate it. The sociolinguist William Labov feels that linguistic-variability studies will lead to an understanding of language change, because language change operates in a social milieu (1962:32). The study of linguistic variability can show how language change works.

Not all scholars who deal with linguistic change agree that social factors are as important as Labov feels them to be. He sees language change as occurring first in a particular subgroup. Then the change spreads to geographically and culturally close groups, carrying with it prestige and social value from the originating group. Next, the change is generalized in the originating group. New social groups are then culturally influenced or actually move into the area of the originating group and reinterpret the change.

One example of such change may be seen at work within the social dialects of American English. Members of the National Organization for Women (NOW) used the term *Ms.* as a title for all women to replace the *Miss/Mrs.* distinction and to parallel the use of *Mr.* in American society. Thus, *Ms.* as a replacement for *Miss* and *Mrs.* is a change first observed in NOW, a particular subgroup. The term is now gaining in prestige and social value in that a number of outside groups such as businesses and universities use it in their correspondence, in application forms, and the like. The question "Is it Miss or Mrs. Blattnatz?" is fading from use.

Ms. is just one term that some NOW members use to mark their group identity as distinct from the larger society. (Other terms are *chairperson, herstory, She* as a pronoun referring to God, and so forth—but the consistency of their use is variable.) The change to *Ms.* from *Miss* and *Mrs.* is becoming generalized in the originating group. NOW members all use the term, and the organization is trying to work toward the elimination of all female-marked vocabulary. While NOW is generalizing *Ms.* for its ends, the larger society is beginning to adopt the term. The larger society does not necessarily see any special "liberated" connotation to the use of *Ms.* The change is beginning to be perceived as sensible and neutral; as a result, it is likely to take place. Had *Ms.* not begun to achieve prestige, Labov's model of language change would predict that it would begin to be negatively stereotyped and would fade away. The implications of using *Ms.* as a title on a par with *Mr.*, a seemingly minor language change, are certainly far-reaching from both a political and social standpoint.

Labov suggests that the very linguistic diversity (whether represented by multilingualism or by numerous social dialects) that sociopolitical language planners confront is of value for preserving cultural differences and maintaining cultural pluralism—the stuff nations and societies are made of! Not all language conflicts result in change, but the changes that do occur have social sanction or else they would not take place. It is possible for planners to make informed judgments as to what will or will not be likely to change by looking at the sociopolitical context of the change.

2.3 SUMMARY

We have seen that language planning has been variously defined in the scholarly literature, with most sources agreeing that it is activity involving "deliberate language change" (Rubin and Jernudd 1971:xvi). There are five basic types of language plan: those that purify, revive, reform, standardize, or modernize languages. The activity of planning requires the attention of scholars in many disciplines, chief among them being the social scientists, particularly the political scientist and the sociologist. Social science, in its emphasis on the study of human behavior, is the ideal locus for language-planning research, since language is a form of human behavior as well as a societal aspect about which people have strong feelings. The political scientist's interest in language planning may be seen in the fact that the authorities who do the planning are quite often governments. Also, the context of planning in many cases is the nation (or some such form of political entity). When plans are formulated relating to the choice of a national language, considerations of loyalty to the nation need to be taken into account. We saw that language choice needs to be related to the type of attachment (sentimental-primordial or instrumental, or both) the speakers of the language have to the political system.

Political scientists interested in studying how national languages (and other language types) are optimally chosen also need to consider whether or not the language at issue is standardized. They need to see where the language falls on a standardization continuum. They need to see how it relates in terms of status to other languages of the area. Is the language chosen indigenous to the nation or brought in from outside, and how will this fact affect the plan to implement a national-language policy? The political scientist also needs to consider whether it is possible to develop a language policy of "one nation–one language"; or whether the plan should allow for national multilingualism, with official di- or triglossia policies. The politician of language also may consider setting up policies to foster the functional use of pidgins and lingua francas in those areas where language choices are difficult to make, as for example in places where several languages are competing within one political context.

As social groups evolve into nation states and languages from different groups come into contact, the function of particular languages within the politically growing unit changes. The political scientist-cum-planner is charged with seeing that the government's choice of a language for a given function is sensible within the context of the nation's goals.

In contrast, the sociologist is interested in language planning to help meet the goals of groups within a nation. Whereas the political scientist choosing a national language in a nation-building situation hopes to establish a primordial cohesion across ethnic boundaries, the sociologist seeks to study how conflict between groups with primordial ethnicity may be minimized in a complex society. To the sociologically oriented language planner, language is a symbol of identity which allows people to see themselves as different from others. People use language not only to separate themselves ethnically from others, but also to keep themselves distinct in terms of sex, age, and social class. Investigators studying social structure and social change and the accompanying effects of language need to look at such social variables when they develop plans for social integration.

Finally, the sociologist, like the political scientist who is involved in language planning, needs to be concerned with multilingualism and with co-occurring social dialects. In this area the two fields of politics and sociology tend to merge, except that the political scientist tries to accommodate multilingualism at a national level and the sociologist works within smaller societal groups. We saw that Stewart's language types may be used as a guide for deciding what language choices are best in multilingual settings at either a national or subnational level. We saw that these types cross cut the ten political situations of choice established by UNESCO as applicable in a national context.

Some of the technical terms and distinctions brought out in this chapter might be usefully reviewed before going on. We have seen that LANGUAGE PLANNING is deliberate language change brought about by means of specific programs or plans. LANGUAGE TREATMENT refers to all forms of attention paid to language problems. LANGUAGE CULTIVATION refers to the ways language is used as an object of attention, reflection, and emotion. In the broadest sense, the three terms refer to the same thing, although, specifically, treatment has to do with how people cope with language problems, cultivation with how they feel about language itself (not just about language problems), and planning with ways to change language in order to cope with or solve problems and to manipulate feelings.

Most language planning goes on either (1) where authorities want to develop a "one language–one nation" policy, or (2) where authorities provide specific roles for a number of languages within a single political unit. These two broad categories of planning occur either in a LANGUAGE-SHIFT or LANGUAGE-MAINTENANCE environment. Language planning directs the effort either to shift (bring in a new language or language variety or extend the use of an existing one) or to maintain a language (see that the status quo is perpetuated).

We have talked about various language-choice situations and language functions that planners may identify. In a multilingual society, four language-type variables may also be identified. An understanding of these variables can help planners avoid situations of potential language conflict. The ten UNESCO-defined situations of choice, on the other hand, are intended as policy options for planners to offer to governmental authorities.

In a political context, when the task is to choose a national language, planners need to look at four linguistic and political variables that affect the language-nation relationship (Kloss 1968). When the question is whether to choose an LWC as a national and official language, for example, planners should consider six sociopolitical variables that characterize three modal types of nation. Whether a nation is modal type A, B, or C depends largely on whether NATIONISM (instrumental attachment and operational efficiency) or NATIONALISM (ethnic authenticity and sentimental-primordial attachment) is the goal (Fishman 1969a).

The following lists may clarify and serve to distinguish the discussed language situations and variables.

Situations of Language CHOICE (National)

1. Indigenous
2. Lingua franca
3. Mother tongue/first language
4. National language
5. Official language
6. Pidgin
7. Regional language
8. Second language
9. Vernacular language
10. World language

Situations of Language FUNCTION (Social)

1. Official language
2. Provincial language
3. School-subject language
4. Group language
5. Language of wider communication
6. International language
7. Capital language
8. Literary language
9. Educational language
10. Religious language

Variables Affecting LANGUAGE TYPE

1. Standardization
2. Autonomy
3. Historicity
4. Vitality

Variables Affecting MODAL NATION TYPE

1. Great Tradition
2. National language rationale
3. LWC rationale
4. Type of LP activity
5. Bilingualism
6. Biculturalism

Variables Affecting the LANGUAGE-
NATION RELATIONSHIP

1. Type of national language (endo-
   or exoglossic)

2. Status of languages within the
   nation

3. Juridical status of speech communities in the nation

4. Numerical strength of speech
   communities in the nation

In Chapter Three we will see how other social scientists (economists, anthropologists, and linguists) are involved in language planning. We will see how language planning is a consideration of educators and others who need to use language in various ways in political and social life.

We will now turn our attention to those aspects of planning in national polities and social groups that also impinge on the interests of economists, anthropologists, and linguists, as well as of educational specialists. We will also see that the use of language for special purposes in other fields relates directly to an understanding of how social dialects function in a politically and socially complex environment.

Chapter Three

LANGUAGE PLANNING AND OTHER RELATED FIELDS

3.0 INTRODUCTION

When people hear the term "language planning," they often assume that the specialist who does the job is a linguist, whereas in actuality the job is really in the sphere of all social sciences, since language planning is a form of social change and is subject to the rules of social change. The scholarly literature on LP so far has reinforced the idea that LP is mostly a matter of linguistics, for it has focused on the product rather than the process of change (Rubin and Jernudd 1971:xiv).

However, it is chiefly on the social-change aspects of language planning—on the *process* of effecting language change—that linguistics and the non-political, nonsocial, yet related fields have an impact. The sociologically and politically oriented planners necessarily must consider the product of planning because their concern focuses on actual societal and political goals. In contrast, economists, anthropologists, linguists, and education specialists provide the people who formulate actual plans (products) with the necessary data so that they can produce feasible plans. We will look at the study of economics, anthropology, and linguistics as areas providing ideas for the language-planning process. We will look at the field of education primarily as it is concerned with the practical aspects of LP, that is, with areas such as literacy, standardization, modernization, second-language learning, and so forth.

3.1 LANGUAGE PLANNING AND ECONOMICS

Much of the theory of planning with respect to language will be seen to have an economic base. This base may be seen in the use LP makes of concepts from management science. Some research has shown what needs to be done for a vernacular language to become a language of instruction in terms of time, money, and effort (Armstrong 1963, 1968). It has pointed out that national planners do not pay as much attention to language problems as they should when they develop what they hope will be economically effective plans (Spencer 1963:26). Jernudd and Das Gupta have suggested, in this light, that language be considered a resource at the national level along with other more usual resources such as money, people power, population distribution, natural resources, and the like (1971). Thorburn has looked at LP from the standpoint of cost-benefit analysis (1971), and Rubin has viewed LP evaluation and criteria for choosing among plan alternatives (1971) (in Karam 1974:112–13).

In this section we will describe how both economic theory and economic variables are important factors in language choice by showing how to delineate and assess viable alternative decisions. In regard to planning policy, economic ideas will also be seen to be useful. For example, they provide guidelines for predicting the likelihood of language maintenance or language shift, given the economic condition of the society or nation and its existing language situation. The field of economics, then, serves in a number of ways as input to LP.

Language can be looked at, then, as a societal resource. If we do look at it this way, as Jernudd and Das Gupta suggest, we might also consider it as an instrument:

> We find ourselves working *with it*, by *means of it*, *on* something else. A linguistic community appears as a sort of *immense market, in which words syntagms and sentences, used as verbal messages, oscillate in the same way as commodities do* (Rossi-Landi 1974:1929).

However, when we look at language from an economic perspective, we are confronted right away with the difficulties as well as possibilities of using economic methods to understand "less obviously pecuniary and sometimes non-quantifiable variables" (Rubin and Jernudd 1971:xx). The dollars-and-cents "bottom line" with language as the resource in question is not always clearly discernible.

Economic analysis can be useful, though, in helping solve language problems and guiding language change. Since LP involves decision-making, certain concepts from the economic study of decision-making are useful. In particular economics suggests the concept of ALTERNATIVE or OPPORTUNITY. People devising language plans have to know what options are available. Economics has the concept of "opportunity cost" which "expresses the loss of opportunity by doing one thing rather than another, by selecting one course of action at the expense of another" (Jernudd 1971:263). To an economist, a decision is defined as a choice of an alternative which has been valued better than another alternative. The language planner might profitably (pun intended!) look at decisions about language choice from the point of view of opportunity cost, that is, from the perspective of a cost-benefit model. Cost-benefit analysis, in whatever sphere, focuses on the change process. Thus, with respect to language, it can be used to assess the consequences of the process of language change.

All consequences of language change need to be related to the preferences of the nation or the society for whom language planning is being done. "This group of people will perceive some of the consequences as *costs*, other consequences as *benefits*. Some consequences are intangible, some tangible" (Jernudd 1971:264). The use of such an economic approach in LP will be examined in more detail in Chapters Four and Five, where we will see it first as a component of general language-planning theory and then as a component of language-planning method.

In addition to the concept of alternatives, the idea of the linguistically HOMOGENEOUS society or nation (with few languages) and the linguistically HETEROGENEOUS one (with many languages) is useful to the economically oriented planner.

3.10 Homogeneity and Heterogeneity

Planners are well advised to take a comparative look at societies when they seek to assess the likely effects of one type of deliberate language change over another. In a number of social sciences such as political science, sociology, and economics, researchers have "undertaken to compile 'cross-polity' files in which data on linguistic homogeneity are included among the many indices that are provided for a large number of countries" (Fishman 1968:54). By comparing the linguistic data from country to country, planners can see how linguistic factors interact with other social, economic, political, and cultural variables. The use of such variables by economists to determine social and cultural homogeneity is a major task where the goal is to foster development. The economist usually refers to these variables as social and economic indicators. Planners feel that economic development proceeds most effectively in homogeneous communities— including those that are linguistically as well as economically and culturally homogeneous. That is, nations are likely to advance economically if there is little ethnic variation, if there is a common religion, if people speak the same language, and if there are minimal class differences. As the linguistic, social, and cultural variables determining national homogeneity contribute to economic development, so also do the variables determining linguistic homogeneity foster language development in accord with the goals of a particular language plan.

Many of the differences between linguistically homogeneous and heterogeneous nations (societies) "also appear to be differences between rich and poor polities" (Fishman 1968:61). Some of the variables distinguishing a linguistically homogeneous nation from a nonhomogeneous one are:

Linguistically HOMOGENEOUS Nations	Linguistically HETEROGENEOUS Nations
1. small area	1. large area
2. large population density	2. low population density
3. low agricultural population	3. large agricultural population
4. highly urbanized	4. low degree of urbanization
5. "medium" per-capita GNP	5. "low" per-capita GNP
6. "developed" economic status	6. economically "underdeveloped"
7. many students enrolled in higher education	7. few students enrolled in higher education
8. religious homogeneity	8. lack of religious homogeneity
9. politically independent for a long time	9. newly independent or not yet independent
10. "non-developmental" orientation	10. "development" the national (societal) goal
11. stable constitutional or totalitarian government	11. authoritarian government
12. noncharismatic leadership	12. charismatic leadership

It appears from this list of variables that the wealthier the society, the more linguistically homogeneous it is. Fishman found that "when differences in per-capita gross national product are controlled," most of the differences between linguistically diverse and linguistically uniform nations are less striking, although still apparent (1968:64). Language differences do not perhaps play an important role in maintaining social and cultural boundaries when a nation or a society is not highly stratified economically.

Linguistic unity or homogeneity usually characterizes a nation that is "economically more developed, educationally more advanced, politically more modernized, and ideologically-politically more tranquil and stable." Homogeneity also characterizes "the state in which primordial ties and passions are more likely to be under control, cultural-religious homogeneity and enlightenment are advanced ... and in which the good life is economically within the reach of a greater proportion of the populace" (Fishman 1968:60).

This strong relationship between economic growth and a movement away from linguistic diversity toward unity is most often seen to accompany MODERNIZATION—another concept used by economically and developmentally oriented planners. The LP researcher Björn Jernudd feels that economic theory might also be able to explain the correlation between linguistic unity and modernization:

> It seems natural that a nation aspiring for efficient use of resources and for self-definition would attempt to rationalize its linguistic resources in order to eliminate such heterogeneity that hinders communication and identification. It is obvious that translations (duplications of personnel or addition of personnel, of print, limited labor, and professional mobility, etc.) are inefficient from the point of view of production as compared with their absence. When an economy is being strongly integrated by division of labor, specialization, and the like into modern structures of production, the pressure on "translations" is increased, and it becomes proportionately all the more desirable to have it eliminated because of increased scarcity of resources. Only certain kinds of political group-problems (e.g., ethnically or religiously based) that are given linguistic expression seem to pull in opposite directions. This latter pull would presumably remain only as long as such linguistic differences correlate with obstacles of access to desired roles in society (1971:272).

Homogeneity (unity) and heterogeneity (diversity) in the jargon of the economist are "macro" concepts: they relate to a large societal system. The fact of one nation having few or many languages as compared to other nations is a MACRO-EFFECT. It is possible that generalizations from a macroeconomic standpoint about modernization might be useful for sociolinguistic theory (Jernudd 1971:273).

An example of one such macro-effect generalization is Fishman's claim that economic growth and progress toward linguistic unity go hand in hand. Relatively little research has been done on macroeconomic generalizations relating linguistic and economic variables, although Jernudd (1971:273–75) reports a number of hypothetical relations for further research. It is suggested that planners look at the relationship of population growth accompanying an increase in per-capita income to the relative strength of speech varieties. They might look at the relationship of the strength of speech varieties (numerically speaking) to an increase in the quality of production, that is, how language contributes to better-produced goods. They might study how language is used to cope with the demands of foreign trade by means of the use of an LWC or second language or lingua franca. Existing language loyalties and educational systems have a lot to do with how a nation adjusts to certain demands of foreign trade. A nation such as Tanzania, which has an indigenous national language, will handle foreign trade quite differently than a multilingual nation that has a language policy of using an LWC (275).

We will take another look at possible relationships between language and economics in Chapter Five, where we will see them as likely assumptions developed from economic theory and applied to language-planning theory.

3.11 Language and Economic Development

As we have seen, new supranational forms of economic organization have developed. We have also seen the field of DEVELOPMENT STUDIES emerge. Social scientists of many persuasions pursue development studies as part of an interest in dealing with questions of regional and national growth. In development studies, there is a well-articulated awareness that a number of issues in development are language issues. For economic development to take place, it is necessary to set up a type of "linguistic infrastructure," so that in areas where many vernacular languages are in use a "common language of wider communication" is also available. This LWC, which transcends local linguistic diversity, is used to ensure that everyone in the developing area can understand the goals of development. To set up such a situation, "Surveys of vernacular languages, contrastive analyses between them and the language of the developing power, and research on more effective methods of second-language instruction are all the order of the day" (Kjolseth 1979:803). In essence, then, there is an awareness that LP is a necessary part of development.

In planning which LWC should be used for development purposes, competition arises among the world powers. We find

each seeking to find more effective ways for its language to gain hegemony as the dominant language of wider communication in different "developing" areas of the world. One also thinks of the competition for primacy among the working languages of the European Common Market (Kjolseth 1979:803).

Planners, working at the behest of such powers, need to be aware of the influence of such competitive urges.

The phenomena of language shift and language maintenance, discussed earlier, are generally influenced by economic factors. Both "are concerned with the relationship between change or stability in habitual language use, on the one hand, and ongoing psychological, social, or cultural processes, on the other hand, when populations differing in language are in contact with each other" (Fishman 1965d:32). An example of language shift in the interest of economic development may be seen in the case of French in Strasbourg, France, after a period of German occupation. Alsatian (a

Germanic dialect also known as Alemannic) had been the first language, German a language of culture, and French the language of education and also the national language. Strasbourg has now become a bilingual city (Alsatian and French) in which an understanding of German is also promoted. The socioeconomic context of the shift from Alsatian as the mother tongue (and major language in the city) to the acceptance of German and acquisition of French has much to do with the social and political history of the area. In Strasbourg, an urban area of the Alsace region, the knowledge and use of French as a second language has prestige. In parts of Alsace where other languages prevail, people have begun to feel that French is desirable, even though Alsatian remains the language of many and "the most widespread means of communication." The relative use of French and Alsatian in Strasbourg depends on what district of town a person comes from. People who live in neighborhoods of tenements tend to be French/Alsatian bilingual. French-versus-Alsatian knowledge and use also relate to what social class people belong to and what they do for a living. Upper-class people tend to command a number of dialects of French, while "very old people and children under six remain dialectal unilingualists." French is used in some homes, places of work, shops, and so forth, while Alsatian is used in others (Tabouret-Keller 1968:111). In contrast, in rural areas outside Strasbourg, Alsatian language maintenance is usually the norm. Despite the industrialization of the Strasbourg area and the accompanying daily influx of people to the city from outlying areas, the linguistic configuration of the countryside has remained stable. "For example, 30,000 people (whose homes are spread over an area of 50 kilometers around the town) come to work in Strasbourg (France) every day; this phenomenon is not accompanied by any notable linguistic shifts in the countryside" (113).

The stability of Alsatian in the countryside outside Strasbourg in contrast to the language shift within the city is considered to be related to the fact that the urban area is a wealthy one, whereas the countryside outside Strasbourg is

> divided up into small plots according to the customary inheritance system of individual ownership. Under such conditions it is economically rewarding to hang on to a small estate while having a regular income from some industrial or administrative job. Any change in economic status is undesirable as is any change in one's way of life, which would be brought about by departure to town. The socioeconomic motivation for using French is clearly not so strong, and the stability of the dialect should not be endangered for the moment (Tabouret-Keller 1968:114).

Decision-making in regard to language planning, then, needs to consider economic factors that (in addition to social and political factors) might be crucial to the likelihood of maintenance or shift. Decision-making studies should emphasize characterizing what behavior accompanies language use and cognition. What people think is very often manifest in what they say and in the language they say it in. Planners need to look at the relationship between language use and such variables as subsistence practices, inheritance practices, and land use. We need to see both *what* people do and *how* *they talk* about what they do. "It is quite clear that language maintenance in bilingual and multilingual situations is related to larger patterns of resource control and distribution" (Brudner-White 1978:153). Because of this, decisions about language choice need to pay attention to how language is used to maximize political, economic, and social situations. On the basis of what we find language to be doing in the interest of such goals, we must realize that we cannot assess language maintenance values by merely looking at language choices. Language choice does not necessarily reflect what people feel about language. Frequently there are "a number of indirect linkages between economic structure and language maintenance that are important to the survival of second and third languages" (182). People may want to maintain a language that they perhaps cannot keep for economic reasons. Thus, it is possible for language choice in a particular situation to be a matter of expedience rather than preference.

Finally, as we consider the role of economics in language planning, we can view language as one of the status factors important in measuring the vitality of a nation or society. Jewish communities all over the world maintain their ethnic distinctiveness by "amongst other things, sound economic control of their immediate environment" (Giles, Bourhis, and Taylor (1977:310). Other groups, in contrast, such as Mexican-American migrant workers and Albanian Greeks, have not done likewise. Thus the consequences of linking or not linking economic factors to the language or ethnicity of a society need to be assessed by planners as well.

Economic theory and economic variables are important considerations that need to be heeded when we try to provide alternative decisions about language choice. These economic considerations are also important when we make language policy, because they point out when to recommend shift or maintenance in the interest of economic development. A state's place in the world also tends to reflect its degree of linguistic unity, a fact that planners recommending change need to understand.

3.2 LANGUAGE PLANNING AND ANTHROPOLOGY

The field of anthropology as a whole, but particularly sociocultural and linguistic anthropology, addresses and incorporates many questions raised in the other social sciences. Anthropology has many subfields, known e.g. as political, social, economic, psychological, and recently ecological anthropology. Often these subfields justify their adherence to anthropology mainly through their focus on the study of other cultures or subcultures. Many of the political, social, and economic studies mentioned in the preceding pages may be seen as part of general anthropological literature as well. Anthropologists examine such issues as development, nation building, ethnicity, social change, and language change. In this section we will discuss the role anthropologists play in LP in a narrower sense, while still bearing in mind that they also address the broader issues discussed. Language planning, after all, occurs in a cultural context (albeit simultaneously political, social, and economic).

Einar Haugen defined LP as "the activity of preparing a normative orthography, grammar, and dictionary, for the guidance of writers and speakers in a non-homogeneous speech community" (1959:8). Later he revised his thinking. In 1966 he saw these activities—often termed language STANDARDIZATION—to be the outcome rather than the definition of LP (1966:162). For our purposes, standardization activities and the related tasks of translation and orthographic reform will be seen as the specific concern of the anthropologically oriented planner. We will also see how language planning requires an understanding of a cross-cultural world view.

3.20   Standardization

Language may be thought of as a tool, which, when standardized, is "cheaper to acquire and maintain" (Ray 1962:754). It should be efficient (concise yet with enough redundancy for communication to take place) and uniform (with a single common form or a number of common forms for different functions). Standardization may be carried out through "unplanned decisions" or accomplished administratively by means of developing approved terminologies, giving awards for "good" writing, subsidizing self-help in literacy, and so forth (754). The anthropologist comes into the standardization picture when language planners have to rely on the use of existing networks of social communication for LP to succeed. Planning needs to consider with whom people need to communicate the most and then see that such communication be done effectively. Communication needs arise because we need what others can give us or because association with others gives us self-respect. "Prestige derives from both utility and honor" (763).

People who communicate to a great extent with each other may be referred to as the MOBILIZED part of a population. The sociologist Karl Deutsch has shown that language changes "spread along the lines of social mobilization" (Ray 1962:763). Anthropology is useful in socially mobilizing or "civilizing" a language in that it is concerned with intracultural and cross-cultural communication. The people who reduce languages to writing, decide how to standardize them, and determine how the standard is to be socially/culturally mobilized are usually anthropological linguists. The job of standardization is an anthropological one in that it requires that a group of people normalize certain forms without impeding cultural communication. A standard is needed in those areas where people use one language, but different forms are used for the same meaning (Ray 1963:54). The language users who feel the commonality of a given language comprise speakers of a number of dialects, some very similar and others widely divergent. The standard is needed for the commonality to be expressed.

The historical formation of dialects needs to be considered by planners seeking a standard. In addition, ethnohistorical accounts of dialect origins must be taken into account. That is, the origin of the diversity to be dealt with needs to be considered. Often, too, planners need to look at earlier attempts at standardization, such as by missionaries who have already written down one form of the language rather than another prior to actual standardization attempts.

The process of standardization is applied to the language itself. The body, or structure, of a language is provided with a writing system, grammar, and dictionary that people can point to as *the* language. Such activity of preparing a language as a standard is referred to as CORPUS PLANNING.

3.200 Corpus Planning

All language planning may be seen to have three dimensions: corpus, status, and economic. CORPUS, or CODIFICATION, PLANNING involves coining new words, making spelling changes, adopting new script. LANGUAGE-STATUS, or POLICY, PLANNING looks at how nations or states see one language in relation to others. The ECONOMIC DIMENSION OF PLANNING "may be called planning for language planning and can include other managerial aspects as well" (Karam 1974:81–83).

So far we have seen that status, or policy, planning is in the domain of the political and social scientists. We have seen economic, or "planning," planning in the domain of the economist. It is in the area of corpus planning that anthropologists figure most prominently. We will also see this to be the major planning area of concern to educators, second-language teachers, and users of language for special purposes.

Three components are involved in the corpus planning activity of developing a vernacular into a standard language: (1) graphization, (2) modernization, and (3) standardization (Ferguson 1968). GRAPHIZATION refers to the developing of a writing system for a language (see Chapter One), thereby providing a "basis for literacy, for formal education, and for modernization" (Karam 1974:114). If a language has no writing system, it is unable to be used in schools to any great extent, nor can it grow easily. MODERNIZATION that depends on graphization refers to the development of expanded vocabulary and ways to communicate "about contemporary civilization" so that the language can be used in all necessary situations. STANDARDIZATION "consists basically of creating a model for imitation and of promoting this model over rival models" (114). A standard language has "a body of spoken and of written discourse directed to listeners and speakers respectively. The body of spoken discourse is based upon the availability of modern speakers while the body of written discourse is based upon the availability of literature in prose" (114, characterizing Ray 1963:70).

A standard is thus a common form of a language that speakers of varying dialects learn to read and write both formally and informally. The preferred standard model may be best promoted through the use of mass communications. If "information pertaining to the events of the world as well as to matters of immediate importance to the local population, such as daily agricultural information" (Karam 1974:114 characterizing Ray 1963:70), is presented in the proposed standard, its acceptance is likely to be hastened (cf. Schramm 1964:151–54). Whereas the anthropologist figures prominently in setting up a standard, other social scientists, as well, are involved in planning for its acceptance.

3.201   *Conventionalizing a Standard*

A language hitherto unwritten and spoken only in a relatively isolated area needs to have a number of things done with it for it to make sense to non-native speakers and for native speakers to be able to read and write it. Anthropologists using linguistic techniques are frequently the first to do this, developing scripts, grammars, and vocabulary lists. Then, educators (in literacy, religion, and so forth) see that the now regularized (or conventionalized) language becomes accessible in written form to native speakers and as both a written and spoken language to others. This process of standardization as seen by Karam

> is an on-going process whereby the formal and informal forms of the language become *conventionalized*. This one area consists of such activities as the codification of the language (in terms of a script, grammar, and dictionary), and the dissemination of this codification to the population through educational and non-educational channels of communication (115).

Anthropologists figure mainly in the codification area of standardization, while dissemination as an aspect of conventionalizing a standard will be seen to be a major activity of the educator.

The definition of a standard usually used in LP is the one attributed to Paul Garvin and Madeleine Mathiot (1956:283): A standard is a "codified form of a language accepted by and serving as a model to a larger speech community." Thus, codification may be considered key to standardization. In codifying a language, grammatical rules and pronunciation rules are made explicit in "official" grammars and dictionaries (Gumperz 1962:466). Codifiers construct a norm for the language in formal grammars and dictionaries and seek to enforce the norm by having an "imprimatur," or official say, on it through style guides and the like.

Why are we considering codification to be in the domain of the anthropologist rather than the linguist? The answer lies largely in the fact that codification needs to be sensitive to the culture in which the codified standard will operate. Garvin and Mathiot (1956) proposed three sets of criteria by which a standard language can be evaluated; these criteria clearly place standardization in an anthropological context: (1) A standard may be judged on its "intrinsic properties" as being both stable and flexible and also being able to make "precise and rigorous" abstract statements if necessary; (2) it may be judged according to the actual functions it has within the culture of the speech community and according to the attitudes members of the speech community have toward it; and (3) within a culture, a standard language may be judged with respect to how well it contributes to uniting speakers of different dialects into a single speech community while simultaneously symbolizing the speech community's identity as distinct from other communities. A standard language endows the speech community it represents with prestige. It allows the culture of the speech community to be communicated intraculturally and cross-culturally. It allows what may be called the "aesthetic function" in language to emerge. A language's aesthetic function is the property a language has to attract attention to its form rather than to its specific messages (Garvin and Mathiot 1956:370). There is something French about French regardless of what is being said in it!

Deviations from a standard language, as in dialect usage, reveal a culture's distinctive features. Such deviations may appear in the literature, poetry, humor, advertising, lyrics, and so forth of a given culture. Without a standard language, we might miss the linguistic character of different cultures.

Standard language functions produce a set of cultural attitudes that the anthropologically oriented planner needs to be aware of when planning the codification of a vernacular as a standard. Standardization leads to language loyalty by unifying dialects yet allowing diversity in creative spheres. The prestige that accompanies a standard leads to linguistic pride. The existence of an orthography, grammar, and dictionary leads to an awareness that there is a common form.

To incorporate cultural attitudes in a standard language, a planner codifying a language has to conceive of the language as a system of speech elements reflecting cultural heritage. The procedure of standardizing a language as an aspect of culture in many ways parallels the procedure involved in reintroducing a language in an area where it has been lost. LANGUAGE REINTRODUCTION differs from REVIVAL (as we saw beginning to take place with Cornish) and restoration (as in the case of Irish) in that the process applies to languages with no written records or few remaining native speakers that can be used as resource material. Such language reintroduction is done so that people who no longer have their language might regain it as an aspect of their ethnic identity. The first step in reintroducing a language is to develop a practical orthography so the language can be written down; the second step is to train people to know and use the orthography so they may become literate in the language (Eastman 1979a:12). In reintroducing a language, these codification tasks reorient people to the language. In standardizing a language, these same tasks reorient people to the dialect chosen to be the standard. In both cases people are presented with a new vehicle of common cultural communication available in written and usable form—in many cases for the first time.

The third step in codifying a language to be standardized or reintroduced is to develop cultural and historical materials and literature in it. Finally, if there are already existing materials written in any dialects, they are made available in the standard to the public. This step aids in the development of linguistic pride and loyalty. Once literacy is achieved and cultural materials are developed, cultural revitalization can proceed more easily. Also, the "frame-of-reference" function of the language begins to operate; that is, the speakers develop a common awareness of "who we are" and "what our language is." The extent to which a language is such a frame of reference is determined by the degree of creative use made of the standard form in new literature, in the conduct of business, and in the media. Standardized languages generally become the main linguistic frame of reference for a society, whereas the function of reintroduced languages usually is restricted to linking a group with its ethnic origins.

The anthropologist as language planner who codifies a language or dialect in the interest of standardization carries out LP in the sense envisioned by Haugen (1959:8); that is, the planner prepares "a normative orthography, grammar, and dictionary for the guidance of writers and speakers in a non-homogeneous speech community." Anthropological linguists (and often today, sociolinguists as well) are persons trained in the analysis of linguistic systems and in the description of language behavior—of language use in context. Their interest in language research and application relates to cultural as well as linguistic variables. They are concerned with how language ties into ethnicity. They are interested in how language is related to political, social, and cultural change. They want to see what influence language has on education. Sociolinguistic training provides people with the necessary skills to produce the materials needed to codify a language. They are able to assist in the preparation of writing systems; they can analyze the situational variables affecting language use. Those that have structural or descriptive linguistic training as well can analyze the languages and prepare grammars. They can develop programs for achieving literacy.

The interest anthropologists have in language behavior or language use is also important in planning. For instance, some anthropologists are particularly interested in how people label cultural concepts from culture to culture, a study that can provide helpful ideas toward devising effective language plans.

3.21   Language Planning and World View

From what we have just seen with regard to codifying a language as a standard (or as a reintroduced language), it is very important to understand the culture in which the standard will function. In Chapter Two, we also saw that language is an important factor in ethnic identity. Language is important in the way we define ourselves in the society we live in. In fact, the form and extent of a language's relationship to the way its speakers see the world have been the subject of much anthropological and linguistic research in this century. Some scholars feel that to become a speaker of a new language means to change the way a person thinks. When we learn a new language, we think the way its speakers think (cf. Pool 1979a:3). It has been suggested along this line that language planning as a form of language change entails planning a change in world view as well. If language shapes a people's perception of the world, then if we want to find out what the "root beliefs" of a culture are, we study its language to gain insight (Laitin 1977:17).

By looking at how a people use their language and by defining what it is that people communicate with it, we can describe what aspects of their group culture a people consider as important. A recent book of essays edited by Roy R. Male and reviewed by the *New York Times* (Broyard 1981), *Money Talks: Language and Lucre in American Fiction*, suggests that "both language and money are currency, that money plays a large part in American fiction." One of the essays contends that money is on a par with sexual-romantic love in modern American writing. Clearly the writing of fiction is one of the things Americans do with their language. And insofar as fiction communicates about money as a major aspect of American culture (as these essays contend), it is not difficult to see what constitutes an important aspect of American group culture!

Group identification is a form of cultural behavior. This type of behavior is of particular importance to language planners since a language associated with a group that people strongly identify with is likely to be more successfully planned than a language that is no longer viable. Language planning generally consists of ways to affect language use by groups of people for communicating group ideas. Thus LP activity may be seen as an effort to alter group ideas or a group's world view.

The relationship of language to world view has been expressed thus: each language has a particular world view and perpetuates it; the speakers of a common language agree to think about the world in a certain way and look at it in the same way. In fact, speakers who share the same environment but speak different languages may think about and look at the world in different ways. The same physical space and social environment can be structured differently, largely due to the influence of the differing structures of different languages (Eastman 1975:78). This articulation of the language-thought-reality connection is known as the Sapir-Whorf hypothesis—after Edward Sapir and Benjamin Lee Whorf. For our purposes we need only note that the Sapir-Whorf hypothesis represents the idea that one's language determines one's world view. If one agrees with this view, then planning to change the speech used in a nation or state is, to some extent, planning to change the perceptions people have of their environment— *what* people talk about and *how* they do it.

When we talk of LP and world view, we refer to LP in its policy-making aspect rather than the normative one we talked about with regard to standardization. That is, we are concerned with those aspects of language about which people have feelings; we need to know what parts of language can be changed and what parts should be left alone (Rubin and Jernudd 1971:xviii). It seems "that policy may be made with respect to the contextual use of language (communication) but not with respect to the parts of language that are innate behavior and something that is with us all the time" (Eastman 1980:8).

Of particular concern to language planners is actual speech used to express cultural and behavioral notions in real-life situations. Such speech reflects cultural or behavioral rather than linguistic concepts. Fishman (1972c:299) distinguishes those who see language as a determinant of thought from those who see it as a reflection of world view. The former represent the LANGUAGE-CONSTRAINT view, and the latter, the LANGUAGE-REFLECTION view. The language-constraint view represents the extreme position with regard to the Sapir-Whorf hypothesis; this view is also known as LINGUISTIC DETERMINISM. It states that we are constrained to think a certain way by the structure of our language; that is, our language determines our thought. The language-reflection view represents the modified view, generally accepted today, known as LINGUISTIC RELATIVITY. According to this view, "language behavior feeds back upon the social reality that it reflects and helps to reinforce it (or change it) in accord with the values and goals of particular interlocutors" (299).

The language planner enters the picture at the point where language is seen as a factor in changing or reinforcing social reality. The anthropological literature on world view is vast. There is general agreement that different languages name and grammatically code different categories, order words differently in sentences, and use different sounds. If a nation decides to make one language its national language, then the people in that nation who are not native speakers of the language will, as they learn it, also learn the way the new language makes distinctions, in contrast to the way the speakers' first language makes distinctions. However, the national language as used by these new speakers will change to reflect their distinctions as well. The English used in India is quite different from American English, which, in turn, is quite different from British English or Australian English.

If English speakers learn an Eskimo language and move to Alaska, they may use a number of words for snow, whereas previously they knew and used only one. But if they learn Eskimo in Florida, they may not learn a single world for snow in that language. In fact, they may borrow new words to describe an alligator or palm tree in the Eskimo language, which, more than likely, has no lexical items to represent them. Planners therefore need to be aware that in choosing a language to be used, for example, to unify a linguistically heterogeneous nation, the language can express any thoughts that need to be expressed.

3.3   LANGUAGE PLANNING AND LINGUISTICS

The structural and vocabulary changes that occur in language planning are the concern of the general linguist. It is only in this relatively small aspect of LP that the "pure" linguist figures. As we saw at the beginning of this chapter, LP is a form of social change. The linguist who is not oriented socially or anthropologically has little to do with LP aside from specifying the nature of language change.

The change-oriented approach to linguistics is a branch of sociolinguistics that complements the work of other LP scholars. William Labov, whom we mentioned earlier in this regard, is perhaps the person who best represents today the linguists involved in the study of language change. To Labov (as also to those interested in standardization), language is an instrument used by the members of a community to communicate with one another. Idiosyncratic speech and speech habits are not a part of language so conceived, nor are random differences in usage from speaker to speaker. Therefore, we can say that a language has changed only when a group of its speakers use a different pattern to communicate with each other.

Whereas LP refers to *deliberate* language change and the evaluation of it, linguists concerned with language change see it as evolutionary. The linguistic stance is that language change is a process that happens but cannot be forced to take place. Clearly, if the planner hopes to introduce change and see that it takes place, an understanding of how change occurs naturally is necessary.

The study of linguistic change aims to find out what variables "permit or incite" the possible forms of linguistic change (Meillet 1921:16). To study language change in progress, Labov suggests that five problem areas that affect language change be addressed: (1) transition, (2) embedding, (3) evaluation, (4) constraints, and (5) actuation. If these problems could be solved, Labov feels, we could understand the adaptive function of language change and also why and how language change occurs.

To address the transition problem, we need to look at how one stage of a language evolved from an earlier one. This allows us to trace the intervening stages of a language and see how the change that took place became the major alternative (Labov 1972:161). To solve the embedding problem we need to find out how elements of the linguistic system correlate with elements of "the nonlinguistic system of social behavior" (162). We need to find out what kind of fit the language has with its culture. We need to see how general the change is in the community.

The evaluation problem refers to how people's attitudes toward language change can be related to their actual behavior with respect to the change. If people say they want to keep their first language in the face of a different national language, for example, we need to see if they are indeed using their first language or have in fact adjusted to the national language. The actuation problem refers to *how* change occurs: How does a national language, for example, actually replace a vernacular? Evaluation and actuation are the two most important areas of the linguistic study of language change, since LP seeks to effect change and evaluate it.

From a linguistic point of view, the constraints problem is at the crux of the study of language change. The linguist seeks to determine the social and linguistic variables, for example, that enhance or impede a sound change in progress. From a linguistic viewpoint, the only way to find out if a sound change has occurred is through "a set of observations of two successive generations of speakers—generations of comparable social characteristics which represent stages in the evolution of the same speech community" (Labov 1972:163).

An example of a successful sound change that represents the solving of all five problems is the change of the /aw/ (phonetically [au]) sound in the speech of residents on the island of Martha's Vineyard (Massachusetts). Admittedly, one sound change can hardly provide a language planner with enough information for proposing large-scale change elsewhere, but the example does show how linguistic analysis of sound change can provide input for LP. The sound represented by the two vowels /aw/ pronounced "ow," as in the slang form of "ouch," occurs in words such as *out, house, about, mount, found, town, now,* and *how.* The sound is treated as a unitary segment pronounced as a low vowel (noncentralized in terms of tongue position) in the speech of many Americans. Other speakers use varying degrees of centralization of the initial vowel, to the point of pronouncing /aw/ as "uhw," where the /a/ of /aw/ sounds like the "uh" in the slang "uh huh" (meaning "yes").

The transition problem is solved when we look at this change through "a detailed examination of the distribution of forms through apparent time— that is, through the various levels in the present problem" (Labov 1972:165). That is, we see how people of different ages in the community today pronounce the words that have this sound. When Labov did this for /aw/ on Martha's Vineyard, he found there to be a continuous development of centralization of "ow" to "uhw," from very little change in the oldest informants to a great deal in the youngest. That is, old Vineyarders would say "h'ow'se" (for *house*) while young ones would say "h'uhw'se."

With regard to the embedding problem, Labov was able to place the change of /aw/ in the context of the use of another diphthong, /ay/ (pronounced as the word *eye*), which was also showing a shift of the first vowel from a low to a central position. That is, the initial phonetic [a] was shifting to [e]; thus /ay/ was shifting from "ay" (*eye*) to "ehy" (pronounced as the name of the letter *a*) just as "ow" [au] was changing to "uhw" [əu]. He found the centralization of /aw/ to be part of a more general change, including the centralization of /ay/, which may have begun as a regional characteristic of the speech of the settlers on the island. Its increase in usage started in a community of Yankee fisherman who were direct descendants of these original settlers. Then its use spread to speakers of the same Yankee ethnic group who had different occupations and lived in different communities. Then, as Labov sees it, the structurally parallel /aw/ variable in Yankee speech began to show similar tendencies: it began to be pronounced as "uhw." Eventually the change was picked up by non-Yankees and was used by a neighboring group of Indians at Gay Head. A generation later, the "ow" to "uhw" change spread to the large Portuguese group in the more settled sections of the island. In these two ethnic groups, the Indians and Portuguese, centralization of /aw/ "overtook and surpassed centralization of /ay/" (Labov 1972:169). The "ay" (*eye*) to "ehy" (*a*) change never went beyond the Yankee community, where we can still hear people say "l'ehy't" instead of "l'ay't" (for *light*). The /aw/ change, in contrast, extended throughout the island and can be heard in the way islanders in general say words like *now, town,* and *house* today. In this example we can see how one change became widespread in the larger speech community while the other remained restricted to the originating group.

The evaluation problem was solved by finding out that the increase in use of a centralized /aw/ was correlated with the successive entry into the mainstream of island life by groups that had previously been partially excluded. As English-speaking Gay Head Indians and Portuguese people began to be more integrated into Vineyard society, they began to use the Vineyarders "uhw" rather than the "aw" of standard English. The centralization of /aw/ was positively valued on the island; it showed the speaker to be a Vineyarder, "to the extent that a Vineyarder abandoned his claim to stay on the island and earn his living there, he also abandoned centralization and returned to the standard uncentralized forms" (Labov 1972:170).

The constraints problem is solved by the linguistic analysis of the change at issue. With respect to /aw/, Labov found that some people centralized /aw/ when it occurred in words ending in voiceless sounds but others did not, or did so to differing degrees. Thus, in certain speakers, centralization might occur more in *house, out, about,* and *mouth* than in *town, found, now,* and *how.* The actuation problem is solved by attempting to generalize the process of change based on the observations of and solutions to the other problems. If we understand what is involved in change, then we can predict other changes and, as planners, perhaps make sensible suggestions for change that can be sensitive to the issues raised by these problems. In this example we saw that groups wanting to be thought of as "in" picked up a linguistic feature they thought had prestige and marked their speech as "insider" speech. This one change was felt to be sufficient, and the generalization of the process of centralization was not extended to other diphthongs such as /ay/. Labov feels that

> It is plain that the noncognitive functions which are carried by these phonological elements are the essential factors in the mechanism of the change. This conclusion can be generalized to many other instances of more complex changes, in which the net result is a radical change of cognitive functions (Labov 1972:170).

That is, change occurs if the group affected by the change feels that the change is in keeping with its goals and the view it has of itself. In Chapter Two, we saw that the term *Ms.* is beginning to gain acceptance in American English. When we discussed that change, we talked about how change takes place. Now that we have looked at the five problems that need to be solved for sound change to take place, you might review the problems yourself and consider how each might be solved with respect to a lexical change such as the use of *Ms.* for *Miss* and *Mrs.* The change to *Ms.* is in progress, whereas other vocabulary that seeks to ensure that women not be labeled by language is not entering the "mainstream" language. Apparently society is ready for *Ms.* but not for some of the other changes stemming from the women's movement.

3.30   Language Change

In recent years, linguistics—apart from some descriptive analyses done by anthropologists—largely excluded the study of speech or social behavior from its sphere of interest. Since the mid-1950s, much of linguistics has dealt with studying a language mainly as a cognitive system rather than a behavioral one.

However, sociolinguists are now attempting to develop methods for analyzing language behavior and the "inherent variation within the speech community" (Labov 1972:204). Such sociolinguists feel that an understanding of linguistic change requires in-depth analysis of the social factors motivating the change. So linguists interested in language change try to find out how differences in language use are socially activated and embedded. American men and women use English differently. Some sociolinguists feel that this reflects the need (conscious or unconscious) American men have to dominate American women. The need is seen, for instance, in the way men interrupt women in conversations 96 percent of the time; and so far, women have been taking it! For men to interrupt women is accepted practice; but women who interrupt men are "babblers" or are "strident" (Battelle 1981). To change this pattern it is necessary to change the social status of men and women in relation to each other. As long as men describe women's language as "gentler," "more emotional," "faster," and "friendlier" than theirs and women describe men's as "more forceful," "boastful," "blunt," and "straight to the point" than their own, we do not have social or linguistic equality (Battelle 1981). If society changes, language changes as a reflection of it.

Not all linguists are interested in the process of language change or its applicability to LP. Labov characterizes linguists as either "social" or "asocial." Those in the social group do pay attention to the social factors underlying language change. They see language use closely enmeshed with the communication of referential information, that is, sensitive to the context of its use. Social linguists describe language change in progress and see it reflected in social and geographical dialect maps. They stress the importance of linguistic differences and of languages in contact, and they see language change as moving from one place to others in waves (1972:264). Clearly, all of the social scientists who study language and are involved in its planning would count as members of this social group, for they approach language as a behavioral system.

In contrast, the asocial linguists consider language as a cognitive system and focus on its internal-structural or psychological aspects to explain change. They look at social communication as being different from the communication of "ideas" and consider it outside their bailiwick. They believe that sound change in progress cannot be studied directly. In their view, community studies and social or geographical dialect maps show only what forms have been borrowed from which locality or which group. To them language change occurs internal to a language. They use a STAMMBAUM model of change rather than a WAVE model as employed by the social group. The asocial linguist's view of change is that it begins in the "stem" or system of the language, that is, in its internal structure, and then extends to its "branches." Change is seen not to reflect or rely on the outside world, being independent of social context.

The Wave model of linguistic evolution, on the other hand, considers language change to take place in a social and geographical space that can be envisioned on a matrix. The vertical axis is social space, and the horizontal axis is geographical space. "The further away one goes in either direction—toward a more distant social class or a more distant locale—the less effect the new change will have at a particular point in time" (Bolinger 1975:457). The Stammbaum model sees different languages as descendants of earlier parent languages in prehistory. The "parents" can be hypothetically reconstructed, showing how they differ from the "children," that is, from the present-day languages, in terms of internal sound and meaning changes, regardless of where and by whom the languages have been or are still being spoken.

The socially oriented Wave model pays attention to language use. Our earlier examples of vowel centralization on Martha's Vineyard and the introduction of *Ms.* to American English represent language changes operating in accord with the Wave idea. The Wave model is particularly useful to planners who want to be able to judge the progress of planned change. The Stammbaum model is far more useful to linguists interested in language classification and comparative linguistics.

The study of linguistic variability by seeing how language changes spread through a language group suffers from what Labov sees to be a lack of precision. He therefore advocates the development and use of instrumental measurements of language change so that future work would be more precise. If we could tell what would be valued and accepted as language and what would be stereotyped and rejected, we could devise more accurate language plans.

3.31   The Sociolinguistic Context

Not all five problems that need to be solved for language change to take place are related to the setting in which the change takes place, even though they are *socio*linguistic problems in the Labovian sense. For example, the CONSTRAINTS in language change are language-dependent. The TRANSITION of a change (that is, the actual change process) is also "asocial." The EMBEDDING problem is both linguistic and sociological.

A change is embedded in a matrix of other linguistic changes or constraints. A change is also embedded in a social complex, correlated with social changes. The change of /aw/ on Martha's Vineyard took place without the extension of the related change of /ay/ to the new group. As the Gay Head Indians and Portuguese became more "in" as Vineyarders in the socioeconomic sphere, they picked up centralized /aw/, which they perceived as marking their adherence to the prestige group, while leaving centralized /ay/ to the "real natives" from whom they were still to be distinguished. Both noncentralized /aw/ and /ay/ were left to the mainlanders, the "outsiders," from whom both the "natives" and the "new Vineyarders" wished to be kept distinct.

Why a particular change takes place—why it is actuated—is closely associated with the society in which the change occurred, as the Vineyardian example shows. The EVALUATION problem has social ramifications in depicting reactions to the change by members of the speech community and in determining what the change actually expresses.

In order to study the social context of language change, we need to describe the speech situations where change occurs. This context should be described in terms of its component parts (participants, setting, and so forth). We need to see whether the language changes reflect changes in how the people interact and how they respond to their environment.

Another "social" linguist, Dell Hymes (1962), has proposed the ETHNOGRAPHY OF SPEAKING as a method to describe speech situations in a way that reveals language variation within a community. The ethnography of speaking is a method of analyzing the use of speech that incorporates a number of factors: attitudes toward the use of speech, the ways in which speech is used appropriately, and the ways in which speech is used in areas such as education to effect social control. Hymes' method of describing language use is to set up a framework that includes language as a part of any description of culture. In a speech community, speech events are behavioral acts involving language. To describe a speech event, the ethnographer needs to say who the participants are; what the setting is; why the event is taking place; what is actually said and in what order; what tone is used; what rules govern who says what, when, where, why, how, and to whom; and, finally, what characterizes the event as a whole (that is, is it storytelling, ritual, conversation, business communication, or something else). From looking at descriptions of a culture's speech events, it can be determined how the culture is socially and geographically stratified. That is, we can describe the culture's variability. By doing this we can see in what direction change is likely to occur.

3.4   LANGUAGE PLANNING AND EDUCATION

Much of what we have said in the previous pages about the relationship of LP to the social sciences can be seen to fit into the area of applied social science. In many cases, LP activity involves the field of education. Chiefly, education figures in LP when there is a need for bilingual training, establishing literacy, and learning a second language—all forms of education that are in some ways types of language planning.

Education is accomplished in bi- and multilingual settings and requires an LP perspective if it hopes to interpret the social aspects of linguistic complexity in deciding the role of each language in the education process. In education circles, literacy is considered a branch of reading instruction. LP affects instructors who are in a position to control the choice of orthography and the form of a language in which people learn to read and write. Second-language learning and LP are also intimately connected. The goals of learning a second language are usually tied to the social or political context of the education system, or to both.

By way of introduction to this section it is interesting to observe that S. I. Hayakawa, formerly senator from California, is a United States politician who recently proposed a constitutional amendment "which would enshrine the English language as the official language of the United States" (Stewart 1981). The idea behind the amendment is to curb what Hayakawa sees as the linguistic fragmentation brought about by the growing population of Spanish speakers in the United States. Hayakawa also wants the Bilingual Education Act recalled, so that Spanish will no longer be used to teach basic skills to children while they are learning English as a second language.

We can see that in the United States the issue of bilingual education has turned into the question of whether Americans are secure enough in their national identity "to risk some relaxation of our earlier prohibition and tolerate the kind of cultural and linguistic pluralism Hispanics are seeking without feeling that the cohesiveness of the nation is threatened" (Alan Pifer, President, Carnegie Corporation, as quoted in Stewart 1981:B2). Senator Hayakawa apparently thinks the answer is *no* (Stewart).

3.40   Bilingual and Multilingual Education

One of the more common LP problems is deciding what language should be the medium of instruction. Should the United States offer English-only education or teach basic skills in Spanish and other languages while non-native speakers learn English as a second language? The question, as we have just seen, is certainly a controversial one. In 1951 the UNESCO Meeting of Specialists conducted a worldwide survey of language in education and recommended that "every effort should be made to provide education in the mother tongue" even where the mother tongue or first language is not the national or official language and even where the first language has no other function in the larger society. The rationale behind this is the assumption that people who continuously have to express ideas in a language other than the one they think in will lose the ability to express themselves or "never achieve adequate self-expression" (Fishman, ed. 1968:690). The assumption that people think in a particular language implies an acceptance of the Sapir-Whorf hypothesis; that is, it assumes that ideas formulated in one language are somewhat different from ideas formulated in another. The conviction that the first language is the best medium of instruction is also based on the assumption that the use of the student's native language in school will foster a good home-school working relationship.

These ideas about the relationship of first languages to learning ability and sociability underlie most bilingual education programs and are the reason that first-language instruction in multilingual societies is thought to be desirable. The validity of the assumptions behind these ideas, however, has not been demonstrated—a fact that does little to help solve the public controversy.

As pointed out earlier in our discussion of world view, it is also possible to make converse assumptions. It may be that all humans have a common innate capacity that allows them to acquire language. Then language might be considered a universal vehicle for the expression of thought. This linguistic knowledge takes a different form in different societies and is manifest in what we perceive to be different languages. Whatever language our particular society uses to express its thoughts is the one we acquire as a "native" language so that we can exhibit appropriate linguistic behavior in that community.

Following these assumptions, if our mother tongue expresses a thought in one language, our national language (if different) expresses the same thought in another. Human thought is thinkable and expressable in any and all languages equally. Insofar as education is concerned with teaching people various ways to express thought, the language they are educated in ought to be the one most in harmony with the goals of the larger society.

Aside from the fact that the implementation of first-language instruction in a linguistically complex society may be based on questionable assumptions, other problems also exist in such implementation. There may be financial and practical problems in supplying first-language educational materials. There may be "too few students speaking certain of the languages" or there may be too many first languages to make instruction in every one of them feasible (Fishman, ed. 1968:694). Another problem with first-language instruction is that the teachers themselves, having been educated and professionally trained in a second language (not the first language), have to learn to teach in the first language. They are thus put in a position of having to do something they have not been trained to do. Still, advocates of the first language as the medium of instruction feel that early training in one's native or first language will act as a bridge for learning the second language in later training.

In education, a second language is necessary in addition to the first when a child's first language differs from the national or official language or when the first language is not an LWC with a technological vocabulary and a written literature. Programs of early instruction in the students' first language(s) and later learning in a second language are referred to as TRANSITIONAL PROGRAMS. The child learns basic skills in the first tongue while simultaneously learning the second language; eventually, in the higher school grades, he or she is instructed solely in the second language. Many of the Spanish bilingual programs in the United States are transitional in this way. The second language allows the child "to feel at home in the language in which the affairs of government are carried on" and provides "access to world history, news, arts, sciences, and technology" (Fishman, ed. 1968:698).

In bilingual and multilingual areas, where a choice of medium of instruction must be made, four options are open to the planner (Mackey 1962:561). The medium of instruction may be chosen according to

1. NATIONALITY—The language of the country is the medium of instruction regardless of the child's mother tongue, religion, or ethnic origin.

2. TERRITORIALITY—The language of the community where the child happens to be living is the medium of instruction.

3. RELIGIOUS AFFILIATION

4. ETHNIC ORIGIN

Nationality is the principle upon which, until recently, United States educational policy was based. In Switzerland the policy is based on territoriality. In countries where religious and linguistic boundaries tend to coincide, the language of instruction is usually chosen according to religious affiliation. The way religious affiliation and the language of instruction interact may be seen in Quebec, where

> there are French Catholic schools, English Protestant schools, and English Catholic schools. The French Protestants in some areas may not be numerous enough to warrant a separate school system, in which case a French Protestant family might send their children to a French Catholic one (Mackey 1962:561).

Ethnic origin is the basis of educational language policy in many parts of South Africa. This is common in countries where bilingual communities are closely intermingled. The best policy is thought to be to teach children in the language normally spoken at home. Also in Kenya, the present language policy holds that primary education is to be in the first language. It is interesting that ethnic origin has become the basis of modern bilingual education programs in the United States (at least it is the stated goal of many of them) and that ethnic origin is the preferred choice according to the 1951 UNESCO survey. The possible complexity involved in trying to ensure first-language instruction based on ethnic origin can be seen from a report in *Time* magazine addressing recent U.S. immigration trends:

> In Chicago, for example, more than 38,000 students are receiving bilingual instruction in a babel of languages from Assyrian to Urdu at a cost of $32.5 million. Even at that level of spending, school officials cannot find enough qualified teachers (May 18, 1981:26).

It is possible, however, that first-language instruction, particularly where materials and current vocabulary in the first language are not available, may have the opposite effect to that intended. First-language primary instruction could cut people off from access to the fruits of education in the dominant language (jobs, advanced training, access to political and social power). This danger exists especially for those who leave school after primary education. In effect, the policy keeps them ignorant of the national or official language, or of the LWC used in the larger sociopolitical context. In South Africa, many people have access to primary instruction in their mother tongues (such as Xhosa, Sesotho, Tswana, Zulu) and then no further education. This fact helps ensure that they do not gain access to the South African power structure that operates in English and Afrikaans. Education in the separate languages also serves to keep the people who speak these languages separate from each other as well as from the government. From a research standpoint, it would be interesting to explore governmental policy and language policy that is specifically designed to support educational policies resulting in certain segments of the population being prevented access to the national and official language.

In the United States, the medium of instruction at all levels beyond early bilingual transitional programs is "standard" English. In addition to the new bilingual programs, some moves have also been made to offer early instruction in nonstandard English such as Black English. It is thought that the child entering the school as a speaker of Black English is confronted by a strange language in the classroom. One of the complicating factors in this situation is that a standard form of any language is actually no one's mother tongue. A certain dialect may be the basis of the standard, but once standardized, the language is something foreigners learn as a second language and students study in school. The language of monolingual education in the United States is a written standard form of American English. It happens to be relatively close in its spoken form to the language used by white middle-class teachers, that is, close to the language spoken in white middle-class homes. To this extent white middle-class students have an edge over others in learning the language of instruction.

There is little doubt that the language spoken by lower-class black children is more unlike the language they will need to learn to read, write, and speak in school than is the language of middle-class white children. But a standard is largely developed especially as a medium of instruction. In many cases it is appropriate to define a standard as the language of the schools. If a child comes from an English-speaking home in the United States, the home dialect (with its childhood vocabulary and grammar and its social and regional dialect markers) is a different language than that which the child will need to learn to read, write, and study in at school.

> Given a moment's thought it is quite apparent that most of the world's school children (rather than our black children alone) are *not* taught to read and write the *same* language or language variety that they bring with them to school from their homes and neighborhoods (Fishman 1972a:341).

Schools in general are places where we all go to have our home dialect (or language or language variety) transformed into the standard language of the society in which we live. Planners need to understand or be able to find out at what point a vernacular (such as Spanish in the United States or a dialect (such as lower-class Black English) is different enough to interfere with learning the language of instruction when the teaching is done in the dominant standard.

Where a standard language is the medium of instruction (but not a child's mother tongue), it is not necessarily the medium of expression. We may read and write a standard yet express ourselves in a form of the standard that is influenced by a dialect or first language when we speak spontaneously. Black American students will still speak Black English even if they do their learning in standard English. In a sense, schools may be seen to foster a kind of diglossia. Educated people have control of two varieties of a single language—their learned standard and their home variety.

If schools are flexible in allowing some language variability in class discussions and student-teacher interactions while still requiring mastery of the standard in reading, writing, and formal speech, it would appear that use of the standard language as a medium of instruction would provide a more socially integrative educational policy wherever possible and feasible.

> The child and the adult deserve to have and to hold their home speech. The home and regional speech can be used for many purposes in school as well. The standard language has serious functions, but it can be enjoyably learned and unashamedly restricted to its prescribed prerogatives (Fishman 1972a:350).

3.41   Literacy Planning

Many of the same issues involved in decisions about medium of instruction have to do, as well, with deciding on what language(s) people should be trained to be literate in. Once again the assumption is made by many that literacy should initially be achieved in one's mother tongue. With literacy, however, the assumption is that once literacy is achieved in one's first language, it is easier to become literate in a second language, the reason being that the process of becoming literate is not thought to depend on the particular language one is becoming literate in. Literacy programs assume that "reading and writing can only be taught in a language that the pupil already speaks" (Gudschinsky 1974:2040). A literate person is one "who, in a language he speaks, can read and understand everything that he would have understood if it had been spoken to him; and can write, so that it can be read, everything that he can say" (Gudschinsky 1968:146). When we talked about language choice in Chapter One, we outlined the considerations that go into deciding on a language or languages for literacy. There the considerations mentioned had to do with deciding on the type of writing system to be developed. Decisions about what language is to be used in reading and writing also rely heavily on considering the attitudes people have about the proposed language, its social status, and its similarity to neighboring languages.

A language planner who is faced with developing a plan to foster literacy, in addition to being involved with the choice of the language of literacy, needs to understand how the read or written language relates to what people in the society actually speak. How does the standard relate to the dialects or varieties spoken by the people who will be reading and writing the language? For example, will people from various backgrounds be able to master the standard with equal or near-equal ease?

The REDUCTION of spoken language to written language has long been held to be one of the goals of descriptive linguistics, particularly as it developed in America. It has always seemed curious to me that people talk about "reducing" a language to writing. Perhaps the implicit assumption is that not everything that can be communicated by language in its spoken form in context can be captured in its written form. Nonetheless, to analyze the structure of a spoken language, it somehow needs to be represented in an analyzable form as data. The descriptive linguist begins the analysis of a language by transcribing the sounds native speakers are heard to make as they use their language. The resulting PHONETIC TRANSCRIPTION is a record of *all* the speech sounds heard by the transcriber. As a tool, the linguist uses the International Phonetic Alphabet (IPA), wherein each sound is associated with one and only one symbol. When it is unclear exactly what sound to record, the linguist has available a number of extra marks called DIACRITICS, which can be used to provide as accurate as possible a rendering of all the sounds in the language. We talked about diacritics in Chapter One—as extra marks needed in certain scripts to make distinctions for which no symbols exist. In that chapter we also made use of phonetic transcription to show how certain spelling similarities in English do not correspond to similarities in sound. Recall the mention of *through*, *bough*, and *cough*—all spelled with *ough* but pronounced [ðru], [bau], [kɔf] respectively.

When we talked about linguistic sound change earlier in this chapter, we referred to the various pronunciations of /aw/ by the people living on Martha's Vineyard. The symbols written in square brackets ([a], [e]) were phonetically transcribed. Generally phonetic transcriptions make finer distinctions in sound than orthographies do. When a spelling system is set up, many phonetic distinctions can only be approximated in the orthography. Whereas the usual English pronunciation of *house* and *town* is "h'ow'se" [haus] and "t'ow'n" [taun], the people of Martha's Vineyard have centralized the initial vowel [a] in [au] to [ə], resulting in [ə u], so that the Vineyard version of *house* is "h'uhw'se" [həus] and "t'uhw'n" [təun].

The descriptive linguist's goal for a phonetic transcription is to gather and prepare language data for further analysis. It is somewhat impractical to consider the IPA as a possible universal alphabet because many of the distinctions the IPA allows the linguist to make are of a technical nature and contrary to the psychological reality of the language as perceived by native speakers. In our Martha's Vineyard example, *all* speakers thought they were saying the same words despite the phonetic differences in their pronunciation! The linguist thus records sounds that the speakers do not consider crucial to their being understood. The IPA makes ETIC distinctions; that is, it allows a linguist to transcribe all sounds by all speakers of all languages. Writing systems, on the other hand, are intended to make EMIC distinctions—to record what is specific to particular languages, what makes a difference in meaning to native speakers. We need separate symbols for the initial sound in *pill* and *bill*, but we need only one symbol, *p*, to use in *pill*, *viper*, and *reap* despite the fact that, to the linguist, these words represent three different *p* sounds in English. The different *p* sounds are not distinctive whereas the *p* and *b* sounds are, and the difference needs to be represented in spelling.

Although ideally writing systems should be emic, representing distinctions perceived by speakers, language change complicates the picture. The writing system for a particular language necessarily reflects the language as it was at the time the writing system was devised. As time passes and language change takes place, the writing system remains the same (unless a movement arises calling for spelling reform). That such change has occurred in English, which has long had a writing system, is quite obvious, since there is little correspondence between the spelling and pronunciation of many words. Read the following sentence out loud: "The *bough* is *tough enough* to go *through* the *trough*." The five italicized words look alike, suggesting that they should sound alike—but clearly do not.

In languages that have been reduced to writing relatively recently, the spoken and written forms seem to correspond much more closely. Thus we see that emically based orthographies, while sensitive to specific languages when devised, are unable to respond to language change. In English today, we can see where this tendency has led. The orthography and speech differ. Even the written grammar and vocabulary are becoming quite different from spoken grammar and vocabulary these days. As we noted earlier in this chapter, the language of the schools is quite different from what most school children speak at home—even when the children's home language is "standard" English. We are reminded that the use of two varieties of a language in different situations represents a diglossic situation; one's language of literacy and one's spontaneous form of spoken language may represent two varieties of a single language.

One of the foremost scholars in the field of literacy was Sarah Gudschinsky, who envisioned a model of orthography that sees writing and speech to be interdependent. Once a person becomes literate, that person's spoken language would then influence writing. She saw this interrelationship as follows:

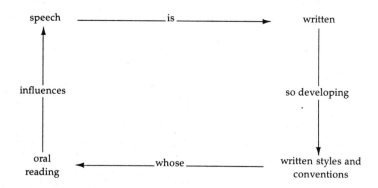

Gudschinsky's model assumes first-language literacy. Speech is written down, then writing styles and conventions develop. When this new written language is used orally in reading aloud, in plays, in newscasting, and so forth, it is, in turn, affected by the speech of the reader. Eventually this speech is written down and conventions grow up around it. In American English we are able to see the influence of such a process when we listen to news broadcasters reading written wire-service news and then begin to hear vocabulary in everyday speech that originated in written news form. It is common parlance today, for example, to *deep six* something one wants to get rid of: also, *-gate* and *-scam* became quickly accepted as allusions to the Watergate episode and the Abscam (Arab Scam) scandals.

It is possible for successful literacy programs to be built on inadequate orthographies as long as in the teaching of writing and reading the differences from speech are pointed out. Although to be truly literate is to be able to read and write everything we can say, literacy is a relative term. Many literacy programs aim for *functional literacy*, whereby a person is taught to "read and write with understanding a simple statement on his everyday life" (Bowers 1968:381). Functional literacy is a way to prepare people for the reading and writing requirements of the social, civic, and economic roles they need to play in the society they live in. People who are functionally literate can read maps, menus, directions, and the like. They can fill out job applications and do most of the routine activities that require a knowledge of reading and writing. In line with this, it is interesting to observe a current movement in the United States to meet this aim halfway. There is a drive underway for establishing the use of "plain" English, urging that people such as doctors, lawyers, and manufacturers use a simplified grammar and vocabulary in official documents so that everyone can understand them.

In 1976, the United States Federal Trade Commission implemented a readability project to teach federal bureaucrats to write in plain English so that consumer contracts and warranty forms could be more easily understood. The idea behind encouraging plain language is to increase the mutual intelligibility of bureaucratese and people language. So far, most proposals to simplify English have centered on reducing sentence length, using the pronoun *you* rather than *he* or *she*, and putting definitions in context. Some scholars feel that what is simple is not necessarily clear and that much more work needs to be done before the government can write for the functionally literate as well as for the specialized literate it now writes for (Goodman 1981).

For a language to be used for literacy at all, the following need to be available:

1. an accepted writing system (see Chapter One) and textbooks written in it

2. basic teaching and reading materials designed to get the language across as a means of reading and writing

3. teachers who can speak, read, and write the language of literacy as well as train others to read and write it (Bowers 1968:388)

If the language in which literacy is sought is unwritten, it needs to be transcribed and analyzed first. Ideally this would be done by trained descriptive linguists, trained in anthropology as well so they would analyze the social and cultural context in which the language is to be used. Such anthropological linguists could then work in conjunction with language planners in devising a good literacy plan.

The LP aspect of literacy is evident in the fact that the teaching of reading and writing in a language yields an end product in the form of a written medium of expression. This medium of expression should be able to be used by educators, it should be conveniently and economically typewritten and printed, it should be sanctioned by the government, and be popularly accepted (Bowers 1968:393). The collaboration of educators with linguists and social and political scientists that literacy training requires might best be achieved through the help of "a national or local language committee (or both), appointed by government, including representatives of government, of interested nongovernmental agencies, of religious bodies, and of appropriate institutes and universities, as well as qualified individuals" (393). That is, literacy training has its most likely chance of success if it is carried out as a language plan. Literacy programs as forms of education imply the existence of a language policy that is guiding the decision to use a particular language or languages for reading and writing. For example, a government might decide to use one official national language for literacy. This policy might have been chosen "on grounds of either cultural unity or economy, though it may be a matter of doubt whether either of these aims will be truly served" (398).

Whatever policy may be behind a literacy program, certain requirements need to have been met:

1. choosing a language or languages

2. deciding which script is to be used

3. analyzing and describing the language(s)

4. making provisions for vocabulary expansion, spelling revision, and the like

5. making provisions for teaching the language of literacy as a second language where necessary

3.42   Second-Language Learning

Just as certain forms of LP may require standardization or literacy in order to produce their desired effects, the learning of a second language by a large segment of the population may also be called for. Whereas anthropological linguists have the skills to standardize a language and educators have the skills to carry out literacy training, specialists in second-language learning can help the language planner in yet different ways. Language planning figures in second-language learning in two areas: (1) deciding what is a second language for pedagogical purposes, and (2) determining the methods for preparing second-language learning materials.

An enormous scholarly literature is available on second-language learning. Teaching a second language may be carried out alone or in conjunction with a bilingual education program. A number of scholars feel that an effective second-language teaching program should be based on an analysis of the native language of the student as contrasted with the second or target language (Troike 1974:2123). This approach is known as CONTRASTIVE ANALYSIS. It is a type of linguistic analysis which focuses on showing sound differences, grammatical differences, and semantic differences between the two languages. The purpose of contrastive analysis is to provide teachers of a second language with ways to predict, diagnose, and overcome likely learning problems students might have due to the differences between the languages.

The process of second-language learning may be distinguished from foreign-language learning. Some people feel that there is not much need to emphasize speech in a second language since the second language is acquired by people who are already speakers in their normal speech situations. That is, second-language learners are already speaking in those situations in which they would be using the language, although the language they use is their first language. Still, they are in a position to hear the second language and can practice using it in real-life situations. In contrast, foreign-language learners are not provided these natural situations and need to be taught what the language sounds like and how they themselves sound while using it (Lewis 1974:2135).

A second language, then, is one already in the learner's world, whereas a foreign language represents a foreign culture. A foreign language is used in a speech community different from the one the learner lives in, whereas a second language is used as another language in the same speech community in which the learner already uses his or her first language. The vocabulary of a second language always becomes associated with concrete referents already in the learner's culture; this may not be true of a foreign-language vocabulary. The person learning Eskimo while living in Florida will have different problems learning that language than would the Spanish speaker living in Florida who is learning English.

Another point of difference between foreign- and second-language learning is that the norms of usage of the second language are less strict than those of a foreign language. We learn a second language to use in a familiar environment and we do not have to be particularly careful of being misunderstood. With a foreign language, correct grammar is more important because we need to rely on the language as a whole to be understood.

In the Soviet Union, all national groups are taught Russian as a second language even though there is a "statutory right of parents to have their children taught in their mother tongue if they wish" (Lewis 1974:3142). As a result, many people in the Soviet Union speak Russian with added characteristics from their mother tongues.

Planning is required in second-language learning in order to ensure that the second language is perceived and used appropriately in the society's political and social structure. Most Soviets of whatever mother-tongue background use Russian political vocabulary whether or not they use the vernacular while shopping or farming. When Thai is taught as a second language in Thailand, the social status of the teachers, their degree of familiarity with the students, their family relationship, and their age play an important role. Cultural factors of second-language learning come into full play only when the language teaching is well underway. When a student begins to attain linguistic mastery and a degree of conceptual sophistication, such cultural factors become especially important (Lewis 1974:2149). Once we begin to be at home in a second language, it becomes very important to know what is sociolinguistically appropriate in that language—which may differ from acceptable norms in the first language.

When we learn a foreign language, we don't have attitudes already established about the society the language operates in. Thus, we don't have prior attitudes about the appropriateness of the teacher; the teacher's status, age, and so forth; and we have only a minimal idea about the sociolinguistic rules of appropriate usage. It is important for planners to understand that whereas a foreign-language teacher has to be sure that the linguistic norm at each intermediate stage of learning conforms to the ideal final product, the teacher of the second language can be far more permissive (Lewis 1974:2150).

Problems of learning what is correct and what is incorrect are not at all as important in teaching or learning a second language as in learning a foreign language. However, learning another language to get along in society is quite different from learning a second language for higher education. In second-language learning for purposes of education beyond the primary level, the student has to be prepared to use the second language in reading and writing abstract material and in reading and writing material from outside the immediate speech community (if the language is an LWC). Second-language learning in this sense, though still different from foreign-language learning, needs to be handled yet differently.

Sometimes the teaching of a second language to students whose primary education has been in their mother tongues may be considered as occurring in a diglossic situation. In Arabic-speaking countries it is common practice to teach Arabic as a second language to people with other mother tongues *and* to people whose mother tongue is some form of colloquial Arabic in order to ensure the acquisition of the classical or "high" form of Arabic. To do well in society, however, a person needs to be able to use a "low" form of the language on the streets, with friends, on the town, and so forth. To the students of Arabic whose mother tongue is not Arabic, a range of extra vocabulary and a set of grammatical features not normally included in the standard classical Arabic course have to be taught so that the social use of the second language—that is, the social use of the "low" form—is also conveyed.

The language planner also needs to realize that translation from a first to a second language is an aspect of second-language learning. Learners use the mother tongue, or vernacular, as a point of reference for comprehension (Lane 1968:109). Since they already understand the culture through their first language, they continue to use that language to interpret many of the situations in which they use the second. The field of second-language learning is a fertile area in which persons interested in testing the Sapir-Whorf hypothesis might operate. What happens when a person uses a first language to interpret a situation involving second-language use, for instance?

One example of how translation from a first to a second language plays a role in a culture with a functioning second language can be seen in Tanzania. Abdulaziz (1978:138) reports a radio broadcast in which the English "He died of acute alcoholic poisoning" was rendered in Swahili first as *alifariki kwa kutokana na mvinyo mkali aliokunywa* (literally, "He died as a result of a strong alcoholic beverage which he drank") and later as *alikufa kwa kunywa pombe nyingi* (literally, "He died from drinking too much booze"). Swahili first-language speakers who have learned English as a second language would understand the second rendering to mean that the person who died was an alcoholic and that alcoholism caused his death. That interpretation would be largely due to the fact that the English idiom is to say that someone "drinks too much" when they mean that the person is an alcoholic. A monolingual Swahili speaker listening to the Swahili news broadcast would understand by the first statement that the person died because of the strength of a particular drink, either poison or alcohol; and by the second statement, that the person died because of drinking a large quantity of beer on a particular occasion.

Such Swahili equivalents for English phrases are produced on an ad hoc basis by people in news rooms who themselves know English as a second or third language (more often than not) and Swahili as a first (or a second) language. These people are under immediate pressure to translate the "hot" news stories that arrive in English directly into Swahili and broadcast them. Available English-Swahili dictionaries are not equal to the task, and it is up to the Swahili readers or listeners to "disambiguate the referential contents" of the news as best as they can. Such a task is almost impossible for an audience which does not know English as a second language! Thus, only those who are first-language speakers of Swahili *and* who also know

English as a second language are likely to get the intended meaning of a Swahili story on the news broadcast.

People who are translators from English to Swahili for the consumption of Swahili audiences are often in the habit of transferring complex journal-istic sentence structures from English directly into Swahili. The result is long, tedious, and hard-to-understand Swahili sentences. Thus, what people learn and use as a second language may influence how they use their first language. Swahili spoken by people who know English as a second language may be very difficult for Swahili monolinguals to understand. The lan-guage planner who suggests a second language as part of a plan needs to understand how second and foreign languages differ, how second lan-guages may influence first languages, and how contrastive analysis can be used as a tool for teaching a second language.

3.5   LANGUAGE PLANNING FOR SPECIAL PURPOSES

Now that we have seen the wide range of fields that impinge on language-planning processes and language-planning results, it remains for us to consider how language planning can be channeled to serve goals that may be narrower than nation building or establishing of ethnic solidarity— but which often ultimately achieve those same ends. Perhaps the broadest umbrella under which to place such activity is to subsume LP for special purposes in the category of modernization, an area we looked at briefly in connection with LP and standardization and LP and development.

In the sphere of modernization are included those aspects of LP that re-sult in the development of special-purpose dictionaries or special-purpose vocabularies for use in fields such as law and medicine (when "plain" language is not being attempted). Such modernization aspects of LP encompass what is generally known in the literature as LEXICAL ELABORA-TION activity.

It is not uncommon when a language policy is being implemented that the language in question cannot fulfill all its prospective roles the minute the policy is in effect. When this is the case, often technical language, scientific terms, philosophical and religious concepts, and the like have to be expressed for some time in a different language, foreign or second. Not only do special lexical items need to be added to the language being modernized so that it can play a number of roles, but also ways need to be found to express certain concepts or perceptions of logic and order that may never before have been expressed in the language (Passim 1968:447-8).

The language planner needs to realize that language processes such as lexical elaboration in the interest of modernization may be linked to other social processes. To advocate new terminology so that chemistry, for example, can be studied in a standard version of a widespread vernacular involves much more than just the activity of lexical elaboration. To so alter a standard means that another code or variety that has previously been used to teach chemistry (that is, a second language) has to be displaced. Thus the second language will no longer be required in order for a person to know chemistry, causing a decrease in power in that segment of the population which identifies with the second language. At the same time, it causes an increase in the power of those who know the standard (Fishman 1974:93).

Modernization of a language is considered in planning terms to be more a part of plan development than a manifestation of the effect the plan is intended to bring about. Modernization is a way of seeing that the desired effect of the deliberate language change being introduced takes hold and flourishes. In Kenya, for example, as part of the modernization of Swahili that accompanied the language policy to establish Swahili as the national language and optionally as an official language, a law is on the books that requires all menus in restaurants to be written in Swahili. At present, most menus are bilingual in Swahili and English; some are trilingual. For example, Chinese restaurants in Nairobi list their fare in Chinese characters, English, and Swahili. One Swahili-English menu in an Italian restaurant there lists "pizza" in this rendering of English into Swahili: *aina ya chapati ya Italia*, which translates back into English, literally, as "a kind or sort of Italian chapati." This translation would mystify both Swahili and English monolinguals, who might not be a part of the East African culinary scene where everybody knows that a *chapati* is a round, flat, unleavened bread made from wheat or gram (e.g., chick-pea) flour and used to accompany much of the Indian food (curries) that is Nairobi standard fare. The mental image conjured up by an Italian *chapati* is a marvel!

3.50   Lexical Elaboration and Linguistic Emancipation

Lexical elaboration may take place in order to equip a language to function in the modern world, aside from the needs dictated by scientific advances. One example can be seen in the way the Japanese language expresses a generic term that in English is paralleled by "the people." Japanese has many terms for referring to people. Some refer to people in particular capacities; others refer their social ranks; still others label people as biological organisms. None of the traditional terms, however, precisely evokes the sense of people as citizens endowed with rights (Passim 1968:447). The word *shomin* has traditionally referred to the common people, while *tami* has referred to subjects who owe allegiance to superiors. Rulers were expected to be kind to *tami*, but *tami* had no rights to benevolence. As modern political vocabulary developed, Japanese had no lexical item that could be used to mean people who have a right to be treated well by their government.

The language has another word, *heimin*, which had been used to refer to "ordinary people" in the sense of being from the lower social classes; so that could not serve the purpose either. *Kokumin*, another people word, is a compound made up of *koku*, "state or government," and *min*, "subject." This word still misses the need, in that its meaning connotes an entity subjugated by the state rather than a people in a cooperative relationship with their government. *Minzoku* is another compound, this time combining *min* with *zoku*, "family, group." It is the Japanese word used in a parallel sense to the English word *nationalism*. We see this word also in *minzoku-shugi*, which refers to the national or ethnic group character of the people, and in *minshu*, which used to describe the Japanese as a racial group. The term *shimin* (from *shi*, "city") has been suggested for "the people," but it would need to be stipulated that in a Japanese context the word should not have the same content or connotation as does the word *citizen*, which means "city people" in the West. Western "citizens" did arise from an experience that was urban—from the medieval city "with its corporate rights as against the king or the feudal power" (Passim, 1968:448), but the Japanese "people" did not develop through this process. In recent times another word, *jinmin* (from *jin*, "person, human"), has been suggested to closely approximate the idea of "the people" as the term is used in leftist societies.

This experience with trying to adapt Japanese to cope with the seemingly simple modern concept of "the people" indicates that lexical elaboration involves more than adding words to a language or extending the meaning of existing ones. It includes expanding a language's lexicon to express concepts that may have never before needed to be expressed in the language. Any language is suitable for expressing any human thought. Problems arise only when concepts from other cultures (easily expressed in the languages of those cultures) need to be expressed in one's language for the first time. In Japanese culture, "the people"—in the particular ideological sense discussed above—is an idea that traditionally had no need to be expressed. Now that it does, the language has no single lexical equivalent. It can either express the idea behind the concept in a phrase or a sentence, or it can try to produce a composite word using ideas expressed by single lexical items combined to express a new idea.

National language policy can be considered to have both an ideological and a technological aspect (Whiteley 1969:110). We have just seen how lexical elaboration may proceed to handle ideological changes in Japanese. Lexical elaboration also forms a major part of any policy's technological aspect since it is concerned with practical problems that affect the implementation of the plan's underlying ideology as expressed by language. For example: (1) new vocabularies have to be promulgated through the educational system, (2) teachers need to be taught to incorporate the new vocabularies in their teaching, and (3) scholars have to be found who can devise special terminologies such as technical or ideological vocabularies not previously available in the planned language.

The devising of terminologies for special purpose is lexical elaboration par excellence. Commonly, the language academy implementing a language policy will set up committees to prepare special dictionaries of legal terms, parliamentary terms, scientific terms, and so forth. One area in which particular attention has to be paid to lexical elaboration is in developing words to express political-economic concepts. "If the country wishes to utilize the resources and enthusiasm of its citizens to the full, then there must be a minimum of misunderstanding of the nature of the political and economic objectives involved in particular polities" (Whiteley 1969:118). In the case of Swahili in Tanzania, a good deal of lexical elaboration occurs via the journal *KiSwahili* published by the Institute for Swahili Research in Dar es Salaam. Issues of the journal have a feature called *Samiati*, "Vocabularies," wherein the latest specialized terms recommended for use in the national language are presented. As soon as specialized vocabularies appear in Swahili, it is expected that they will be used from that time on, replacing the technical vocabulary hitherto in force (usually English). It is felt that each new appearance of *Samiati* serves to make Tanzania more "free" linguistically from its British colonial past.

The idea of linguistic emancipation, then, is directly related to lexical elaboration. While the academy is in the process of modernizing the planned language, it may, either implicitly or explicitly, try to rid the language of linguistic traces of former rule as it works on extending and expanding the vocabulary. This desire for the political and social liberation of language goes back many years. In the eighteenth century, attempts were made in the case of Welsh to develop special vocabularies without the taint of English, Latin, or Greek. An eighteenth-century lexicologist admonished people making up words for shells in Welsh as follows:

> You must make your cregyn [shells] Welsh names. I'll send you a catalogue of the English names of some sales here . . . and it is an easy matter to invent new names, and I warrant they will be as well received as Latin or Greek names. Tell them they are old Celtic names; that is enough (quoted in Lewis 1978:345).

3.51   Extended Lexical Elaboration

Language planning may also be seen to apply to situations in which SPECIAL-PURPOSE LANGUAGES are devised and used. We may see this to be a kind of extended lexical elaboration. Business English, Caterpillar English, and technical English are examples.

Caterpillar English ("Caterpillar" refers to the company by that name that produces construction equipment) is a simplified form of English taught to Caterpillar Company (and other construction companies') employees with overseas contacts to use to communicate to the local non-English speaking employees in the host country. Technically the language is known either as Caterpillar Fundamental English (CFE) or as the SMART system, after the company that now markets the program. It is a technique for writing maintenance manuals in the construction-equipment industry. As a language, it has a limited vocabulary of job-related technical words, such as *bolt, blade, capscrew, generator,* all geared to equipment maintenance. A person writing in CFE uses only the fundamental vocabulary and follows the guildelines set out for keeping sentence structure simple, style consistent, and writing clear. Then, the vocabulary is taught to the personnel who will be servicing the equipment, wherever they live and whatever language they speak.

SMART Inc. now recommends CFE to other international companies for "product support." The company is expanding it as controlled English to Japan, the Middle East, and Asia while simultaneously devising computer programs to translate CFE into French, Spanish, and Portuguese. There are also plans to translate CFE into Japanese so it will not have to be exported to Japan as a simple form of English. Originally CFE was geared only to the Caterpillar brand of construction products, but SMART Inc. asserts that it is ready to adapt the language to other products or technology as necessary.

The Caterpillar Tractor Company, which exports a great deal of its construction equipment, originally devised CFE in 1971 because it "experienced all the problems that arise from communications with non-English speaking dealers and customers" (von Glasenapp n.d.:80) and wanted a solution that would make translation unnecessary. People who work on Caterpillar equipment learn to read and understand only CFE vocabulary and are not taught by the company to write or speak English for general use. By not requiring that everyone who uses Caterpillar products know English, the company greatly expanded the labor market of its distributors. Any person speaking any language could learn CFE, the idea goes, in order to service the equipment. CFE vocabulary does not exceed 850 words and thus is small enough to be easily learnable. No vocabulary exists for parts that can be illustrated. Vocabulary is taught to be recognized rather than read as language. However, a person who uses CFE needs to be literate in some language and must be a trained mechanic, familiar with Caterpillar products. The person also must be familiar with the illustrated Caterpillar parts and have taken the 30-lesson CFE course. In a somewhat chauvinistic vein, the company article on CFE as a special-purpose language states:

> The mechanic does not need any knowledge of proper pronunciation or grammar, or words like "babies, apples, milk, or sex." He could not go home and talk to his wife over supper in English" (von Glasenapp n.d.:82)

The people who devised CFE, though, feel that

> if and when this man would like to advance his knowledge of English, he will find that everything he learned is *correct, simple English* (82).

Caterpillar English can be considered to be a kind of lexical elaboration plan to provide a technical vocabulary of a certain type to a population that needs the vocabulary to handle an imported technology. From a planning standpoint, however, it would seem that a system of mutual exchange might better serve the public-relations aspect of international business in the language. Caterpillar employees learning CFE could teach English-speaking Caterpillar employees some of their local language as well.

Another type of special-purpose language is Business English. It is a simplified general form of English, a sort of constructed lingua franca taught to people who need to do business in English-speaking areas. Its vocabulary is geared especially to the particular business involved. Whereas Caterpillar English is geared to servicing equipment, Business English is more broad and is geared to conducting transactions. There is also "technical" or "scientific" English, a form of English used by international scientists to communicate with each other. To call this language English is a bit of a misnomer, since many of the scientific terms in English are borrowed from other languages such as Greek and Latin. Scientific English consists of a set of agreed-upon technical terms for worldwide use.

Special-purpose languages are simplified pidgins, in that their domain of functional usage is restricted to the specific task at hand. Tourists in Kenya, for example, use the Swahili of guide books. Employees of beach and game park hotels now use this special *safari* vocabulary in turn. This guide-book Swahili is a special-purpose language not common to the rest of East African culture. It is responsive to shifts in the tourist trade as well and lately has borrowed a number of vocabulary items from German, due to heavy traffic in German tourists especially on the Coast (Crampton 1979).

Also of interest to planners is the kind of special-purpose language that one group uses for its own interests, often unintentionally excluding outsiders. True linguistic emancipation would be achieved when everyone in a speech community had the "freedom" to understand everyone else. We mentioned earlier that certain professions, like law and medicine, keep the client/patient linguistically distinct from the practitioner. Such language use by professionals or technocrats (Rubin 1978, 1979) limits the accessibility of language to the rest of the population and is therefore "undemocratic." In the United States, the problem of "bureaucratese" has now been recognized and is being addressed by calls for plain English. In fact, former U.S. President Carter signed an executive order (number 12044, March 1978) "directing that federal regulations be written in 'simple and clear' language" (Rubin 1978:3). As long as it is recognized that "simple" and "clear" are two different things and that both are goals, such a move could be generally beneficial to American culture. It is now accepted quite commonly that professional jargons of any kind may go against the purpose the profession is trying to serve, particularly if interaction with nonprofessionals is involved. While professional jargons may foster a feeling of belonging to the in-group among the members of the "club," they may also isolate the "club" from the community it serves.

English for special purposes is a growing field, and efforts are being made to adapt English to an international context via CFE, Business English, scientific English, and so forth. However, little attention has been given so far to the need for Spanish for technocrats or for communicative competence in French by English speakers, for example. It is likely that LP and LP research in the coming years will be devoted increasingly to such areas of interlanguage competence.

3.6   SUMMARY

Economic theory and economic variables have been seen to serve as input to the language-planning process. Likewise anthropology, in showing how the linguistic and cultural milieu of planning is crucial in language choice and policy formation, serves as planning input. If LP ignores world view, it cannot succeed. The linguist's explanation of how language change takes place is also useful to planning changes that will actually occur. These LP-related fields of economics, anthropology, and linguistics not only provide theoretical input to LP but also contribute to the planners' knowledge of what the effects of LP are and how they may be brought about.

We saw how the anthropological linguist provides the planner with the means of language standardization. We saw how educators and linguists have arrived at techniques for bringing about literacy and second-language acquisition. We also saw how planners can find out how to modernize languages by looking at new "applied" areas of linguistic and cultural concern, such as the field of developing special-purpose languages.

We saw how language planning needs to be concerned with the language-related areas of social change. We saw how planning for linguistic homogeneity may relate to economic development and modernization. We also saw that language shift may be a desirable goal in the interest of economic development, whereas in other sociopolitical contexts a plan to maintain the linguistic status quo may be the best path to modernization. We saw that maintenance is often preferable to shift in rural areas, with the reverse case being true in cities—largely due to differences in rural-urban economics.

In the interest of social change, we examined the role of the anthropological linguist in standardizing languages so that they may be used by literate people in the modern world and so that literacy (and thereby modernization) may be brought to nonliterate people for the first time. We saw this particular aspect of LP to be corpus planning, that is, doing something to the corpus, or body, of a language. The term CORPUS PLANNING extends to most areas of planning for social change—to literacy training, standardization, second-language teaching, and lexical elaboration. LP for social change as corpus planning takes three forms: graphization, modernization, and standardization. Modernization in the corpus-planning sense is generally lexical elaboration; for most purposes, the two terms do not need to be distinguished.

Language standardization is primarily a process of codifying a language. To standardize a language it is necessary to analyze and describe it and provide an acceptable writing and spelling system for it. The codification process also requires that the standard devised be sensitive to the cultural complexity of the area in which it will be used. Codification was seen in Chapter One to be part of the policy aspect of LP. When a language is codified as part of the standardization process so it can be used as part of a language policy, it is also necessary that historical and cultural materials be prepared in the language to record traditions representative of the area and the people. This process provides that a continuous culture accompany the language, contributing to the development of an ethnic or cultural identity (with a primordial basis) for the language users.

Language planners need to consider the question of language and social change as related to attempts to change the way people construe their world. When language communicates culture, language change may be seen to communicate culture change.

Language changes that occur as a form of social change are the concern of a certain group of sociolinguists who study exactly how systematic language change takes place. It has been found that language change is closely related to social values. People adopt forms that have prestige. It has also been found that language change takes place far more rapidly than people used to think it did. When the linguist looks at language change, the change needs to be seen as a transition, embedded in a social class context, which becomes evaluated as either prestigious or not. If prestige is attached to a form, it is adopted, otherwise it dies out. Prestige forms picked up by one group are then generalized throughout the speech community.

All language choice and language policy is promulgated through a society's educational system. Overt language policy figures most prominently in education in multilingual settings and in areas where second languages, as opposed to foreign languages, are functioning. Language planning is an aspect of all education—in the form of literacy training, a universal school responsibility.

It has been the purpose of this chapter to show that the language planner who carries out a plan with certain political and social implications (as discussed in Chapter Two) needs to also be aware of the change-related aspects of the plan that impinge on the schools, the culture, the economy, the language itself, and the people who will use the language for their own special purposes and personal ends.

So far, we have seen that LP is the study of how language is used as a tool in nations and states and how it behaves when it occurs in the context of social change. The discussion to follow of how language planning developed as a complex interdisciplinary form of language study will serve as a background to Chapter Five and Chapter Six, where we will examine the nature of LP theory and LP method, respectively.

Chapter Four

THE HISTORY OF LANGUAGE-PLANNING STUDY

4.0 INTRODUCTION

The field of language planning is just a little over twenty years old. Since it is such a new field, the practice of LP and LP theory have not had time to come together. As we have seen so far, one of the biggest names in this developing field is Joshua Fishman. Fishman was at the University of Pennsylvania in 1958–59 when he responded to a U.S. Census Bureau questionnaire by suggesting that the language questions be revised for the national census of 1960 (Fishman 1972:xii). With this suggestion began his campaign to see that data on the status of non-English languages used by United States ethnic and religious groups be systematically collected. If such data were available, Fishman thought, we could find out what language-related problems existed in the United States and what workable recommendations could be made to the government for preserving the country's linguistic resources.

This suggestion led to Fishman's 1966 book *Language Loyalty in the United States*, one of the first works of scholarship to consider language planning as a scientific endeavor in a social context. Ever since the publication of *Language Loyalty*, Fishman has worked in conjunction with a number of other scholars to carry out language-planning projects at both the national and international levels.

Prior to the 1960s, the languages used in social and political contexts were assumed to be accidents of fate—facts or situations that simply exist and about which nothing can or should be done. The concept of *planning* language use had not yet been born. The idea that language problems might underlie social and political problems had not gained currency, particularly insofar as anyone thought solutions to language problems might lead to the alleviation of sociopolitical conflicts.

This is not to say that language planning was not an implicit area of concern before 1960. In the pages to follow we will see what types of studies provided a background for the field of LP. We will then look at the development of LP practice between 1960 and now and sketch a history of LP theory, to be discussed in more detail in Chapter Five.

The ongoing history of LP is being documented in a series of books on *Language Science and National Development* edited by Anwar S. Dil and sponsored by the Linguistic Research Group of Pakistan. There is also a *Language Planning Newsletter,* edited by Joan Rubin and published by the East-West Center of the University of Hawaii. The "Guide to Information Resources in Language Planning" appended to the present book is taken from a 1979 issue of that Newsletter. In the series edited by Dil the works of notable LP scholars are collected and reproduced. All contributors to the series provide "Author's Postscripts" in which they comment on their careers in historical perspective. Three volumes that appeared in 1972 are of particular importance to LP history. One contains the writings of Einar Haugen and is called *The Ecology of Language.* Another has a collection of Fishman's essays and is titled *Language in Sociocultural Change.* A third, which contains articles by Wallace Lambert, is called *Language, Psychology and Culture.* As we trace the growth of LP, we will be relying heavily on the ideas of Haugen, Fishman, and Lambert as collected in these books.

In the work of Lambert, the importance of LANGUAGE ATTITUDES affecting language planning in bilingual and bicultural settings is stressed. Lambert's work contains a basic *credo,* as Dil calls it: Bilingualism is not a handicap but an advantage; people can successfully become both bicultural and bilingual. It is important to understand, though, that people's attitudes toward the group whose language they are learning have an important effect on the acquisition of the language. These attitudes are related to *why* people are learning the language and *what* they expect to gain from having learned it.

Styles of language use need to be understood also. In those areas where people use a second language, the situations of first- versus second-language use may constitute arenas of "social prejudice and unfair discrimination." Language planners need to see how to build antidiscrimination safeguards into educational, social, and political systems. To do this they must realize that "the study of bilingualism as a personal and social phenomenon, especially in situations of conflict, is a critical area of psycholinguistic and sociolinguistic inquiry" (Lambert 1972:xiii–xiv).

Lambert's notion of language attitudes as changeable, that is, plannable, underlies the definition of LP that guided research during the 1970s. To deliberately change language, it is necessary to change the attitudes people have toward language. In accord with Lambert's credo that language barriers can be overcome, it is necessary to alter educational, social, and political contexts of language use in such a way as to generate attitudes toward language that are favorable to change. We can prepare a nation's people to receive and accept a national language, and we can alter a community's social structure to shift prestige values among different language varieties.

We can also trace the beginnings of LP and predict its future course by consulting the twelfth volume of the series *Current Trends in Linguistics* (edited by Thomas A. Sebeok), the section entitled "Linguistics and Adjacent Arts and Sciences." That volume appeared in 1974 and contains a discussion of language planning up to that point in time. It refers to language planning as an emerging branch of sociolinguistics that draws on fields that hitherto had been seen as distinct from linguistics. Such fields include sociology, education, and the other areas we have already looked at, especially in Chapters Two and Three.

When we regard LP as being a mere twenty years old, we are referring to the role of scholars and of linguistic-oriented research in the planning process. In Chapter One, we looked at the role of language academies in codifying, cultivating, and elaborating language policy. Language academies, in one form or another, go back for centuries. Grammarians and governments would make pronouncements as to what should or should not be admissible new words or officially sanctioned languages. The Welsh case cited on page 99 above in which seventeenth-century lexicographers were urged to use Welsh words for shells in preference to borrowing words from English, shows an implicit form of LP that has undoubtedly been with us as long as diversified languages have been known. Swahili language policy from 1890 to 1940 has been traced through documents attesting to the variable use of the language during that time (Wright 1965).

4.1   BACKGROUND

Whereas LP as we now know it is a twentieth-century endeavor, the activities of LP may be construed to have a much longer history. Reese asserts that "one may speculate upon such an ancient artifact as the Rosetta Stone as an example of the recognition of a need for coexisting official languages" (1981:40). Pre-twentieth-century activities suggestive of LP can be seen to be of two types—"the rashly ideal" and "the starkly pragmatic" (40). The ideal-type plans are represented by the many early efforts to come up with international languages as universal systems of communication. The pragmatic type of LP activity may be seen in the work of the language academies, which go back as far as the sixteenth century.

Language academies all performed standardization activities and provided an institutional means to deal with changing needs in the language, whether those needs were lexical elaboration, orthographic simplification, textbook creation, or others. The range of language needs served by an academy end up being precisely the goals of modern LP. In today's terms, these goals include standardization, simplification, codification, elaboration— in other words, the basic concerns of the language planner (Reese 1981).

The people seeking ideal languages hoped to replace natural languages with totally new symbol systems that might represent ideas more directly. This goal still persists, particularly in the current move to develop Loglan, a logical language. There is also a recent attempt to devise an international gesture language called Gestuno, aimed at being culture-free. The nineteenth century saw a number of efforts to devise auxiliary languages for world communication. These languages tended to be made up of "pieces of natural languages and bits of inspiration" and designed to be used as universally understood second languages (Reese 1981:43). Esperanto is one of the few languages of this kind that has had a long-standing following. It is too soon to know whether special-purpose languages such as Caterpillar English, intended to be universally applicable, will succeed. The attempt to devise the international gestural Gestuno is likewise too new to be evaluated.

Most of modern LP owes its recent history to the language academies. It is thus more a child of its practical ancestor than of its idealistic forebear. Its practical ancestor gave rise to its parent discipline, linguistics, which has merged in modern approaches with sociology.

Today, LP, unlike the broader aspects of the sociology of language, is "a byproduct of very recent and still ongoing developments in its two parent disciplines, linguistics and sociology" (Fishman 1968d:3). One such development is the discovery that linguistic differences that were hitherto considered random, unsystematic, and not scientifically interesting are now being understood to follow rules. These variable rules state under which situations certain forms are used or prohibited. The discovery that language use is patterned and that it varies with behavior and context led to the idea that something could be done to language to avoid or solve language-related social and political problems. Linguists could become "even better prepared to struggle with literary problems, problems of nonstandard ('dialect') speakers, problems of societal second-language learning, and problems of language planning and language policy than they might otherwise be" (4).

The further discovery that patterned or rule-governed language use covaries with patterned social variation led sociologists to begin to think that language might provide clues to social change and to think of language change itself as a form of social change. The field of LP may be seen in this light to have started with a concern for language problems in multiethnic settings. This is the area of concern expressed in Fishman's desire to see what problems in the United States stemmed from differential language use in various ethnic and religious communities.

In a different vein, in the 1930s members of the Prague School of Linguistics in Czechoslovakia were showing concern about the kinds of language problems that arise as a nation or state develops. According to the Prague linguists, when the nation-building process occurs language becomes an object of people's attention, reflections, and emotions. It begins to be "cultivated." When LANGUAGE CULTIVATION is taking place, it is accompanied by "an increase of systematic interventions by society in language development" (Johnson 1978:35). That is, language planning takes place. "Language law," "language pedagogy," and "language perfection" are labels used by the Prague School to refer to types of social intervention in language development. A type of intervention (that is, a particular plan) would be chosen depending on what particular problem needed to be addressed in a given sociopolitical context "with the gradual democratization of culture in general and language in particular" (35).

The Prague linguists of the 1930s saw themselves in the role of a Czech language academy. The introductory issue of the journal published in the thirties by the Prague Linguistic Circle states that

> Czech linguistics must take the initiative in solving the immediate problems of language cultivation. The scattered efforts of individual linguists do not suffice here: the urgency of the tasks call for a collective organized unity of scientific forces. Isolated activity on the part of linguists is insufficient; their close cooperation with pedagogues and lawyers, with philosophers and psychologists, with psychiatrists and phonoartists, with historians and theoreticians of literature and art in general, with professionals in sociology, history, geography, and ethnography is indispensable. Primarily, however, cooperation is needed with the practical agents of language cultivation, with writers and translators, with agents for theater, film, and radio, both artistic and technical, with professionals in education and workers in administration and technology, all those who have practical experience with questions concerning terminology (Johnson 1978:37).

This Praguian concern with language cultivation lies behind many later efforts to standardize language. In fact, many of the Prague School recommendations about how to cope with language problems in changing societies "are remarkably up-to-date and are clearly applicable to many language-planning situations in today's world" (Garvin, trans., 1973:102). Prague linguists in the thirties consciously sought to foster the development of a Czech language and, by so doing, provided a number of insights useful to language standardizers elsewhere in the world.

The standardization of a dominant language (as advocated in Prague) and attention to minority language problems in their social settings (as advocated by Fishman in the United States) are the two main strands of LP research undertaken from the 1960s on. Haugen's 1959 definition of LP sees standardization as the main focus of LP. Jernudd and Das Gupta saw the LP of the 1960s as placing a primary emphasis on solving multilingual problems. We will see that in the 1970s the thrust of LP research shifted. LP came to be regarded as a conscious, predictive approach to changes in language and language use (Rubin and Jernudd, 1971). That is, LP was defined as the efforts made to effect deliberate language change. The 1980s began with research finally beginning to heed Haugen's 1966 plea that LP ought to focus on the evaluation of linguistic change as well as on ways to bring it about.

Thus, during LP's twenty-year history the orientation moves from seeing planning chiefly as a tool of standardization (1935–1959), to seeing it as the study of language problems and their solutions (1960s), to the study and practice of managing language change (1970s), to an awareness that it is necessary to evaluate language change, given the nature of the context in which it occurs (multiethnic, supranational, and the like).

From the outset, LP looked both at language standardization (in keeping both with Haugen's definition and with the Prague idea of cultivation) and at language problems in complex societies where a standard already prevails.

Once LP became a field in its own right in the 1960s, emphasis began to shift to actual language planning, both in its problem-solving and standardization aspects. It quickly became clear that Europe and the United States were not alone in their need to deal with language issues, and attention shifted to include research in developing as well as developed nations.

We will see that in the 1970s, when emphasis changed to planning for change rather than planning for problem-solving purposes per se, research looked both at developing, or emerging, nations *and* at established political entities in order to see how different language varieties might figure in prospective plans and how planning could be accomplished by religious, ethnic, and political authorities.

A pioneering LP research effort is Einar Haugen's 1938 work entitled *Language and Immigration.* Haugen bemoaned the fact that the "homelessness" of immigrants straddling two cultures is largely due to linguistic difficulties: "even linguists have often regarded the dialects of the immigrant as beneath their dignity" (1938:2). The few studies done on immigrant dialects before the 1930s were surveyed in H. L. Mencken's *American Language* (1936), and the general finding was that each language had "taken over elements from American English" and had "been forced to adapt itself to new conditions" (2). Haugen documents the "usual" reaction to the linguistic adaptation of immigrants as "scorn or amusement." People either looked down on or made fun of people with foreign accents. Haugen called for full and adequate treatments of the linguistic experiences of immigrant groups as a way to find out how to combat the adverse reactions.

In his research, Haugen analyzed the speech of Norwegians who settled in America. He undertook this study as a step toward seeing that the "living sources" of foreign speech in our country are "tapped" before "it is too late" and they are dried up. He urged investigators to "prepare a list of words which will bring out the chief features of the Norwegian dialect of the speaker, so that it may be possible to determine the extent of its change in America, and its relationship to other dialects" (Haugen 1938:3). This plea has become a basic methodological tenet in the study of language change in multiethnic communities. That is, we need to know what characterizes the native dialect of the immigrant in order to see how those characteristics are carried over into the immigrant's English as well as how certain features change in the native dialect.

In Norway, as in many other parts of the world, language is and has been an index of social situation. Haugen's observation that "forms that smacked of the country" (1938:5) were ridiculed is one of the first enunciations of the notion of PRESTIGE as a factor of LANGUAGE ATTITUDE, a value prominently heeded in the LP research of today. Most Norwegians who immigrated to the United States spoke a modified country dialect (circa 1850). Those who were also literate in Norwegian used "the official Dano-Norwegian of the nineteenth century." Haugen referred to this as LINGUISTIC DUALISM, and he saw the spoken and institutional language varieties to be "one of the outstanding facts about the Norwegians in America" (8). Since Haugen's pioneering study, such dualism has been seen to be an outstanding fact in a number of other planning situations elsewhere in the world, especially where mother tongues exist alongside a different school language and where diglossia is present.

Another major LP fact brought out in Haugen's work is that early immigrants in the United States had few linguistic or social problems because they kept to themselves. More frequent contact with people speaking other languages plus increasing complexity in the social structure of the immigrant communities themselves led to changes in language attitudes. People have ideas about the worth of their own language vis-à-vis the languages spoken by others, and they develop views about the relative position of their social dialect as well. The idea that language problems arise only when language and social contacts take place lies behind the Fishman distinction between linguistically homogeneous and linguistically heterogeneous societies (discussed earlier).

Language contact and increasingly complex social organization within the immigrant community led to Norwegian being replaced by English among the Norwegians living in the United States. One of Haugen's main findings was that it is possible to "trace the parallel development of language and social circumstance in practically every phase of life" (1938:11) and that more such studies should be done in order to understand and solve the types of language problems that occur in multiethnic communities.

Language is one of the most serious problems an immigrant has. By seeing how immigrants use language in a new environment, we can see how they gradually move, in social terms, to a point where their former national identity or sense of group membership blends into American society. As Haugen sees it, the process is not easy on the people involved:

> Many heartaches and bewilderments have assailed the immigrant, and no one can wonder that he has often resisted the melting pot. The social life of his native group has given him a home and a standing in the new nation and has been a solid protection to his mental health (1938:12).

Thus, in addition to observing that language and society covary, that prestige and language attitude relate to language change, that linguistic dualism exists, and that language problems arise as social structure becomes more complicated, Haugen's 1938 work also enunciated the importance of language as a factor of ethnic identity.

Haugen credits the idea of the importance of language in ethnicity to Michael West, an early scholar of bilingualism who worked in India. Back in 1926, West stated:

> The small group is the natural protection of the individual soul, and the small language or dialect is the natural and important distinguishing feature of the small group, anything which, while common to the group, tends to differentiate it from other groups tends to intensify the sense of solidarity and of distinctness. Of all instruments for the intensification of group individuality, language is undoubtedly the most powerful (quoted in Haugen 1938:17).

The Norwegian-American situation also brought to light a number of features of language change that figure in planning. One of these is LEVELING. With the younger generation of immigrants, contact with others takes place in school, at play, and eventually at work. The older immigrants, on the other hand, tend to stick together. As the younger people would interact more with the outside world, modification of their original dialect would begin to take place and their speech would start to diverge from that of their elders. Immigrants from many different dialect areas in the "old country" would come to know each other in the "new country"; eventually, one dialect of Norwegian would begin to prevail over the others as the one immigrant dialect. What Haugen calls "conspicuous forms" would begin to be phased out or "leveled." The forms that people would agree to use in place of those leveled out "would not be book forms but such popular dialect forms as would have the greatest prestige on account of their wide currency" (Haugen 1938:16). When we discussed Labov's work, we saw that he also found that people adopt speech usage according to what they feel to be prestigious or popular regardless of what stratum of society the usage may have originated in.

Another phenomenon related to leveling is that of language SHIFT, whereby words in one language are totally replaced by words from another or whereby part of the meaning of a word in one language is taken over by another word. For example, an English word might enter Norwegian, not replacing the Norwegian equivalent but displacing part of its meaning:

> The Norwegian *kjeller*, like English "cellar," referred to a dark, damp place and was obviously inappropriate when referring to a church basement; so English "basement" was adopted, but not "cellar" (Haugen 1938:20).

Processes such as shift and leveling realigned Norwegian vocabulary in the direction of English. By noting the categories of words to which shifts apply, we can see culture change in progress and make predictions about the path of likely culture change; for example:

> It is a matter of course that words for all types of machinery that had come into general use since the beginning of immigration were overwhelmingly English, from the reaper and the binder to railroad, automobile, and radio (Haugen 1938:22).

If an immigrant comes in contact with a radio for the first time in his life in the United States, there is no reason to come up with a word for it in Norwegian. As the radio becomes a part of immigrant culture, the word for it becomes part of the person's language.

Haugen, again foreshadowing Labov's views on language change, noted that "The social-linguistic shift of the immigrant may best be observed by taking a single activity and watching its transformation through the years" (Haugen 1938:24). The reconstruction of the process of linguistic assimilation through time is possible if we "find informants whose language dates back to the first generation of Norwegian settlement and who are admirable fossil specimens of the language of those years" (29).

Labov's ideas about how language change took place on Martha's Vineyard (see Chapter Three) were based on a number of the ideas first expressed in Haugen's study of language and immigration. Labov studied three generations of Vineyardians and found that the old-timers centralized *aw* and *ay* while the new people ("immigrants," in a sense) adopted only a centralized version of *aw* and outsiders used *aw* and *ay* as in standard English. In both Labov's and Haugen's studies language change was observed as it happened. To see language change in progress we must consider successive generations of speakers, members of different social groups, and speakers from different geographical areas.

A significant contribution to LP development after 1960 was Uriel Weinreich's work entitled *Language in Contact* (1953). This study stresses the importance of describing what takes place when two or more languages impinge on each other. Weinreich is credited by Haugen (1965:209, n. 1) as being the first person to use the term LANGUAGE PLANNING. "Language planning" was the title of a seminar Weinreich gave at Columbia University in 1957. But Haugen is the first person to use the term in scholarly literature. In his article "Planning for a Standard Language in Modern Norway" (1959), he used the term LANGUAGE PLANNING "to describe the efforts in Norway, over the past century, to achieve a language expressive of nationalistic individuality" (Karam 1974:104–05). Norway's efforts to develop a national language were seen as an "experiment in language planning." In this article Haugen provides the definition of LP as "the activity of preparing a normative orthography, grammar, and dictionary for the guidance of writers and speakers in a nonhomogeneous speech community" (Haugen 1959:8).

In 1959, LP was conceived of as normative linguistics (compare with applied sociolinguistics as discussed in Chapter Two). By describing how Norway dealt with reconciling *Landsmål*, a "national language" designed to be entirely Norwegian, and *Riksmål*, a "state language" with Danish and Norwegian components, Haugen showed "that social pressure for linguistic change can be created and channeled through official organs" (Haugen 1959:142). Literally, *Riksmål* refers to the "language of the realm" (Dano-Norwegian) while *Landsmål* is "country language." Today these terms have been replaced by *Bokmål*, "book language," and *Nynorsk*, "neo-Norwegian," respectively. Haugen knew that the idea of language planning or engineering would be anathema to many linguists, but he believed that a sensible approach to effecting language change by conscious planning could solve a number of sociopolitical problems hitherto ignored:

> Although linguists generally bridle at the suggestion that language can be tampered with, it is here shown that given sufficient motivation, written and possibly spoken language like any other social phenomenon can be deliberately guided and changed. Whether the effects of government planning in this field, as in other parallel fields of social life, will be permanent and thoroughgoing, or only superficial, remains to be seen. About all the government can do is to create an atmosphere favorable to certain kinds of linguistic change, and recognize that there are forces that escape government regulation (Haugen 1959:142–43, as in Haugen 1972).

Just prior to the 1960s and the years in which LP took off, the 1951 UNESCO report on world language situations also appeared on the scene.

The ten language situations defined in that report with regard to language choices in mulilingual societies (see Chapter One) guided much of later LP research in that area. That UNESCO report entitled "The Use of Vernacular Languages in Education" also figures significantly in LP history, since it sets out to allege the *universal* "reasons why education should, if at all possible, be provided in the Mother Tongue" (Jernudd and Rubin 1971:318) and also delineates the variables constraining the implementation of such a policy.

Finally, by way of background to the rise of LP as a scientific field, we have the practical point to make that, like all new disciplines, LP is necessarily interdisciplinary during its early phase, and has arisen in many respects in response to limitations in its antecedent disciplines. The world of 1960 was ripe for LP. In the 1960s there were many complex stratified societies that had given rise to social differences laden with "covert conflicts of interest" (Kjolseth 1978:800). These conflicts of interest were becoming transformed into "overt social issues," which became problems needing solutions (800). LP arose as a way to solve such problems that involved language. In the post-1960 world "with the development of new supra-national forms of economic organization, the whole question of regional and national development has arisen, and there appears to be a well-articulated awareness that many of the problems involved are related to language" (803).

Thus the history of LP must record the fact that its origin lies not so much in the fact that problems of language as it relates to society are "intrinsically interesting," but that they "are related to large and pervasive social issues as currently conceived" (Kjolseth 1978:803).

4.2   THE 1960s: LANGUAGE PROBLEMS

In studying language-planning processes, we can consider language as something subject to manipulation by a vast array of people, ranging from language-change specialists to the general population, whose attitudes, myths, and reactions to language bring about change (Rubin 1973:v). One of the main foci of LP research in the 1960s was the relationship between language and ethnic relations, an inquiry spurred by Fishman's desire to see how language figured as a "problem" or "resource" among various groups in the United States. Fishman felt that by studying various stages in the development of feelings of ethnicity we could determine the relationship of that development to forms of language behavior (1965:105). This phase of LP research consisted mainly of studies showing the parallels between socially complex and linguistically complex situations. In these years developed the idea that different types of linguistic communities exist

(Gumperz 1962). Later this notion of linguistic-community types emerges in the concepts of endoglossic, exoglossic, heterogeneous, and homogeneous linguistic communities (discussed in Chapter Two).

In our earlier discussion of types of linguistic communities, we saw that LP and ethnicity concerns center on sociologically based considerations of language (1) as a factor of ethnic identity, (2) as a marker of social class, and (3) as a reflection of status and mobility in a multilingual context. The study of LP in the 1960s became the study of how societal language problems might be solved. LP was no longer primarily the activity of preparing a language to serve a social function (in a national, official, or other role, à la Haugen 1959) as it had been earlier. The problem-solving aspect of LP in the 1960s was more theoretical in nature. The study focused first on multilingualism within a constituted nation or state (as seen in Fishman's *Language Loyalty in the United States*) and later on the language-related issues faced by developing nations (as seen in Fishman, Ferguson, and Das Gupta's *Language Problems of Developing Nations*).

The activity-oriented practical LP of Haugen's approach that aimed at creating standard languages gave way to the problem-solving policy or outcome-oriented approach of the 1960s. Problem-oriented LP served more to generate ideas about problem-solving procedures than to create solutions. Some of the theoretical concepts of LP developed so far came from proposed alternative solutions to language problems in multiethnic communities in developed or developing nations. The LP scholars Björn Jernudd and Jyotirindra Das Gupta called for "organized efforts to find solutions to societal language problems" (Fishman 1974:1758). Thus, research since the 1960s has yielded a number of case studies identifying societal language problems and documenting how they were handled. Einar Haugen's 1966 case study of LP in Norway yielded the concepts of selection, codification, elaboration, implementation, and evaluation that are central to all forms of LP acknowledged today. The 1960s was a period of growing interest in seeing how language policy is formed and implemented and how language development proceeds as a kind of development planning.

In 1966, a conference on language problems was held, and in 1968 the papers from that conference appeared in a volume edited by Joshua Fishman, Charles Ferguson, and Jyotirindra Das Gupta entitled *Language Problems of Developing Nations*, which is a good reflection of what the field of LP was like in the 1960s. The rationale for the collection of papers was to rectify the "sad fact of American academic life" that at that time no American university had a program to train students for "either theoretical or applied involvement in the language problems of developing nations" (Fishman, Ferguson, and Das Gupta 1968:x). The editors of the volume bemoaned the fact that most American linguists of the 1960s were "only

marginally interested in language development (language policy, graphization, standardization, modernization, planning)" (x). They lamented that
"most sociologists and political scientists are just becoming aware of
language as an aspect of societal and national functioning." They saw sociolinguistics as "still a very fragile flower" (x). They hoped that their book
would stimulate the growth of LP as a branch of sociolinguistics. Many of
the language problems that came to light in the 1960s have, as yet, no
solutions.

First, the role of political authorities in language planning needs to be
understood. Colonial rulers were not bothered by LP problems because
they had little interest in establishing communication ties throughout their
territories. As national political authorities began to replace colonial ones, it
became desirable to foster national communities and "this naturally involved the politicization of selective group loyalties, including language
loyalty" (Das Gupta 1968:23).

In addition to the emergence of problems relating language loyalty and
political authority, it also became clear that languages that are to be
politically sanctioned in the interest of development need to be purified,
reformed, and modernized in order to keep pace with the nation's development. As a consequence, the concepts of graphization, modernization,
and standardization as language development emerged as important "although the factors making for success and failure in such planning [were]
not clear" (Ferguson 1968:34). The work of the 1980s will be to attempt to
measure planning success or failure. We can see graphization, modernization, and standardization as extensions, in the planning arena, of the
Prague concept of language cultivation.

Another LP problem that began to be faced in the 1960s was how to
choose a national language in ethnically complex states where no obvious
choice exists. In some cases it might be found appropriate to use a lingua
franca as a solution. Fishman saw that many developing "new nations" will
need to stress "nationism (rather than nationalism) and *diglossia* involving an
LWC (language of wider communication) rather than monoglossia" (Fishman 1968f:47). The choice of an LWC or a lingua franca and the maintenance of two or more varieties of a language are practical responses to
efforts to avoid ethnic rivalries in the process of nation-building. The
language/nation typologies discussed in Chapters One and Two were
intended as guides to planners needing to make these decisions.

The 1960s also saw a number of efforts toward determining the factors
that contribute to likely language maintenance and language shift as nations
develop on a continuum from ethnicity to nationality (also see Chapter
Two). The notion of shift was seen to be opposed to that of maintenance,
and both phenomena were seen to be related to factors of linguistic
complexity or uniformity.

Another idea that developed in the 1960s is the distinction between ABSTAND and AUSBAU languages. This distinction was made by Heinz Kloss in 1967 and characterizes languages as being distinct for either linguistic or social reasons. Speech varieties that constitute distinct languages on linguistic grounds are ABSTAND (from the German, meaning "different, contrasting") languages. Speech varieties that constitute distinct languages on sociological grounds are AUSBAU ("improved, extended") languages. Ausbau languages, then, are those that have been subjected to planning; they have been "reshaped by deliberate action in order to become distinct standardized tools of literary expression" (Jernudd and Rubin 1971:312). In other words, ausbau languages are cultivated languages in the Prague sense.

According to Kloss, DIALECTIZATION is "the reversal of the status of an ausbau language" (312). In a sense, dialectization is a contraction rather than an extension of a language. Thus, dialectization may be seen, in many instances, as the source of language problems in multilingual societies. The development of social dialects (as discussed in previous chapters) within a centralized polity exemplifies dialectization of an ausbau language. In contrast, abstand languages are those that exist where planning is not yet an issue, in the sense of functionally allocating different languages or different varieties of languages. Abstand languages are generally found in linguistically homogeneous areas and often in areas where no central political authority nor a need for one exists. In the modern world, abstand languages—as pure, distinct, and unaffected by contact with other languages—are becoming increasingly rare.

The kinds of problems developing nations have, then, center on the conflict between the acceptance of an ausbau (or planned, extended) language for the society as a whole and the pull of various dialectization processes from a number of different ethnic, social, and religious spheres seeking to achieve or maintain distinctiveness.

India provides a good example of the language problems that were seen as needing to be addressed by LP research of the 1960s. Post-independence India encountered a number of problematic situations in regard to language: a national language had to be chosen, questions about the status of all languages in the country with respect to each other had to be answered, the choice of orthography presented problems, and many minority groups desired linguistic autonomy. Such problems are usually seen to be mainly cultural or political issues unrelated to "mass communication, social mobility, social control, and other aspects of socioeconomic development" (Das Gupta and Gumperz 1968:151). It became the task of LP to show how such language problems can be solved only by seeing them in their social context.

Thus in the 1960s, sociolinguists recognized that any planned political or

social development involves a language choice, that one or more languages
need to be promoted and accepted.
The issues of the LP research of the 1960s may also be seen in West
Africa, where

> in the great area between Yaoundé, the capital of the Cameroun Republic, and
> Dakar, the capital of Senegal, from 500 to 1,000 different languages are spoken,
> and that these languages are typically divided into many different dialects. These
> languages are important to the people who speak them and who, speaking them,
> become complete human beings. So important, indeed, are their respective
> languages that people make them the very symbol and banner of the cultural and
> tribal differences that today rack Africa, as they have done and still do in other
> places as well. Thus it is obvious that when we discuss language problems of
> developing nations, we are not merely discussing cabinet and ministry decisions,
> the recommendations of international conferences, the statistics of examination
> results, and the experience of pilot teaching projects. People still kill each other
> over language questions, and not merely because of their failure to understand
> each other as they are thrust into closer contact by the conditions of modern life
> (Armstrong 1968:227).

Language-planning research of the 1960s focused not only on problems
of standardization as opposed to linguistic ethnicity in centralized societies,
but also sought to understand the factors underlying language attitudes in
complex societies in order to find clues to solving language problems.
Wallace Lambert is well known for his approach to multilingualism from a
social-psychological perspective. He developed a technique for measuring
language attitudes that "calls out the stereotyped impressions that members of one ethnic-linguistic group hold of another contrasting group"
(1967:222–23). These identified attitudes may be used by planners to
suggest directions of policy. That bilinguals have incorporated these language attitudes can be seen in their ability to predict the reactions of others
when they use one language in certain contexts and another in different
ones. Bilinguals know how they are seen or stereotyped by others when
they use each of their languages. One language is good for some purposes,
the second one is proper for others. Bilinguals receive "social feedback"
that allows them to realize that they are perceived differently depending on
which language they use (223).
    National language planners or people seeking to standardize language
and solve language problems in developing nations are well advised to
foster favorable stereotypes for the chosen language(s) and engineer prestige as social feedback. Lambert's language-attitude work introduced the
idea that both INSTRUMENTAL and INTEGRATIVE MOTIVES for learning and
using a second language are important. People with instrumental motives
want a second language because it can be used as a tool to get them what

they want; for instance, helping them get ahead in their occupation. People with integrative motives want the second language so they can fit into the larger society better or learn more about the other cultural community (1967:225). If we want to foster language development in line with planned policy, we need to see that the people the plan involves are appropriately motivated to accept the plan. We need to be sure that they have positive attitudes toward the chosen language(s). Positive attitudes are tied to whether instrumental or integrative motives underlie language learning. According to Lambert, if we are to successfully learn a language spoken by a different social group, we have to be willing and able to adopt various other aspects of that group's behavior as well. Our feelings for our own group and our preconceptions of the other group will determine our success in learning the new language.

Language, as we saw in Chapter Three, is a vehicle for expressing the cultural concepts we share with others. Thus, integrative motives involve a desire to be culturally as well as linguistically assimilated into another group. Lambert, in a study of English-speaking Montreal high school students who were studying French, found that "students with an integrative orientation were more successful . . . than were those with instrumental orientations" (Lambert and Gardner 1959). It is generally thought today that whereas people may attempt to acquire a second language for its perceived utility, they do not successfully acquire it until they also have developed a desire to know more about the culture that accompanies it.

Lambert has also done work on the problems bilinguals have vis-à-vis language and ethnic identity. In settings where a language policy is being devised, he found that efforts to solve language problems by proposing language change need to be cognizant of the social and psychological factors that accompany bilingualism. A person who, because of an LP decision, will need a second language, is subject to pressures that will affect that person's "self-concept, . . . sense of belonging and . . . relations to two cultural-linguistic groups, the one [the person] is slowly *leaving*, and the one [the person] is *entering*" (Lambert 1967:229).

People who are bilingual and try to maintain both of their languages usually compartmentalize the languages according to the situations in which each has prestige. Thus, bilingualism is usually accompanied by biculturalism.

These ideas—that attitude toward language and motivation for language learning are planning considerations—dominated much of the problem-oriented work of the 1960s. Today, although it is generally regarded that both instrumental and integrative motives for second-language learning are necessary, the current thought also emphasizes the idea that attitudes toward modernization may be as important as attitudes toward language in fostering the adoption, acceptance, and use of another language (Webber 1979).

The decade of the 1960s saw LP as a field concerned with language situations (national, official, first language, and so forth); language types (see also Fishman's a-modal, uni-modal, and multi-modal languages discussed in Chapter One); language attitudes; motives for second-language learning (nationistic and instrumental; nationalistic and sentimental, primordial, and integrative); diglossia; standardization concepts (the Prague concept of cultivation; Ferguson's graphization, modernization, and standardization); and factors of language maintenance and language shift. Many of these concerns arose in the 1950s (and even before) to be studied in the 1960s in the context of how they relate to problems of language loyalty in developed nations and to language planning in developing ones, that is, to ausbau situations.

We will now look at LP in the 1970s, at which time emphasis shifted to effecting deliberate language change by means of planning, rather than just identifying and classifying situations and problems.

4.3   THE 1970s

Though much of LP in the 1970s was still definable as the "organized pursuit of solutions to language problems, typically at the national level" (Jernudd and Das Gupta 1971), the field in general was consolidated such that all solutions pursued involved language change, generally by means of language choice and language-policy formation (as we saw in Chapter One). By the beginning of the 1970s the field had a two-pronged emphasis: standardization (cultivation, development) in national settings, on the one hand, and solving problems in multiethnic communities, on the other.

4.30   Language Standardization

In Chapter Three we saw standardization as an area of LP in which the fields of anthropology and education play a significant role. In the context of LP history and with regard to ideas about standardization, the 1970s appears as a period in which a number of similar ideas were proposed for how to go about standardizing a language. The LP literature is replete with overlapping and confusing terminology in this area.

In general, standardization is the branch of LP concerned with unifying underlying linguistic diversity, often in the interest of making a chosen language fit to be a national or regional language. A language that has been standardized has been written down (graphized), normalized, and refined as representing an amalgam of its dialects. That is, it has been standardized in the sense that Ferguson (1968) has delineated. It has been updated to express contemporary issues (modernized).

Prior to the 1970s, the scholarly literature in LP essentially held that standardization is the way to make language an efficient and functional tool of development (Ray 1962). Ferguson's model of how to bring about standardization was the prevalent one: we should graphize, standardize, and modernize (1968) in order to conventionalize! A standard language had been defined as far back as 1956 as a "codified form of a language accepted by and serving as a model to a larger speech community" (Garvin and Mathiot 1956:365). The activities of conventionalizing a standard were LP activities par excellence given the 1959 Haugen definition of LP as the preparation of "a normative orthography, grammar, and dictionary for the guidance of writers and speakers in a nonhomogeneous speech community" (8).

To standardize a language, (1) a dialect of it had to be selected as a norm, (2) the norm had to be codified, (3) the codified norm had to be extended throughout the area to use it, and (4) the standard had to be put into use in the schools, government, press and other areas (Haugen 1966:80). But in the 1970s this relatively straightforward picture became blurry due to differing views by scholars as to what planning stages are necessary in order to achieve standardization. Haugen's four stages of norm-selection, codification, elaboration, and implementation were meant to accomplish the same goals as Ferguson's three-step approach to language development (graphization, standardization, and modernization).

In 1970, a scholar named Jiři Neustupný added more confusion to the picture by defining his own set of necessary components of standardization, which we will outline below. His word for standardization was LANGUAGE TREATMENT—a 1970s version of the LANGUAGE CULTIVATION defined by the Prague linguists in the 1930s.

Recognizing the jumble that standardization approaches had become, Fishman (1974b) set out to compare the stages of each approach to each other. All approaches advocated in the 1970s had the common goal of preparing a common language to be used throughout a multilingual area in the interest of linguistic unity over linguistic diversity. Fishman sought to compare Haugen's four stages of standardization to Ferguson's three stages of development to Neustupný's stages of cultivation.

One way to conceive of the situation is to see Haugen's stages of standardization as processes of LP and Ferguson's stages of development as results of LP. To come up with a standard it is necessary to select a norm and then codify, elaborate, and implement it. A selected and codified norm is one that has been graphized. A selected and codified norm that has been implemented has been standardized. A codified norm that has been implemented and elaborated is generally modernized as well.

According to Neustupný's view (1970) of language treatment (cultivation), LP processes such as Haugen's norm selection, codification, implementation, and elaboration are regarded as LP PROBLEMS. He sees LP results such as graphization, standardization, and modernization as PROCESSES. Therefore much of the confusion! What is a result in the Ferguson model is a process in Neustupný's. What is a process to Haugen is a problem to Neustupný:

DEVELOPMENT RESULTS (Ferguson 1968)	CULTIVATION PROCESSES (Neustupný 1970)
graphization	codification
standardization	cultivation
modernization	elaboration

STANDARDIZATION PROCESSES (Haugen 1966)	CULTIVATION PROBLEMS (Neustupný 1970)
norm selection	implementation
codification	codification
elaboration	elaboration
implementation	treatment or cultivation

Whether one calls it standardization, treatment, cultivation, or development, a major thrust of the LP activity of the 1970s had to do with efforts to unify linguistic diversity in national contexts. It was clear that certain stages are involved in the process, each with problems that need to be solved and with desired results to be achieved. Common to each approach is the need to do corpus planning, that is, to do the "real" work of being sure that a writing system and grammar for the selected dialect are available. Each approach also recognized the need to make sure that the standard is popular, acceptable, and widely known. Each approach also considered it necessary for the standard to be up-to-date and fit for the contemporary world.

4.31   Multilingualism

The other main thrust of LP research in the 1970s was in the area of multilingualism. In the literature, this area of LP is referred to as the "study of societal multilingualism" (Fishman 1968b) with an emphasis on sociopsychological aspects of language behavior. The fields of sociolinguistics, anthropological linguistics, ethnolinguistics, the ethnography of speaking, the ethnography of communication, the sociology of language, and the like—with overlapping and often coinciding interests—have been involved in varying degrees in this research. In 1979, Fishman produced a collection of articles entitled *Advances in the Study of Societal Multilingualism.* These articles give a good idea of where that interest led in the 1970s. We saw earlier that efforts toward either language maintenance or language shift characterize most studies of societal multilingualism. Maintenance and shift studies look at

1. What languages are habitually used in *contact* situations

2. What "psychological, social, and cultural processes" are linked to *changes* in habitual language use

3. What kinds of conscious *behavior* foster language change (toward maintenance or shift) (Fishman 1968a:110–111)

This focus by societal multilingualism studies on maintenance and shift among languages in contact reflects the operational definition of LP activity that was used in the 1970s. The LP of the 1970s may be seen as an approach to changes in language and language use that aims to predict the direction of deliberate language change (Rubin and Jernudd 1971). To conduct LP in this way, planners need information about the sociolinguistic traits of the population they hope to change (Rubin 1973:v).

Whereas most LP in the 1960s centered "on the language code—its choice and standardization" (Rubin 1973a:1), the 1970s witnessed a broadening out of LP concerns to also include problems of multilingualism in a changing society. The 1970s needed to plan change in the context in which a language is used as well as the structure of the language itself.

Neustupný is credited with the idea that a cultivation, or standardization, approach to language problems is desirable in national contexts, but a policy approach is preferable in "developing" societies. In those areas where linguistic homogeneity prevails or is the goal, cultivation is the branch of LP most relevant. To Neustupný, the two-pronged LP approach in the 1970s amounted to a split between the standardization thrust of language planning in the 1960s and a new kind of planning in the 1970s. He saw pre-1970 LP to be the best approach to use in modern industrial societies, where it is possible to choose one language to be the focus of a nationwide plan. That language could then be spruced up by a cultivation approach, a synthesis of all the problem-solving processes of standardization we looked at in the previous section.

In areas where linguistic heterogeneity exists, Neustupný prefers a policy approach tied to the analysis of socioeconomically less-developed speech communities (Rubin 1973a:7). In such a situation no obvious language choice exists, and statehood or nation-building is just beginning.

Thus, in most multilingual developing areas, a policy approach would be preferable. In Chapter Five we will see that from the perspective of LP theory, the policy approach is at one end of a language-treatment continuum, being a low-level treatment (a T_1 approach), while a cultivation approach is at the other end, being a rigorous approach (T_r).

The study of multilingualism in the interest of LP, then, is generally from the perspective of a policy approach. Emphasis is on finding out what linguistic varieties exist and how they are distributed rather than on questions of style, correctness, efficiency, and the like. In a policy approach, *what* languages are used is the primary focus of study, while *how* they are used is secondary (Neustupný 1970:39).

In his edited collection of articles on societal multilingualism (1978), Fishman arranged the articles under subtopics in a progression that obtains in the "real world." Many of the studies focus on language contact, language maintenance, and language shift. Other studies examine the spread of LWCs and describe the re-emergence of smaller languages in national language contexts. After a national language or LWC has taken hold, often other languages in a nation begin to be used anew for specific purposes. Thus, other languages may be allocated certain uses in societies that now have an LWC or national language. So both language contact and the functional allocation of languages are major emphases in the study of societal multilingualism. These two categories of multilingualism study reflect changes in the world over the past twenty years that the field of LP is beginning to respond to. While national languages were being developed in the interest of establishing linguistic homogeneity within political boundaries, simultaneously national barriers were beginning to break down in the interest of supranational homogeneity. The emergence of functional allocation as a new category of multilingualism research refers to the development of a unique situation within national entities: After a standardized language has been instituted, becoming the official and national language (often as an LWC), a number of ethnic groups for various reasons seek to maintain their own languages as well. The use of Cornish in weddings in Cornwall, England, and of Irish in primary schools in Ireland are examples of the functional allocation of language for ethnic purposes in contexts of English as an LWC and national/official language. In Chapter Three we saw that functional allocation occurs also with some groups of American Indians (specifically, the Alaskan Haida). Multilingualism studies now include descriptions of the function of Amerindian bilingualism, for instance. Kari and Spolsky (1978:658–59) detect a growing "interest among linguists in the studies of language in use; studies of context, of diversity, and of the sociological aspects of language which are no longer considered uninteresting." Further, they see "evidence of an increasing sense of responsibility towards the speakers of the language" as witnessed by scholarly interest in bilingual-education programs and in training native speakers as linguists.

It is interesting that the presumed solution in linguistically homogeneous communities (that is, standardization) can now be seen as a new problem on two scores. Successfully standardized national languages may exclude their speakers from access to an LWC. Where national multilingualism has been solved in the interest of national unity, the nation may have isolated itself (as Tanzania may have done) from international communication via an LWC. Moreover, in nations where linguistic diversity has been stifled in the interest of implementing a national language, the citizens are now asserting their right to their ethnically based languages. Members of nations need to respond linguistically both to the larger world and to the smaller groups that compose them—as well as to speak for themselves!

As we enter the 1980s, LP is becoming a field that seeks to foster ethnic interaction, world communication, and national identity by means of the policies proposed. In the halcyon days of the 1960s, the fostering of national identity seemed to be enough.

An entire section of the IXth World Congress of Sociology in Uppsala, Sweden (August, 1978) was devoted to the topic "Language and Ethnic Interaction." In an international spirit and also in an interdisciplinary vein, the Comparative Studies in Ethnicity and Nationality (CSEN) program (University of Washington School of International Studies) devoted its 1979 ten-week seminar to language planning in relation to ethnicity.

Languages that are not dominant within a society or polity but have been allocated functions in it may be vehicles of ethnic interaction. In fact, allocating certain functions to nondominant languages is a way to see that groups within a nation are given recognition. LANGUAGE RESURRECTION (or reintroduction, as mentioned earlier)(Eastman 1979b) is an example of a possible plan to functionally allocate to a language the role of preserving ethnicity while simultaneously fostering modernization in a multilingual setting.

Language resurrection refers to the LP activities involved in bringing a group's language to its members in the form of a culture-loaded vocabulary, practical orthography, and folk-historical materials. The oral traditions of a group are gathered and put into writing as a way to preserve the group's language and culture and teach it to both the group members and to interested members of the dominant society. Group members have their "resurrected" language as an aspect of their ethnic identity, and members of the society at large have the benefit of learning something of the complex richness of the culture that the language describes.

Meisel (1978) sees multilanguage use in Canada as a link to the value systems of the different cultural groups there and as an indicator of how each linguistic group has now become somehow identified with either

English or French values. Linguistic diversity is hard to escape, even if we wanted to, as Whiteley (1974a:31–32) saw in Kenya. There, within the community of a completely homogeneous group, the Turkana, the few shops and stores are owned by people from other areas (such as the Meru, Kikuyu, and Luyia) and a similar diversity exists among the civil servants stationed there (Scotton 1978:748).

The 1970s era of LP ended by scholars asking questions about the patterns of language use in politically homogeneous areas: What happens to national languages after they have been implemented? How does a complex multilingual society now with a national language affect that national language? In Kenya, the Swahili that is spoken in Nairobi, used in the media, and written in newspapers is often quite different from the standard of textbooks. What relation does LP have to this type of language change? How may a plan to institute a language such as Swahili as a national and official language be evaluated if—concomitant with the implementation of the plan—ongoing language change is taking place? What *really* does become a national and/or official language? Can we really say that a language such as French or English, once it has become the national language of a new nation and is used in that new context, is still French or still English? Many would argue that the language of England is English but that the language of the United States is American. We know that English in India and English in Kenya have their own characteristics and perhaps it will one day make sense to think of those languages, if they are used widely in those countries, as Kenyan and Indian rather than English.

The other area of LP concern to emerge in the 1970s was the role of planning in the context of LWCs, which were gaining in prestige and utility. Researchers are now beginning to look at the relationship between the spread of lingua francas and the use of LWCs. For example, Cooper (1978) describes the situation of Amharic in Ethiopia, where modern Amharic is expanding both as a lingua franca and as a first language. At the same time, the increase in both varieties of Amharic is accompanied by the increasing use of English as an LWC, particularly in areas of education and technology. Cooper found that "although English may lose ground to Amharic as a medium of instruction, it is likely to maintain its position as Ethiopia's most important nonindigenous language" (1978:474). We have seen elsewhere in these pages that the situation of Swahili in Kenya is similar. Also, Kachru (1978) describes certain aspects of South Asian English as a potential LWC in India, an area of well-documented linguistic diversity.

Ethnic interaction within tolerated linguistic diversity and the changes in LWCs resulting from their contexts of use are areas of planning research with which we enter the 1980s. How nations resolve the conflict of the vernacular versus the national language versus the LWC will be a question with us now for many years to come.

4.4   THE 1980s

We began the 1970s with LP emphasizing the study of how language policy is formed and how language development, or standardization, takes place and is implemented. In the early 1970s, LP was developing more as a practical than an ideal field (Reese 1981). As we enter the 1980s, LP is seen to have a theoretical base derived from case studies in multilingual contexts.

Much of what is important in LP is also important in development planning, a fact that may be due to "the emphasis in the case study material so far on language problems in developing nations" (45). Fishman (1974:92), while admitting the utility of making parallels between LP and other types of planning, feels that we should use caution in viewing language, a creative endeavor, as a quantifiable, allocatable resource.

LP, as a form of cultural or development planning, is lagging behind other types of planning in the area of evaluation of results. Reese considers that this deficiency stems from an almost total neglect of operationalizing its goals:

> The ostensible aim of a language plan may be to "facilitate the use of a simplified orthography," for example, but any means of measuring what the increase may mean in terms of shorter learning time, improved communication, increased literacy rates, etc., are not put in quantifiable terms (Reese 1981:45–46).

It is to be expected that work in the 1980s will see actual plans being produced and implemented. In addition, it is hoped that LP theory will be put increasingly into practice. Whereas the 1960s identified language problems within and among nations and the 1970s considered how change may be carried out by means of policy or cultivation, the 1980s is expected to be the decade in which we see the first results of planned change so that evaluation can take place.

Recent contributions to planning scholarship and reviews of books on planning appear in the journal *Language Problems and Language Planning*, first published in 1977. The *International Journal of the Sociology of Language* also provides an outlet for current planning-research results. Moreover, increasing numbers of general publications in social science are beginning to look at language issues as being within their scope.

In Chapter Seven we will look at samples of different plans produced so far. It is up to the 1980s to evaluate them. Haugen's 1966 definition of LP as the evaluation of linguistic change should finally come to flower: more and more research is expected to provide examples of real plans put into effect such that it will become possible to evaluate their success or failure. Not of undue interest in this regard will be the results of current policies with respect to bilingualism in Quebec, the position of Basque in Spain now that the Basques have received partial autonomy, and the fate of bilingual education in the United States.

As reported in the *Language Planning Newsletter* (1979:5/2:4), a national conference on "Progress in Language Planning: International Perspectives" was held in New Jersey in April, 1979. A number of papers examined the problem of evaluation and implementation and talked about perspectives for LP in the future. Also, the series of publications entitled "Contributions to the Sociology of Language," edited by Fishman, will be continuing into the 1980s. At this writing twenty-one volumes are out and more are in preparation. A number of the volumes have already dealt with many LP-related issues, particularly the volumes *Advances in Language Planning*, *Advances in the Sociology of Language*, *Advances in the Creation and Revision of Writing Systems*, and *Advances in the Study of Societal Multilingualism*. Many other works in the series are also useful to people interested in LP. The most recent volume is called *Language Planning Processes*, edited by Rubin, Jernudd, Das Gupta, Fishman, and Ferguson. This volume results from an International Research Project on Language Planning Processes, which we will see in Chapter Six as being an example of a wide-ranging broadly based sociolinguistic survey.

4.5 SUMMARY

In this chapter we have tried to trace broad outlines of the field of LP as an area of scholarly endeavor. We have seen it as being responsive to the times both in terms of socioeconomic support for actual research and in progress made in how the field defines itself. We have seen LP change, in twenty years, from an emphasis on unifying linguistic diversity to standardization to a stress on evaluating language change in the interest of respecting linguistic diversity, yet simultaneously fostering international communication. The following chronology, by way of summary, indicates some of the major steps in the development of the field. This chronology is to be seen within the history of sociolinguistics in general; thus many landmarks of that broader discipline are not included.

4.51 Chronology: The History of LP Study

1926   Michael West sees language as "the most powerful component" of group individuality.

1930s   The Prague School of Linguistics develops the notion of LANGUAGE CULTIVATION.

1938   Einar Haugen observes that patterned language use covaries with patterned social variation and that people's ATTITUDES toward language are tied up with PRESTIGE factors. The processes of linguistic LEVELING and SHIFT characterize the language of Norwegian immigrants in the United States.

1951   The UNESCO Report on "The Use of Vernacular Languages in Education" is published.

1953   Uriel Weinreich's *Language in Contact* appears.

1957   Weinreich coins the term LANGUAGE PLANNING.

1959   Charles Ferguson develops the concept of DIGLOSSIA.

1959   Einar Haugen defines language planning as the activity of preparing a normative orthography, grammar, and dictionary for the guidance of writers and speakers in a nonhomogeneous speech community.

1960s   A decade of many language/nation typologies.

1960s   LP is operationally defined as the organized pursuit of solutions to language problems.

1966   Joshua Fishman's *Language Loyalty in the United States* appears.

1967   Heinz Kloss distinguishes ABSTAND and AUSBAU languages.

1967   Wallace Lambert discerns instrumental and integrative motives for second-language learning.

1968   Fishman, Ferguson, and Das Gupta edit *Language Problems in Developing Nations*.

1968   Fishman edits *Advances in the Study of Language Planning*.

1968   Charles Ferguson envisions LANGUAGE DEVELOPMENT as consisting of GRAPHIZATION, MODERNIZATION, and STANDARDIZATION.

1970s   LP focuses on the PROCESSES and RESULTS of STANDARDIZATION and on the description of language use in bi- and multilingual settings.

1970   Neustupný distinguishes a cultivation versus a policy approach to LP.

1970s   From 1971 onward, the definition of LP as "deliberate language change" is in effect.

1971   Rubin and Jernudd edit *Can Language Be Planned?*

1971–   The series *Language Science and National Development*, edited by
1972   Anwar S. Dil, publishes the collected essays of Fishman, Lambert, Haugen and other scholars in fields related to LP.

1973   The International Conference on Language Planning Processes (in Skokloster, Sweden; October) recommends that a *Language Planning Newsletter* be established and that meetings on special aspects of LP be held.

1970s   Toward the middle of the decade, the *Language Planning Newsletter* under the editorship of Joan Rubin begins to appear.

1974   LP appears as a section in Vol. XII of *Current Trends in Linguistics*, edited by Thomas Sebeok.

1975   The International Conference on the Methodology of Sociolinguistic Surveys is held in Montreal from May 19–21 as recommended by the 1973 International Conference on Language Planning Processes in order to focus on special aspects of LP.

1976   Fishman edits *Advances in the Creation and Revision of Writing Systems.*
1978   Fishman edits *Advances in the Study of Societal Multilingualism.*
1980s   Haugen's (1966) definition of LP as the evaluation of linguistic change begins to become operative. The continuing series *Contributions to the Sociology of Language* that brought us the *Advances in . . .* volumes (edited by Fishman) will allow us to trace the growth and development of LP in this coming decade as well. It is expected that in the coming years LP will focus on LWCs and the role of language in ethnic interaction. It is likely that actual language plans will be put into effect so that in the not-so-distant future evaluation can take place.

In this chapter we have said little about theory and method in the development of the field outside of certain concepts dominating the work in the past few decades. In the next two chapters we look at what planners have done so far and what theoretical notions have been guiding their work. We will see, for instance, that cost-benefit analysis has been used as an approach to the quantification of certain LP variables. We will also see how LP theory is beginning to be based on ideas about decision-making, development, and social relations. To use LP theory also entails familiarity with a broad range of techniques of research, and these will be our focus in Chapter Six. The well-prepared language planner can carry out survey research and participant-observation approaches, conduct interviews, and use quantitative methods. In addition, the planner needs to be familiar with policy analysis and social psychology. Some of the techniques geared specifically to LP theory (Chapter Five) will be the focus of our discussion in Chapter Six.

Chapter Five

LANGUAGE-PLANNING
THEORY

5.0 INTRODUCTION

As we saw in the last chapter, the history of language planning so far has been characterized by a number of different guiding definitions—and by a number of different theories often related to these definitions. Essentially, theory-building efforts have had to do with planning in the context of

1. alternatives or decisions (language choice)

2. modernization (language development)

3. ethnic-group relations (bilingualism, multilingualism, diglossia, and so forth)

LP, defined as standardization—that is, activity planning in accord with Haugen's definition (1959)—involves decision-making theory geared to choosing the best language for the situation at hand. As such, "The study of *language planning* describes decision-making about language" (Rubin and Jernudd 1971:xii).

Modernization theory underlies much of the language planning that is defined as deliberate language change. Planned changes in language structure or use by planning organizations center on problem solving. The approach to problem solving is to find and evaluate alternative solutions in order to come up with the best decision. LP, both as standardization and deliberate change, relies on decision-making theories. LP as deliberate change, however, is also future-oriented (Rubin and Jernudd 1971:xvi), which means that "the outcomes of policies and strategies must be specified in advance of action taken. Since such forecasting implies uncertainty or risk, planning must allow for reformulations as new situations develop" (xvi). The way language planning takes reformulation into account is to allow for the language's development, that is, to provide for modernization.

Planning must also take into account the effect a plan has on the future of ethnic-group relations, since it occurs in complex contexts, not in a vacuum. LP as the evaluation of linguistic change (Haugen 1966) is the definition underlying theories of language in ethnic-group relations (for example, Giles, Bourhis, and Taylor 1977; Fishman 1977). Because LP does not take place in a vacuum, the context in which it occurs also changes as a result of the change brought about by planning. As the evaluation of change, LP thus also rests on theoretical concepts used to understand language, social, and cultural change in the form of shifting relationships among ethnic or national groups.

In this chapter we will also see how linguistic attitudes, feelings, and beliefs are actually changed as a result of the different language-planning definitions and their related theories. To trace this change we need to look at each of the seven general elements of any language plan: codification, regularization, simplification, purification, elaboration, implementation, and evaluation. The reader will notice that much of LP theory and method has already been addressed in previous pages, insofar as LP's conceptual framework derives from its history and its interdisciplinary connections. Now we will see what LP theory *per se* has come to be. Then, in Chapter Six, we will turn our attention to LP method.

5.1 LANGUAGE-PLANNING ALTERNATIVES AND DECISIONS

In the Chapter Three discussion of LP and economics we mentioned that a great deal of LP theory has an economic base, particularly with respect to the theory behind the decisions and to the alternative courses of action considered in LP. In what follows we will look at not only those aspects but also the use of cost-benefit analysis as a theoretical approach to language planning and additional factors that operate in decision-making and in implementation.

Most LP researchers conceive of LP as a practical, action-oriented field (as applied sociolinguistics), which would necessarily rest on theoretical concepts of how decisions involving language are made so that they reflect "a composite urge articulated in the community" (Jernudd and Das Gupta 1971:198).

In contrast, Tauli (1968) identifies planning with "abstract linguistic thought" and sees it as sensitive to what the linguists or authorities want, regardless of what the community wants. In his opinion, LP should not do what the people want. He believes that LP "is identified with an expert enterprise motivated by abstract ideals of a selected, albeit deeply concerned, group of linguists" (Jernudd and Das Gupta 1971:198). Tauli's approach to LP is quite different from the generally accepted approach of Haugen/Fishman. Their community-based, rather than expert-based, approach is the one also implicitly adopted throughout these pages. In line with Jernudd and Das Gupta (198), we find it desirable to approach language problems "on their social reality, with scientific methods and with a desire to acquire knowledge that may help mankind to improve communication."

For the prescriptive or "language-pure" form of LP, the reader is referred to Tauli's *Introduction to a Theory of Language Planning* (1968). Tauli conceives of LP as a methodical way to improve and regulate existing languages, to create new languages for a nation or a region, or even to devise new international languages (Tauli 1974). To him, an ideal language is one that can do what any natural language can do but also be "economic" in form and pleasing aesthetically; that is, it should sound good and match expression with content. It should say what it means. Tauli believes that voiced sounds are more beautiful than voiceless ones, so the ideal language should have more of those (Tauli 1968:29–39). To him, a b, d, g, or z is better than a p, t, k, or s! This belief is not thought to be widely shared. The reality of consonant systems flies in the face of his aesthetic claim unless we are to conclude that natural languages are not aesthetically pleasing. In natural languages, for a language to have a particular voiced consonant it must also have its voiceless counterpart. Thus, no natural language has b, d, g, or z unless it also has p, t, k, or s. A Tauli-type consonant system— whether it sounds better or not—is not natural.

Most of LP today is concerned not with ideal language construction but with how to cope with language in a multilingual milieu. These language-in-context approaches are not based on theories with goals of abstract linguistic ideals. Most language planning in a modernizing, multiethnic world needs to provide decisions and choices about language that make practical sense. The prevailing concept of planning is that courses of action need to be found "within limits of given amounts of resources . . . in order to reach the goals that have been approved by the political authority" (Jernudd and Das Gupta 1971:198–99). Thus, one theoretical assumption of modern LP is the following:

> Language planning seeks to provide conscious alternative decisions
> and anticipate their consequences, making use of available resources
> that can be used to solve language problems that involve a change in
> the language behavior of a group of people.

Thomas Thorburn has made suggestions for decision-making about language based on general approaches used to evaluate other types of public decisions with wide-ranging effects. He reasons that the "regulation of floods, fluoridization of drinking water, care of animals, community planning and language planning" all involve decisions followed by plans that are put into effect. In all these cases *planning* occurs, and it occurs with language "when one tries to apply the amalgamated knowledge of language to change the language behavior of a group of people" (1971:254).

Planners predict the consequences of alternative proposals to change language behavior. Some people say planning can be thought of as just another word for forecasting (Thorburn 1971); that is, we can forecast language as we can forecast the weather. Given certain conditions, language is likely to change in certain directions. Thus, LP theory can perhaps be based "on a systematic forecast of consequences or alternatives" (255). The alternatives generally have to do with which language or languages are to be used as written and oral communication in a particular geographical area. According to Thorburn, four language-use alternatives can be considered for planning options. Language may be used

1. to communicate among inhabitants of a country, either throughout the country or in just one region

2. to communicate between inhabitants of one country and those of other countries

3. for written communication in official publications, literature, public education, newspapers, or handwritten documents

4. for spoken communication with public authorities, on radio and television, or in everyday conversation (254–55)

In these alternatives the reader will recognize most of the language situations that result from language choice—those identified by the UNESCO report discussed in Chapter One. These alternatives also encompass related language functions noted by scholars such as Stewart (1968), Fishman (1969a), and others in their efforts to define shared spheres of language use and potential planning activity.

5.10   Cost-Benefit Analysis

Cost-benefit analysis allows us to compare consequences of proposed language-use alternatives. It may be begun once the language problem is stated and alternative solutions have been proposed (Thorburn 1971:255).

Cost-benefit analysis takes place by means of a CALCULATION made within a FRAME. An example of the approach would be to consider the problem of adopting a language in a national (temporal and spatial) context. The context is the frame within which the calculation takes place. A frame is adopted for analysis in order to avoid uncertainty:

Uncertainty increases with (1) time and (2) new consequences. When uncertainty grows too great, it becomes meaningless to try to follow further consequences. This means that our analytical sight should be limited by the decision-maker's time-sight and by a cutoff point in space, as well as by his resources etc. (Jernudd 1971:268).

If we consider competing alternatives within a frame, we can be sure that each is suited to the situation at hand. The set of alternatives considered within a frame is called a calculation.

The adoption of a language in a country may be planned in such a way that the alternative approaches are subjected to a cost-benefit analysis. A sample calculation regarding language choice in a national context would have as the MAIN ALTERNATIVE the adoption of an LWC for official written publications and for use on a par with other languages in other spheres. The ZERO-ALTERNATIVE would be the adoption of the country's national language in all official written communication and for use as the main language in all spheres *within the region* of the country where it is a mother tongue. Elsewhere it would be used on a par with other languages in other spheres. The cost-benefit analysis would calculate whether choosing an LWC as the official language would work better than choosing one of the country's indigenous languages within the frame at hand.

> The cost-benefit calculation aims at identifying, quantifying, and evaluating the differences in consequences that may be expected if one decides to choose the main alternative instead of the zero-alternative (Thorburn 1971:258).

Another aspect of cost-benefit analysis is the TIME-HORIZON. The expected or calculated alternatives need to be evaluated not only in context but also in respect to time—for an ongoing, yet reasonable, length of time. The plan's consequences need to be predicted, for example, for the first five years the plan is in effect, then for the first ten, and so forth, up to the first twenty years; the total time-horizon analysis should view all the time segments put together. The twenty-year time-horizon figure is just an example to illustrate that whatever time period is chosen, it has to be sufficiently long yet must end before the point where uncertainty would render prediction meaningless (Thorburn 1971:258) The time-horizon in which a calculation occurs must not exceed the duration of the frame.

A cost-benefit analysis to decide between choosing an LWC or a national language (NL) as a country's official language would, then, have three essential components: (1) each plan as INPUT; (2) the results of each as OUTPUT; and (3) an analysis of the CONSEQUENCES of each. In general, if the beneficial consequences of a plan outweigh the consequences seen as costs (monetary or otherwise), that plan or alternative would be the wisest choice. We may schematize a cost-benefit calculation as shown in Figure 1.

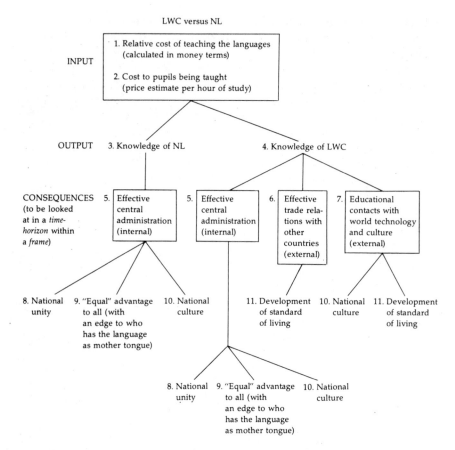

Figure 1. Cost-Benefit Calculation (adapted from Thorburn 1971:259)

A cost-benefit analysis of a choice between an NL and an LWC in a country will come up with relative monetary values for the input features (1 and 2). We can know how much it costs to teach the national language versus the cost of teaching the LWC throughout the country, and we can calculate the person-hour cost in training as well. We can also figure monetary costs incurred by the central administration (5) if an LWC versus an NL is chosen in terms of the need of interpreters for civil servants, for example. A monetary figure can also be arrived at for costs to foreign trade (6) and for the development of a higher standard of living (11) if an NL rather than an LWC is used. But an evaluation in monetary terms is probably *not* possible for items 7, 8, 9, and 10. We cannot attach a real value to the access a people may obtain to educational materials and world technology through knowledge of an LWC. We also cannot figure out the real value of an LWC in such areas as national unity, equality, and the growth of national culture. Still, we can state the probable direction of these planning consequences.

Cost-benefit analysis theory, as well as its application in practice to LP, is a useful way for planners to provide support for the final decisions they recommend and for authorities (such as politicians) to back up the choice made as the chosen language plans are implemented. In short, a cost-benefit analysis of language-choice alternatives shows which language will cost less money when implemented. It shows what measurable future quantification of further differences between the choices will be—at least for the near future. Cost-benefit analysis also provides some indications of which language is best, given the goals of the authority requiring a choice (Thorburn 1971).

The actual nuts-and-bolts method of cost-benefit analysis accompanying a calculation model will be described in more detail in Chapter Six as part of a general presentation of planning techniques. There we will see how to quantify consequences and measure costs and benefits against each other. We will see that it is difficult to calculate the profit maximization of a language decision because so many intangible consequences are involved (such as items 7 to 10 on the chart). Also, monetized costs and monetized benefits for those consequences that have them cannot often be compared meaningfully.

Recently, in the area of language choice within an actual context or frame, a method has been proposed called GLOTTOECONOMICS ("language economics"). Glottoeconomics seeks to relate language use to profit maximization. Glottoeconomists, such as Vaillancourt (1979), feel that an understanding of the relationship of language and profit helps explain natural-language choices and can assist planners in deciding what language choices can be planned. It may be that language choice is as much a function of profit maximization as ethnicity is; at least this idea lies behind the assumptions made by glottoeconomics: Just as people identify themselves with a particular ethnic group because they believe that being a member of it is in their best interests, so people are motivated to use the language they consider as the one that will give them the most benefits. The method of glottoeconomics will also be described in Chapter Six.

5.11   Spread Hypothesis

In addition to taking a cost-benefit perspective, decision-making theory as a concern in LP also rests on a conceptual basis defined as the SPREAD HYPOTHESIS. The word SPREAD refers to the degree of actual use of "language products" resulting from decisions about language. An example of a spread decision about language would be the determination as to which forms are to be standardized and which not in a multidialectal context. In proposing this hypothesis, the language-planning scholars Björn Jernudd and Jyotirindra Das Gupta felt that language planning is required to judge alternatives for the suggested language products or spread alternatives. The spread hypothesis holds that for planning to be successful, alternatives must be chosen to ensure that the decision has an effect on the social use of the language products. It also holds that successful planning will forecast *what* language products will spread and *how* they will spread, so that uncertainty about how the decision will affect language use will be reduced. The rationale behind judging spread alternatives is to come up with a language plan that is the best alternative allowing people to recognize, accept, and use "certain language products" (Jernudd and Das Gupta 1971:206). The spread hypothesis sees LP as the making of orderly decisions that will have public social effects. The plan needs to work—to "spread"—as well as to be cost-effective.

Both the spread hypothesis and cost-benefit analysis view language planning as rooted in decision-making. Both approaches to decision-making forms of planning are necessarily goal oriented. Decisions about language (in common with many other forms of decision) have three types of goals: (1) allocation of resources (for example, raising the standard of living); (2) distribution (for example, seeing that all people have equal access to the language; and (3) stabilization (for example, using the language for national goals). In Figure 1, these goals were seen implicitly in the various consequences of choosing either an LWC or an NL. Cost-benefit calculation by means of cost-benefit analysis and the spread hypothesis constitutes a theoretical basis for the kind of LP that is dependent on language choice.

The models so far designed to forecast consequences of language decisions, however, fail to consider that language choice also has to take into account pressure on planning authorities from a variety of special-interest groups such as professional associations of educators, manufacturers of typewriters, textbook publishers, literacy advocates, journalists, ideological groups, and so forth (Fishman 1974:1758, citing Das Gupta 1969). Governments or educational bodies that need LP are subject to lobbying by these kinds of pressure groups. Wise planning still needs to find a way to help authorities evaluate special-interest claims as well as proposed plans.

5.2 LANGUAGE PLANNING AND MODERNIZATION

We have seen that language planning often occurs in the context of economic development. Also, we have seen that to a great extent economic development rests on concepts of modernization. Not surprisingly, then, a number of theoretical concepts useful in LP derive from modernization theory as well as from the kinds of decision-making theory just discussed.

Both decision-making and modernization theory as used in LP are derived from the field of economics (see Chapter Three).

The modernization-theory aspects of LP, in contrast to the decision-making theory aspects, respond to social pressures and forces in effect *after* a plan has been implemented, that is, after the decision has been made. Modernization theory seeks to account for the interaction of sentimental and instrumental attachments to a nation or state as integrative or disintegrative forces in the language-planning process (Fishman 1974:1758).

Modernization theory is also used to understand language maintenance and language shift. Further, it is useful in seeing the role of language in development.

5.20 Maintenance and Shift

As we saw in Chapter Two, language planning relates to language maintenance and language shift; in those areas where more than one speech variety is used within or among groups, the planned degree of change (or stability) in the use of a language has to do with psychological, cultural, and social processes (Fishman 1968a:76). We linked maintenance and shift to the sociologists' and the social-psychologists' interest in language attitudes and to the political scientists' concern for policy implementation; in Chapter Three, we saw these ideas in relation to the anthropologists' concern with language and one's sense of group identity. Here we will see how the ideas of maintenance and shift figure in the evolution of LP theory.

We saw that there are three major subdivisions of the sociolinguistic study of maintenance and shift: People look at (1) the habitual use of a language (at more than one point) in time or space; (2) the psychological, social, and cultural processes that occur before, during, or after maintenance or shift has taken place and relate to either stability or change in habitual language use; and (3) the behavior toward language that is directed at either maintenance or shift (Fishman 1968a). It is with this latter subdivision that LP theory is concerned. That is, LP theory seeks to assess the way people behave with and about language as a guide in deciding whether to adopt a plan of maintenance or shift. The habitual use of language and the sociopsychological and cultural factors surrounding it are tangential concerns of LP. These areas are more the concern of second-language and language-change studies than of planning research. The related issue of language attitude, however, will be discussed in this chapter when we look at the role of language attitudes in modernization.

Planners seeking to recommend either linguistic stability or change need to consider the effect their plan will have on the status quo. One notion of particular importance here is that of language *domain*. Another is the idea that there are different sets of domains in which a language is used. By domain is generally meant "arena of use"; that is, language is used differently (in terms of style or variety as well as of particular language choice) in the family, school, government, church, media, and so on.

> Domains such as these . . . attempt to designate the major clusters of interaction situations that occur in multilingual settings . . . [they] help us to understand that *language choice* and *topic* . . . are themselves related to widespread sociocultural regularities. Language choices, cumulated over many individuals and many choice instances, become transformed into the processes of *language maintenance* or *language shift* (Fishman 1968a:80).

If the topics discussed in one language become more common than topics for which another is used, the language of the increasingly prevalent topics will be used with greater frequency. Children who speak a mother tongue and use a second language in school eventually talk about school matters in the second language and domestic matters in the first language. As the school and nonhome environment begins to dominate their lives, they use the mother tongue less and less. Beardsley and Eastman (1971) found that in conversations among Swahili-English bilinguals, the topic of conversation influenced language choice. Further, they observed that the speaker's concept of the relevance of the topic to the particular language used influenced the choice for that topic. The speakers in their study who were attending a U.S. university had had their primary education in Swahili in Tanzania. It was observed that when the topic of conversation was related to education back home, predominantly Swahili was used, but English was dominant when the topic was racial prejudice, which was seen as a problem in the English-speaking rather than the Swahili-speaking world (1971:24).

According to maintenance and shift theory, such language choices, "cumulated over many individuals and many choice instances, become transformed into the processes of *language maintenance* or *language shift*" (Fishman 1968a:80). Children in school who talk increasingly less about their preschool days at home will shift to the second language, because their new and ongoing experiences take place in the context of that language and not in their mother tongue.

As Beardsley and Eastman concluded, a particular topic is most likely handled in a particular language because that topic relates to a domain in which the language is dominant in the given society.

> Certainly it is a far different social interaction when topic *x* is discussed in language *Y*, *although it pertains to a domain in which language X is dominant*, than when the same topic is discussed by the same interlocutors in the language most

commonly employed in that domain. By recognizing the existence of domains it becomes possible to contrast the language of topics for particular subpopulations with the language of domains for larger populations (Fishman 1968a:81).

A domain (such as government, church, family, or home) is

a sociocultural construct abstracted from topics of communication, relationships and interactions between communicators, and locales of communication in accord with the institutions of a society and the spheres of activity of a culture in such a way that individual behavior and social patterns can be distinguished from each other and yet related to each other (82).

To show how the concept of domain may be used to study language change, Fishman tells of a study of urban bilingual New Jersey children of Puerto Rican background born in Mainland United States who were asked to name as many kitchen, school, church and neighborhood objects in 45 seconds as they could. The kitchen was to represent the home domain; school, the educational domain; church, the religious domain; and the neighborhood, the community domain. It was found that the school, family, and neighborhood contexts were equally salient for the naming of lexical items, but the religious context less so. That is, they could name an equal number of items in the school, family, and neighborhood areas but fewer in the religious context. The greatest number of overall words were produced in English. But whereas English was found to be favored over Spanish in the neighborhood, education, and religious domains, a difference was seen in the proportion of English to Spanish words in the home domain.

The importance of this study is that it allows the planner to see that if these trends were to continue, one would expect Spanish to disappear from all but the home domain—and consequently to be absent from all arenas of interaction except for the roles, topics, and settings closely related to the home domain (Fishman 1968a:85).

A concept related to that of domain in the context of maintenance and shift is the idea of *dominance configuration*. It is a way to show the direction of differential changes in language use through time. From studies of maintenance and shift we may see a second underlying theoretical assumption of LP emerging (the first assumption was given on page 135 in section 5.1):

Languages used vary with respect to the number and overlap of domains in which their speakers habitually employ each of their languages (Fishman 1968a:86).

That is, people who use more than one language use each language in particular situations. It is important for planners to see that proposed language policies take this fact into consideration. The idea of dominance configuration was first introduced by Uriel Weinreich (1953) and adopted later by Joshua Fishman as a way to predict the status of maintenance or shift. A dominance configuration for a language is a "syndrome of characteristics on which the language is rated" (Weinreich 1953:79). The characteristics of a particular configuration pattern have yet to be worked out by scholars in the field; but, in general, a dominance configuration for a language would include the way it is used (its *mode of use*) and various types of use-frequency data. Dominance configurations are meant to be represented on tables, which should provide (1) a summary of multilanguage-use data for a particular group of people at two different time/space points, and (2) a summary of role relations (parent-child, teacher-student, and the like) relating to the language and the situation of its use.

By analyzing the data of dominance configurations, it is expected that researchers will be able to see, in a much more refined way than is now possible, how maintenance or shift is proceeding. According to Fishman (1968a:91), the only way to analyze such a trend now is to study census statistics on reported first languages as compared to what is observed as language use.

Fishman (1968a:92) gives an idea of what a partial dominance-configuration table would look like for Yiddish-English maintenance and shift in the United States between 1940 and 1970. Figure 2 is an adaptation of his table in tree form. From the tree, insofar as it has been filled in, we may see that between 1940 and 1970 English was being used more than Yiddish by Yiddish-English bilinguals in the United States and that consequently Yiddish use has declined, particularly among friends and acquaintances. In 1970, as in 1940, Yiddish was the language of the home and English the language on the job. Domain analyses such as this Yiddish-English study— just as the New Jersey Puerto Rican example looked at above—provide planners with an opportunity to observe trends in shift and maintenance, information that can be profitably used in planning.

In addition to studying domains of language use and setting up dominance configurations, planning relative to maintenance and shift rests on a concept of LANGUAGE REINFORCEMENT as a form of "overt behavioral implementation of attitudes, feelings, and beliefs" (Fishman 1968a:105). Language reinforcement *is* language planning in a situation of maintenance or shift. The languages positively reinforced stay, those negatively reinforced shift. Language reinforcement involves the "control or regulation of habitual language use by means of reinforcement, planning, prohibition, etc." (111). In Chapter Two, we saw how behaviors that have to do with reinforcing attitudes about language are often the business of scholars of language and politics.

To see what the concept of language reinforcement means in LP theory,

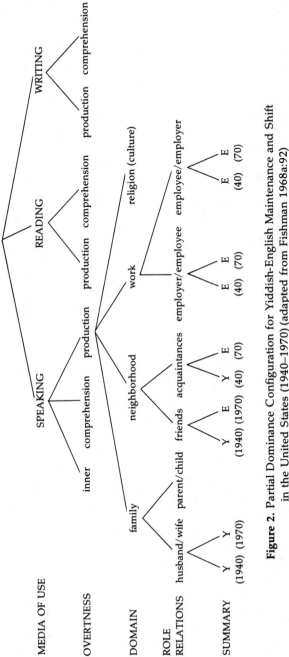

Figure 2. Partial Dominance Configuration for Yiddish-English Maintenance and Shift in the United States (1940–1970) (adapted from Fishman 1968a:92)

we may look at how each type of LP activity has a reinforcement function. In an effort to outline a theoretical framework in which comparative studies of LP might operate, Jernudd (1971) included a list of the language-reinforcement activities that could be used to change linguistic attitudes, feelings, or beliefs:

1. CODIFICATION
   Codification is a method of putting a policy into effect while simultaneously considering the loyalties, preferences, values, and habits of the persons affected by the policy. If codification is wisely done in this way, it will reinforce the aim of the policy by fostering acceptance of the planned language change.

2. REGULARIZATION
   Regularization is the technical side of codification, the busywork of "normalizing" variations in usage that are to be leveled out by a policy. To regularize a national language in order to reinforce its acceptance, the differences between its dialectal variants need to be regularized in a way sensitive to the accompanying social and geographical differences. By preparing "official" grammars, dictionaries, and the like—that is, by standardizing a chosen language, it is possible, via regularization, to reinforce the adoption of a language in accord with planning goals.

3. SIMPLIFICATION
   The simplification of a language being planned may also reinforce its acceptance and use by larger numbers of people. If its orthography is uncomplicated and printable and its spelling system up-to-date, a language has a better chance of success.

4. PURIFICATION
   Like simplification, purification makes a language change more acceptable. In contrast to simplification, purification removes prior associations of a social and cultural nature the language may have had and strives to see that the language is truly a language of the nation (in the case of a national-language choice) or of the group (in the case of an ethnic-based choice). By pruning the language of extraneous cultural stigmata (in loan vocabulary or script, for example) and thereby making it more "*of* the people," the language is thought to be made more usable, thus reinforcing the proposed change.

5. ELABORATION
   Elaboration is the extending of the decided-upon language change to all contexts in which the plan envisions the language will be used. Whereas codification incorporates attitudinal aspects that would be encountered as a policy is being put into effect, elaboration is that phase of language

reinforcement in which the codified language is used for the *first* time in all intended areas. In earlier chapters we saw many instances of the importance of language academies in reinforcing change by means of policy elaboration.

6. IMPLEMENTATION

Implementation is both the continuation of elaboration and the maintenance of the codified change in accord with planned goals. A language change is reinforced by governmental, educational, and social agencies that see to it that the elaborated change is maintained.

7. EVALUATION

The reinforcement of a language change needs to be assessed. We need to know if what has been carefully codified, regularized, simplified, purified, elaborated, and implemented in order to produce and reinforce language change has actually done that. We need to find out if the plan works: Is the language reinforced? Has the change been accepted?

In Chapter One, we considered the codifying (including policy formulation), elaborating, and implementing aspects of language reinforcement to be part of the policy aspect of planning. Three other activities of reinforcement—regularization, simplification, and purification—are more involved with the technicalities of the plan itself. The activity of evaluation applies to the whole process. In Chapter Six we will see that formulation, implementation, and evaluation are often done by means of SOCIOLINGUISTIC SURVEYS. Decisions about language-policy formulation may require prior information about what languages or language varieties are intended to be used for various purposes. Basic information may need to be gathered about the preplanning language situation; later, the evaluation of the language policy's effectiveness may also be aided by further survey results (Cooper 1975:32–34).

5.21   Development

Emerging LP theory also owes a debt to development research for its conceptual framework. The well-known political scientist Karl Deutsch (1953) observed that as countries develop they tend to become more centralized. This centralization leads away from linguistic heterogeneity to linguistic homogeneity. In Chapter Three, we examined homogeneity and heterogeneity as ideas related to the economics of development rather than to political centralization, although often these are but two sides of the same coin. Both government centralization and perceived economic good are aspects of modernization that development theory tells us lead to linguistic unity—*if* both involve the same language.

We also saw earlier that economic development is useful to the language planner attending specifically to the direction of maintenance and shift. Relying on both economic and centralization generalizations from the development field, Jernudd (1971) (based on Kuznets 1966:490–502) finds it possible to provide some development-based assumptions for language-planning theory, which may be added to the two already cited above (the economic assumption behind alternatives and decisions, page 135; and the modernizing assumption underlying maintenance and shift, page 143).

The development assumptions of LP are:

- In a developing area, people with language skills are favored over those without; people with linguistic disabilities are held back in economic advancement.

- In a developing area, population increases via birth rate *or* migration affect the relative strength of languages or speech varieties.

- In a developing area, a quality increase as well as a quantity increase in per capita growth requires an expansion of linguistic knowledge; that is, people need to know and use more of a language as they acquire more and better goods.

- In a developing area, people need to be aware of, and know how to use, different language features (such as social dialects, special vocabularies, argots, jargons, or special-purpose languages) to adjust to changes in professional and industrial growth.

- In a developing area, international trade requires people to be able to use and have access to LWCs.

- In a developing area, linguistic homogeneity adds to the ability of people to cross occupational, industrial, and status lines.

- In a developing area, where the spread of modern economic growth is sequential, modern linguistic growth is also sequential. The need for vocabulary development makes it likely that the world languages will be chosen for adoption in preference to attempts to enhance local languages.

As with the other two potential assumptions of an emergent LP theory discussed in this chapter, hard data are needed to support or refute the above assumptions before any solid theory based on them may be derived.

5.22   Ideas of Attachment to a Nation or a State

So far in this chapter we have seen that some ideas and background assumptions of language-planning theory have come from economics and development research. LP theory is also beginning to employ some of the concepts from political science that we looked at in Chapter Two. To understand the nature of language planning, we have to understand the effect language loyalty can have on national loyalty. Here we will see how Kelman's (1971) ideas about sentimental and instrumental attachment to a nation or state fit into another likely LP assumption. We thus propose an assumption about the need for LP to occur in a politically legitimate and well-integrated context:

Language policies need to meet the needs and interests of all people in a nation or state effectively and fairly. Language policies must foster instrumental attachments both to the language and the state out of which sentimental attachments will arise later.

Kelman (1971:48) asserts a number of ideas related to this assumption about political integration and legitimacy. People in high places in the educational and socioeconomic arenas who also have political power are IDEOLOGICALLY INTEGRATED into the political context. That is, powerful, wealthy, educated people believe in what the system stands for. In contrast, others believe they ought to conform to the system and its dictates but don't particularly want to. These are the people NORMATIVELY INTEGRATED into the political context. The legitimacy of a political system depends on the ideological integration of elites. This conclusion implies that cultural values and social institutions need to be reviewed from time to time to see if they meet the ideal needs of the population.

Legitimacy ultimately rests on ideological commitments, but if normative commitments are shared by the masses of the population, government policy will still be accepted.

These ideas of ideological integration and normative integration to the nation are reminiscent of the notions of sentimental and instrumental attachment, respectively, which we talked about earlier. People who are ideologically integrated into a political system have a sentimental attachment to the state. People who are normatively integrated into a political system have an instrumental attachment to the state.

People who are normatively integrated and instrumentally attached gradually begin to become ideologically integrated with sentimental feelings in certain roles. In certain areas, they begin to feel that they belong to the larger political context. This is referred to as ROLE-PARTICIPANT INTEGRATION to the nation, a sort of symbolic attachment to the state. People who pay lip service to the nation and use its institutions but do not yet "love" it begin to be committed to certain national policies they perceive as helpful to them. People who begin to be ideologically integrated into a system, having begun as role-participants, very often have been encouraged by political leaders who have identified and used national symbols and roles of the normatively integrated for the purposes of bringing about eventual ideological integration (Kelman 1971). Wise politicians can amalgamate the symbolic and instrumental forms by manipulating the varying ideological and normative commitments that accompany people's roles in different domains.

In language-planning theory, it is important to understand the degree of personal involvement people have in the national system as a basis for another likely LP theoretical assumption:

> A common language is a potential unifying force, because it strengthens sentimental/ideological, instrumental/normative, and symbolic/role-participatory attachments people have to a nation or state and plays a major role in reinforcing these attachment processes.

> *Corollary:* Linguistic diversity in a national system can give rise to conflicts due to sentimental, instrumental, and symbolic considerations that are likely to reinforce one another.

The degree of sentimental attachment to a state or the ideological integration of a nation can also be related to the concept of PRIMORDIAL ETHNICITY mentioned in Chapter Two. The more we feel that a nation or group is "ours," the more sentimentally attached to it and ideologically integrated into it we will be. We can designate as primordial this feeling of "ours" and "us" versus "theirs" and "them." *We* are sentimentally and ideologically *nationalists*; they are instrumentally and normatively *nationists* (see Fishman 1969a:193–94).

By seeing the role of languages in relation to one's commitment to a state from an ideological/sentimental, normative/instrumental, or symbolic/role-specific viewpoint, the planner will be able to make recommendations about language that can lead to (or, conversely, that can lead away from) sociopolitical integration. The idea of sentimental and instrumental attachments has also been adopted by Lambert as a way to designate people's motives for learning a second language (Lambert 1967). We will see these ideas to be important in LP theory as well, specifically in the context of planning and ethnic-group relations in multilingual societies. People will learn a second language for both ideological and practical reasons. It is thought at this time that those with ideological goals as well as instrumental needs do better. The planner can use this knowledge in efforts to direct language change.

In this section we have seen that another aspect of the growth of LP theory is the importance placed on the feelings people have about the political context in which they find themselves and the language(s) that represent it. We will next see how existing language situations can be correlated with different stages of national development.

5.3   TAXONOMIC APPROACHES

We will now see how the field has categorized or classified some of the theoretical concepts it has used so far. We have already seen that a number of the assumptions of planning theory are derived from CONCEPTUAL CATEGORIES, such as homogeneity and heterogeneity or the idea of domains and dominance configurations. We have, for instance, categorized kinds of attachment to a nation or state. In previous chapters we looked at how to break up a standardization continuum. We also described a number of lists of language situations. Categories appear in the literature as lists, typologies, and continua. The LP conceptual categories proposed are a kind of classificatory analysis of LP. In a sense, introducing classifications, or proposing taxonomies, could be seen as a theoretical approach. Taxonomies imply the imposition of organization on data. The taxonomic approaches to LP that we have looked at are the many efforts to relate language change (development) to social change (development). Those who introduced these classificatory models have assumed that language and social modernization occur in stages, and they have sought to describe those stages.

In the preceding chapters we have discussed many different sets of classificatory analyses of LP material. In Chapter One, we talked about the four categories of co-occurring social change and spelling-reform relationships proposed by Fishman (1971a:363). His idea is that social change may or may not accompany spelling reform and that it is useful to compare the relative success of the reform in the four possible situations. Another classificatory approach to planning may be seen in Jack Berry's (1968:738) principles for deciding what constitutes an acceptable writing system.

The ten possible language situations delineated in the 1951 UNESCO report (Fishman, ed. 1968:689–90) have provided valuable input to planning theory, particularly as it involves proposing alternatives and decisions. In the same vein, Fishman's proposal for deciding which features of language choice foster nationism and which foster nationalism in developing countries (1969a:192) provides input to proposals for language-choice aspects of planning.

Where reading and writing constitute the planning goal, Bowers' (1968) list of factors for deciding what languages to use provides input to developing literacy theory.

Nahir (1977) classified the functions of language-planning agencies and suggested that those functions might be seen as a way to categorize plans. In Chapter Seven, we use this view when we set out examples of each type, that is, purification, revival, reform, standardization, and modernization. Within each plan category, theories are being proposed for how best to realize each. LP theory has been based mainly on modernization ideas (as we have seen earlier in this chapter) and on standardization ideas (as we will see in Section 5.4). We will see below that modernization plans also partake of theories behind planning and development in general and that purification, revival, and reform are often chosen plans in the interest of a group's social psychology and its need to have a language plan in respect to ethnic interaction.

In Chapter Two, where we looked at the relationship of language to nation building, we discussed Heinz Kloss' (1968) proposed variables for deciding if a language has an endoglossic or exoglossic relation to the nation. Kloss also provided a way to measure a language's status from preliteracy to maturity, so that planners who wanted to use a mature language in a certain context could do so. He also proposed a continuum for seeing how a language is used. Kloss' ideas sought to provide planners with a way to decide where a language fits into a political context in regard to three dimensions: Is it native to the country or not? Is it mature? Is it recognized (officially sanctioned or not)? By not proposing discrete categories, his approach to classifying planned languages allowed languages to shift at each dimension, providing planners with latitude in the area of language choice.

Stewart (1968) proposed a set of language types, which, he says, influences their acceptance in a nation. Each language type has a set of attributes or features, and any language can be analyzed according to its degree of standardization, vitality, history, and so forth. Each language type also has one or more functions, or categories of use, that is, as a mother tongue, regional language, and the like.

Other taxonomic analyses of language-planning material that we have looked at so far include Fishman's (1968) characteristics of linguistic homogeneity and Ferguson's (1968) components of language corpus planning: graphizing, modernizing, and standardizing.

In examining language change, Labov (1972) discerned five categories of problems to be solved in order to understand change. He asserted that language change is analyzable if we know how it is constrained—that is, the situation prior to and after change (its transition), the social context of the change, how people perceive or evaluate it, and how it took hold. This set of categories clearly has direct input to the developing theory of planned language change.

In a sociolinguistic vein, Hymes' (1962) components that describe speech events in a speech community is a taxonomic/descriptive approach to seeing the role of language in society. This approach, known as the ethnography of speaking, proposes to show how language variation is patterned in society.

For choosing a language as a medium of instruction, Mackey (1962) suggested four options: teaching people in the language of the nation, of the territory, of their religion, or of their ethnic affiliation.

These are only some of the lists, category sets, and typologies discussed so far. They have an influence in any emergent LP theory in that they represent the way scholars organize their observations of language in the context of national development and social mobility.

In scientific inquiry, once facts have been observed and recorded it is common practice to analyze and classify them. The above examples represent this analytical, classifying phase of LP study. The next expected step is to derive generalizations from these taxonomies which can then be later tested. Many of the theoretical assumptions developed in the earlier sections of this chapter are such tentative generalizations. As we study emerging LP theory, we should keep in mind that

> Theories are usually introduced when previous study of a class of phenomena has revealed a system of uniformities that can be expressed in the form of empirical laws. Theories then seek to explain those regularities, and generally to afford a deeper and more accurate understanding of the phenomena in question (Hempel 1966:70).

For the most part, LP is still at the stage where empirical laws are being formed; some of the theoretical assumptions we are advancing may, in fact, turn out to be empirical laws. Some may not.

5.4   STANDARDIZATION

Language planning is defined by many scholars almost exclusively as standardization. This occurs particularly in a modernization/development context. When we talked about standardization earlier, we made reference largely to the ideas of P. S. Ray (1963). Another planning scholar, Valter Tauli, the language idealist mentioned earlier in this chapter, has also tried to place standardization in a larger framework by providing a model for research and development. A third scholar, Neustupný (1970), whose name has also come up earlier, wanted to provide a way to "treat" language standardization problems. And we have also alluded to Ferguson's three categories of corpus planning: graphization, modernization, and standardization.

Tauli's idea of LP is that it should be a matter of *language* planning more than *language-and-society* planning; in this respect, he differs from most other planners and approaches viewed in the present study. Tauli feels that language can be planned without heeding the social variables that affect it.

Jiři V. Neustupný's POLICY APPROACH and the INSTRUMENTALISM HYPOTHESIS (Haugen's term) behind the work of Tauli and Ray will be discussed here as the major conceptual approaches underlying an LP theory of language standardization. These approaches subscribe to our next LP theoretical assumption:

> The linguistic aspects of language planning should begin with the idea of standard language as a point of reference.

So that planning could use the idea of a standard as a point of reference, Paul Garvin and Madeleine Mathiot set up a number of characteristics of a standard language. Their characteristics incorporate the outcomes of Ferguson's modernization and standardization components of corpus plan-

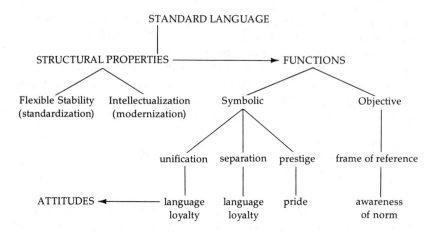

Figure 3. Garvin/Mathiot Standard Language Characteristics
(adapted from Garvin 1973:72–73)

ning. To Garvin and Mathiot, a standard has two structural properties and four functions (three symbolic and one objective) that foster three language attitudes—loyalty, pride, and awareness. A standard has been subjected to planning and, as such, is a thing quite apart from folk speech (Garvin 1973:26).

As can be seen in Figure 3, a standard language needs to be flexible and modernizable. It can then carry out the symbolic functions of unifying the area it is used in and the people who use it. It can also serve to distinguish the area and its people from neighboring people and places. Its structural flexibility and intellectualizing potential give the standard prestige, so it is something of which people are proud. A flexible standard that can keep up with the times also has the objective function of providing a frame of reference for its speakers; they know that the standard exists and that it somehow represents them. Thus, a standard is associated with public attitudes of loyalty to the language, an awareness that a norm exists with respect to the language, and a feeling that there is a real language of the people of which they can be proud.

A standard language brings a diverse speech community together while at the same time distinguishing the community from another speech community of which it may once have been a part. Standard Dutch is an example, having broken off from German (Garvin 1973) sometime after the thirteenth but before the sixteenth century. A speech community with a standard has prestige, as do the people who know a standard. A standard is also a formal model of good usage and "a frame of reference for literary creativity" (73).

These (symbolic and objective) functions of a standard give rise to just those language attitudes (pride, loyalty, awareness) that coincide with national modernization and devlopment aims as well, that is, with attitudes of national pride, loyalty, and awareness. The Garvin-Mathiot characterization of a standard language, then, provides a theoretical conception underlying the process by which a standard comes about. Their model of the structure and function of a standard sets the stage upon which the linguistic aspects of LP take place. We will now look at those aspects of LP theory that address the linguistic aspects of standardization.

5.40   Neustupný's Language Treatment

In 1970, Jiři Neustupný proposed a language-treatment system. When we talked about standardization earlier (Chapter Three) as corpus planning usually done by anthropological linguists, we pointed out that the context the standard is to be used in needs to be considered as well and that the standard must be "conventionalized." A language-treatment system is an approach to conventionalizing a standard. According to Neustupný, there are two kinds of language-treatment systems: RIGOROUS (T_r) and LOWER LEVEL (T); that is, $T_r =$ "Treatment Rigorous" and $T_1 =$ "Treatment Lower Level." The reader might recall at this point that language treatment is another way of referring to language cultivation as espoused by the Prague linguists in the 1930s. Treatment, like cultivation, is an effort to solve language problems through systematic social interventions in language development; in other words, it is LP. The "cultivation" of the 1930s has given way to the "treatment" of the 1970s. To the extent that treatment is rigorous, it is:

1. SYSTEMATIC—It responds to plan rather than merely reacts to history.

2. THEORETICALLY BASED—It is based on sociological and/or linguistic models.

3. DEEP—It responds to the linguistic situation responsible for the language problem rather than just the surface manifestation of the problem.

4. RATIONAL—It has specific long-term goals and objectives and also tries to solve the problem at hand.

To the extent that treatment is lower level, it does not display these characteristics. A language-treatment system, then, may be viewed on a continuum:

$T_{rigorous}$ ——————————————————————————————— $T_{lower\ level}$
(cultivation)   (policy)

A T_1 approach corresponds to what Neustupný refers to as POLICY while T_r generally refers to CULTIVATION.

In Neustupný's view, problems in need of a treatment system are, for example, choosing the language to be cultivated (treated, standardized) and then codifying it; putting the language into practice and then extending it throughout the area. To do this one can take a rigorous or lower-level approach or something in between. The less rigorous approach is a tacit policy solution. A T_1, or policy, approach would be that taken, for example, in a "journalist's attitude toward the language problem of India or a puristic attitude toward Czech" (Neustupný 1970:40). Lower-level treatments appeal to governments and administrators while rigorous treatments, or cultivation approaches, interest the linguist. A T_r approach is usually used where an implicit policy is in effect and would be exemplified by an attitude such as, "We should not borrow words from other languages and should speak "good" English." A T_r cultivation approach rests on the idea of a STANDARD or NORM that represents the Garvin-Mathiot features of FLEXIBLE STABILITY and FUNCTIONAL DIFFERENTIATION (see Figure 3 above). A T_r approach does not start with a standard as a frame of reference but, instead, with a sense that something ought to be done about language. According to Neustupný, different language situations call for different types of treatment on a T_r–T_1 continuum.

A policy, or T_1, approach is useful in "*less developed* modern (or modernizing) societies . . . characterized by a high degree of arbitrary . . . social and linguistic heterogeneity" (Neustupný 1970:43). So far, the policy approach has prevailed in LP, since language planning has had its origins for the most part in the study of developing languages. A cultivation, or T_r, approach is useful in situations "of functional . . . stratification of language which appears in the foreground in *more developed* communities" (43). A T_r approach can be taken in those areas where it has become clear that certain languages have specific functions vis-à-vis other languages.

The policy—cultivation continuum of approaches to language treatment takes the stance that language-use differences need to be considered; and that once a speech community is developing and modernizing, concrete cultivation rather than abstract policy is required. Both the language and the speech community are essential considerations in language-treatment systems. In the next section we will look at Tauli's idea that language treatment or standardization is best accomplished without heeding context of use.

5.41   Tauli's Language Improvement

Neustupný's idea that the context of language use determines the best form of treatment (rigorous, lower-level, or in-between) is quite different from Tauli's view that context is not necessary. In fact, Neustupný (1970:45) asserts that approaches that do not consider the stage of development of a nation needing a language plan and not taking into account the use functions of language are going out of fashion. But Tauli has a very different view of what standardization ought to be.

To Tauli, the linguistic NORM or STANDARD is "inherent in the nature of language" (Fishman, ed. 1974:50) and not in the society it is used in. Further, language users "want to use good language" and are "anxious to improve . . . language, like other tools and even social institutions" (50). As a contemporary language planner, Tauli exemplifies the idealist approach (Reese 1981). In his view, LP or standardization is "the methodical activity regulating and improving existing language or creating new regional or international languages" (56). He contends that both existing and new languages need to and can be aesthetically pleasing, euphonious, harmonious, and symmetrical regardless of function or milieu. Any language and all languages can be kept pure and continuously improved.

Tauli sees language as a tool or instrument which, as such, can be manipulated:

> A language and its components can be evaluated, altered, corrected, regulated, improved, and replaced by others, and new languages and components of a language can be created at will (Tauli 1974:51)

He sees no reason for imperfections in languages. The only reason imperfections occur is because languages that contain them (which he calls "ethnic languages") were not planned. Instead,

> They originated and developed by infinite momentary groping attempts of individual members of thousands of generations to communicate with each other. These individuals had no consciousness of the whole system of language but only the needs of the moment (Tauli 1974:51–52).

To Tauli, the role of language planners and standardization (LP) theory is clearly to make up for the errors of such "infinite momentary groping attempts." Planners should be people with a "consciousness of the whole system" who can prevent linguistic imperfection. This idea of language improvement is a controversial one and also a relatively unpopular view among most planners and planning theorists. Not many planners see the task of linguistics as Tauli sees it. Few agree that linguistics ought "to spread the existing better forms [of a language] and to construct new better forms" (54) without heeding the attitudes of the speakers.

Most of Tauli's linguistic-improvement approach is presented in his book *Introduction to a Theory of Language Planning* (1968). When referring to language policy, Tauli means general governmental linguistic policy rather than aspects of planning policy. Planning language improvement *is* standardization to him, and standardization to him *is* LP. LP seeks "to establish linguistically sound principles for creating new common and literary languages where none yet exist" (1974:58) or to improve and regulate existing languages. Further, when a new language is being created or an existing one improved in the interest of such goals as efficiency and harmony, linguistic considerations are paramount. "Extralinguistic political factors or chance" are relegated to the back seat (58).

Standardization (and consequently LP in general) is the "prescription of linguistic norms by an official or authoritative private institution that decrees what is correct and what is incorrect in a language" (Tauli 1974:62). Tauli's instrumentalist, prescriptivist, context-free idea of how a language should be standardized leads him to make statements such as, "All kinds of diglossia are uneconomic, and the aim of language policy should be to work for its elimination" (64); and to favor the development of an *inter-language*, "a universal language to be used as a means of communication by individuals belonging to different language communities" (64).

Tauli's desire to develop LP as a way to aspire to ideal and efficient language use by looking at language as a tool that can be manipulated leads one to conclude that language needs to be regulated. But this view fails to recognize that "Language is much more than an instrument; among other things it is also an expression of personality and a sign of identity" (Haugen 1971:288). And our identity and personality do not exist in a vacuum.

Standardization theories and practices, in the view of most LP scholars, are better off if they consider societal and attitudinal factors as well as linguistic structure. Most researchers reason that the more practical, less ideal views of Garvin and Neustupný provide a more realistic basis on which to build LP theory with respect to language standards and standardization than Tauli's idealist approach.

5.5　DEVELOPMENT PLANNING

In a modernizing, developing social context, LP is involved with both (1) maintenance and shift ideas and (2) standardization approaches. It is also receiving impetus in its conceptual development from other than language-planning areas (Fishman 1973), usually known as "development." Planning, in general, whether language directed or otherwise, operates on an assumption that

> What more developed entities (be they states, societies, nations, languages, or economic systems) have experienced can be helpful in charting the future course of less developed entities.
>
> *Corollary:* What less developed entities have experienced can help reconstruct those experiences undergone by more developed entities in the past (Fishman 1973:84).

These developmental assumptions suggest that any LP theory should look at indigenous language situations, those that are emerging as well as those that appear to be entrenched, in order to make recommendations for the future. In the study of developed and less developed entities, general development theory tells us, one may distinguish primary development from secondary development. PRIMARY DEVELOPMENT applies to units that arose where few other units "previously-more-developed" existed; SEC-ONDARY DEVELOPMENT applies to units that were "either hindered or assisted in development by the existence of many previously developed units" (84).

In addition to being concerned with the effects of both primary and secondary development, planners are also concerned with an entity's predevelopment or TRADITIONAL STAGE. Certain factors of an entity's traditional stage determine whether it is "change-prone or change-receptive" and whether change should be viewed as modernization or development or westernization (88).

The reader is cautioned here to note the confusion in terminology. Recall that in one approach to standardization, the term STANDARDIZATION is used to refer to a stage in the process. We saw this to be true in Ferguson's three-stage standardization scheme, which he called, ironically, LANGUAGE DEVELOPMENT. Now, from a developmental theoretical viewpoint, we see that a language (or other entity) may go through three types of development, and that one of these stages is referred to as DEVELOPMENT itself, the others being MODERNIZATION and WESTERNIZATION. It is perhaps of no help to the reader to know that as the field of LP grows, the early stages of competing jargon will most likely be replaced by a common shared terminology in the discipline as a whole (much as dialects merge once societies grow and change).

A change-prone, traditional, or predevelopment nation, state, or society is characterized as having a landed elite in contact with the outside world. These people control a military elite and a secular group of educated people and educators. Both the military and intellectual sectors, which are beholden to the landowners within a changeable entity, have free rein with respect to permission to adopt new things. That is, in societies where we can expect change to occur, the first signs of impending change are that the landed elite allow the military access to modern technology and give the intelligentsia access to modern ideas, reasoning that in this way they would be better served. As Shils (1960, as cited by Fishman 1973:88) has stated it, the power elite (the people with land) give the military and educated "modernization dispensation" in order to "maximize their usefulness."

As long as traditional power controls the military, the secular intelligentsia, and the non-landed elites, change processes remain under control and lead, at best, to *development*. However, wherever the "unholy alliance" between military and secular intelligentsia gains power, or one or another power group acquires the assistance of the masses in order to maximize its grip, the outcome is likely to run toward modernization (Fishman 1973:88, citing Shils 1962).

Thus, modernization may be differentiated from development when change is no longer controlled by the landed power elite. Planning is concerned with all stages of development, pre-, primary, and secondary. Developmental stages of a language, state, or other entity lead to changes that may be characterized from the perspective of technological and social change as (1) DEVELOPED (the power elite is still in charge), (2) MODERNIZED (the scholars or military, or both, have had an impact), or (3) WESTERNIZED. A westernized entity is not only technologically changed (developed) and socially changed (modernized) but also similar to foreign entities with which it interacts. Thus, planning may result in

1. DEVELOPMENT: Technological change predominates and social change is minimal.

2. MODERNIZATION: Moderate amounts of both technological and social change occur.

3. WESTERNIZATION: Social change is widespread, accompanying technological change "based upon methods and social relations borrowed from successful foreign models" (Fishman 1973:90).

We thus have a development continuum ranging from development itself through modernization to westernization. If we look at development ideas with respect to language planning in particular, Fishman sees the analogy as follows:

"Development" might refer rather more to lexical elaboration, particularly when conducted on the basis of indigenous roots, whereas "Westernization" might refer to more fargoing changes, e.g., those touching upon the writing system, the pronouns and honorifics in verb-forms, etc. (1973:90).

Modernization is the stage at which we may see the "development" of Hebrew today. Modernization of language is evidenced by a growing popular identification with a standardized national language on the part of the public, an increased accessibility of all social varieties of language within that community to each other, and the more rapid diffusion of linguistic innovations across social classes. The difference between modernization and westernization is more of degree than kind. Modernization implies an increased sharing of a common social membership and identity after new technologies and ideas have appeared. Westernization implies all this, with the added implication that the substance of modernization as social change has come from a predictable source and that the entity within which the change has occurred can communicate with the source of that change (Fishman 1973:91).

The reader is undoubtedly aware by now that LP, as it has developed so far, is a field of the Western academic world; its ideas reach the Western academic world and those societies which that world considers to be "developing." When we use a term like WESTERNIZATION, we should be aware that the process it represents could as well be called "easternization"— if we knew enough about the potential influence of the eastern world on developing, modernizing societies and their cultures. WESTERNIZATION is a term with a built-in bias based on the fact that LP and development planning have so far been fields of endeavor undertaken by scholars and planners of the Western world.

Language planning and development planning, in addition to leading to comparable results, are also analogous in that both types of planning may come up with unexpected consequences. The results of either can lead to COUNTERPLANNING on the part of rival (national or language) groups.

> Planners try to mobilize all of the populations under their control and the very process of mobilization and dislocation from linkages to former authorities and conventions makes possible counter-mobilization on behalf of power elites and identity symbols of a more immediately indigenous or otherwise commanding sort (Fishman 1973:94, citing Deutsch 1966, Wriggins 1961).

Both language-planning and "other-than-language" planning activities are also value-encumbered. Thus, planners need to take language attitudes and values into account. Language planners and social planners need to direct their efforts to "finding the most rational use of resources with respect to the achievement of specific goals" (Fishman 1973:96). Planners need to find solutions to problems. Their clients are responsible for implementing the solutions. Likewise, when a planned change has been implemented, evaluation and feedback are required "for the purposes of improved (more effective) planning" (97, citing Friedman 1967).

The need of planners to be aware of potential counterplans and the influences that existing attitudes and values have on whether or not a planned change can succeed, and the emphasis placed on goal-orientation and problem solving are all common concerns language developers and national developers have. Also common is the need to evaluate the plans, given the fact that implementation is the job of the client. Once a national or language plan is in effect, the planner is out of the picture and cannot know whether the goals have been reached—if evaluation and feedback are not available.

In comparing LP theory with development theory, evaluation is one area in which LP falls short (Reese 1981), prompting Rubin (1971) to call for more concrete evaluative criteria, As was noted in Chapter Four (4.4 above), LP as it enters the 1980s suffers from lack of both goal operationalization and of ways to measure the likely effects of practical plans. There is also a general inability to look at planning results in a quantifiable way (cf. Reese 1981:46).

True, it is hard to quantify factors such as social cost; however, social planners have faced these problems, whereas language planners have yet to come to grips with them. Language plans, again unlike development plans, rarely have operational definitions of positive and negative results built into them. How can any constructive modification of a plan be made if we cannot figure out the source of its success or failure?

Still, disappointments are also common in the development planning process: "the entire planning enterprise is considerably disillusioned by the gap between target plans and demonstrable attainments" (Fishman 1973:98). The areas in which both types of planning seem to be weakest are implementation and evaluation. With respect to evaluation, LP is in somewhat worse shape than development planning. In both areas, a need also exists for "more formal training and comparative experience for the personnel involved in planning functions and their removal from political dependence insofar as possible" (99).

Rubin (1979) looked at the possibility of applying theory from such areas as city planning, health planning, and transportation planning to developing a theoretical model for LP. In doing this, she noted that so far the prevailing model used in LP has been taken from the field of economic planning. She suggests that planners might gain some insights from other areas as well. It may be that in some cases approaches such as cost-benefit analysis would not apply. LP is primarily social planning; as such, it is not always possible to decide what alternatives are best or which decisions are "right" and which "wrong." In social planning, Rubin suggests, you cannot consider all alternatives and choose the best because by the time a plan has begun to be implemented, the social milieu has begun to be altered in response to the plan. To think of "making a plan" may be an illusion! Rather than seeking the best alternative, language planners should take a page from the book of city planners and find a satisfying alternative that will do, says Rubin. She points out that businesses seek to stay in business first and cope with long-term plans secondarily. Planners who are faced with solving language problems should realize that their task is a *wicked* rather than a *tame* one—for which no rule is available that will eliminate all problems. A planner cannot know when a plan is right. In LP as in social planning (such as city, health, or transportation planning), implementation is part of the policy-making process. In LP, language policy is intended to be formulated, codified, elaborated, and implemented. However, in actual practice so far, policy formulation and implementation have been kept quite distinct. If we take a social rather than an economic planning perspective, it may be possible to incorporate implementation into the policy-making (determination, formulation) process.

Rubin feels that planners need to begin to spend less time and energy on the technical aspects of language change as a means of solving language problems and to look more at the social aspects. In other words, status planning rather than corpus planning needs emphasis. In a nation seeking to establish a national language, is the goal to get people to use the language or is it to build a nation? If the goal is to build a nation, then a "good" language plan should foster that goal by addressing the language's sociopolitical components. A less appropriate plan in such a case would be one that had as its main task the standardization of the language or the technical establishment of it as the medium of instruction.

The relationship between a policy and its implementation is an area, like that of evaluation, about which language planners know very little. Most discussions of policy focus on its determination, or else on aspects of codification and elaboration. Rubin calls for a less "rational" and more "action-oriented" model for LP theory in which (1) the people whose language behavior is to be changed are involved, (2) the political nature of implementation is recognized, and (3) the goal, setting, and technological aspects of putting a plan into effect are coped with.

In the next years, LP research may be expected to explore some of these newer avenues of theoretical development and benefit from ongoing research in both economic and social spheres of other-than-language planning.

5.6   ETHNIC-GROUP RELATIONS

So far in our discussion of emergent LP theory we have seen it in light of modernization theory, in respect to language-maintenance and language-shift concepts, and in respect to ideas from social and economic development. We now turn to LP theory with respect to concepts of ethnic interaction. As societies develop, change, and modernize, what can language planning learn from ideas of group behavior in contact?

Language planning has to take into consideration the group affiliation of the persons the plan will affect, for language attitudes and beliefs accompany sociocultural divisions. Language factors and group membership interrelate on a number of dimensions such as location, native-ness (whether the people and language are indigenous to the area or not), status, relationship to religion, sex, age, and occupation. Fishman (1968a:94) offers a number of "questionable generalizations" that seem to apply to language in relation to ethnic interaction. These generalizations are a by-product of the study of maintenance and shift characteristics in modernizing societies:

1. Intact groups and those with a sense of group loyalty (for example, those with a "national spirit") maintain their languages.

2. Urban groups are more likely to give up their languages than are rural groups.

3. "Prestigeful" languages are kept, those without prestige are given up.

The three generalizations overlap. For example, intact urban groups with a sense of loyalty may foist their language onto other groups they are in contact with as they move from ethnicity toward nationality. In this case, the tendency of the group to undergo language shift is counterbalanced by its power vis-à-vis other groups. Power is often accompanied by prestige, leading to language maintenance rather than shift. Ethnic-group relations become a concern only when the groups (and their languages) come into contact. Fishman suggests that one conceptual framework in which to study both planning and ethnicity is a typology developed by R. A. Schermerhorn (1964). Schermerhorn classifies contact situations "in accord with differences between them that we sense to exist" (Fishman 1968a:101). Schermerhorn's typology makes use of the following features to classify each group in a contact situation:

1. power (equal versus unequal)

2. control (incorporated versus colonized)

3. plurality (high versus low)

4. immigration (recent versus nonrecent)

5. social mobility (high versus low)

6. acculturation (high versus low)

7. industrialization (high versus low)

When two groups are in contact, we may compare the values each has for these seven features in order to see whether maintenance or shift is likely. For example, a group that is on an equal footing with another group from the point of view of power, is incorporated with that group, has many people in it, has been in the area a long time, is socially mobile, is highly acculturated, and is highly industrialized is hardly likely to undergo language shift! In contrast, consider American Indian groups in most of the

United States from the perspective of these features. Most of them have a plus value only for having been in the area for a long time, and some are highly acculturated; however, for all other features they have negative values. No wonder that the American Indian languages are rapidly dying out.

According to Fishman (1968a), another way to conceive of ethnic relations among groups in contact is to assess whether, in historical terms, the groups came together

1. as new *settlers* by invitation from the host group

2. as *daughter settlers* who immigrated later from the original homeland of the new settlers and/or the host group

3. as *special-purpose settlers* who came to work for the host group

Crosscutting these three categories of settler groups is their respective degree of cultural maturity or development. This typology arose as a way to analyze German groups established outside Germany. In this typological approach we may look at groups in contact thus:

Culturally developed	New	Daughter	Special
Culturally undeveloped	New	Daughter	Special

A culturally undeveloped new group would be exemplified by the Chinese workers brought to Tanzania to build a railroad; a culturally developed special group would be German scientists in the United States after World War II (Fishman 1968a:102).

Group-contact typologies such as the above or such as the Schermerhorn one can be useful to LP in providing insight with respect to intergroup contact situations and in making it possible "to meaningfully assemble and analyze language maintenance and shift files" (Fishman 1968a:103).

If we know the group-contact situations and the resulting language situations in complex societies, we can make generalizations about likely future happenings when particular attributes accompany language-group contacts. In Chapter Six, where we will look at attempts to formulate LP methods, we will talk about proposals made by Charles Ferguson (1966, 1967) for coming up with national sociolinguistic profiles and for sociolinguistically oriented language surveys. In the rest of the present chapter, we will see how sociopsychological ideas about language and ethnicity might be useful to LP theory and describe a proposed theory of language and ethnic interaction.

5.60   The Social Psychology of Bilingualism

In our discussion about Lambert's idea that language attitude is important in the historical development of LP (Chapter Four), we saw that language change is furthered or impeded by people's feelings about the language to which the change refers. Now we will describe, in somewhat more detail, what Lambert calls "the social psychology of bilingualism," a framework within which planners can see the psychological and social influences and repercussions that surround multilingual behavior.

In addition to the typological characteristics of language and culture contact described above, groups, as they interact with each other, also display attitudinal characteristics that affect language. Jessel stresses the fact that social and language behavior has a strong ethnic component. He feels that outside of communication,

> the major function of language is to reflect the social and behavioral conditions of its group, its life and experience, its manner of thinking and its world view, both of the group as a whole and, specifically, its intrinsic institutions (1978:85).

When we talked about language and world view (Chapter Three), we mentioned that language may function as a reflection of group culture. As a reflection of a group's social and psychological self, language may and often does play a significant role in how people see themselves. Planners seeking to implement language policy need to see how the policy will affect the perception group members have of themselves and of others. In this regard, the sociopsychological characteristics of ethnicity as well as the typological sociocultural ones (as in the Schermerhorn approach or the historical approach just described) need to be looked at together. As the linguist Joshua Whatmough asserted back in 1957,

> Language is the expression of the attitude of a certain speech community toward its culture. . . . Language mirrors the psyche, and it the culture, of a language community (quoted in Jessel 1978:88).

The idea of language as a symbol of ethnicity is extremely useful to the planner, particularly when ethnicity factors are being developed into nationality feelings. Levic Jessel has proposed the ETHNIC PROCESS as the way language and cultural evolution takes place. Jessel takes the position that Whorf's "world view" idea that language determines the way a people see the world was actually the "outlook of an ethnic community." Jessel thinks that it had probably occurred to Whorf that linguistic and cultural observations "need to be directly correlated with ethnic considerations" (1978:95–96). Jessel sees ethnicity to be related to language in the following way:

Although the innate faculty for language is universally human, every language tells a special story: the origin, experience, use, and development of each one invariably fall within an ethnic framework. In some measure, then, and in some manner, language changes are the consequence of ethnic pressures; in turn, these changes affect the cognitive system and create a characteristically ethnic world view (96).

Jessel understands ethnicity as the symbolic expression of social behavior "reflecting the dynamics of the ethnic process" (1978:119). The ETHNIC PROCESS is "a dynamic current of primordial origin" that flows from "a pristine group to modern society"; it is "the combined effect of the primordial ethnic stimulus and the corresponding ethnic setting in the changing environment" (18). To Jessel, then, ethnicity *is* world view. Language as a factor of ethnicity changes in response to the ethnic process.

Jessel's idea of the ethnic process as sociopsychological input to developing LP theory needs to be looked at from the perspective of Fishman (1977) and in relation to what was said earlier about LP and world view when we looked at world view as the concern of the anthropologically oriented planner. In Chapter Three, we pointed out that some scholars think that when we learn a new language we learn to think the way its speakers think. Jessel's view is that the way we think is what makes us members of a group, and part of becoming a member of a group is to know its language. Language planning as an effort to change what language people use is an attempt to change what people talk about in their world. To the extent that LP is also an effort to see that people talk about the same things in the same way, LP is an attempt to see that people share group membership or world view. The process of group membership change and accompanying language change is labeled by Jessel as the ethnic process.

Fishman's (1977) analysis of language and ethnicity (discussed in Chapter Two) sees both social and psychological intergroup factors as related to language. His idea that primordial ethnicity prevails before groups come into contact is also relevant to our analysis. Once the ethnic process has begun, a new sense of common origin needs to develop. No longer can we think that *we* are the people with a right to exist, and *they* are not. As part of the ethnic process, groups in contact need to reconcile each other's right to be. If we take the position that language may function by means of a "culture-loaded vocabulary" to foster ethnicity as well as nationality, the sociopsychological components of ethnicity could be related to language planning. The planner should consider changing the cultural (external) aspects of language (such as special vocabulary expressing group characteristics) as well as its structural (internal) aspects.

For example, to make Swahili the national language of Kenya while having the national cultural vocabulary represented by loan words or direct translations does not work. When words referring to government, science, medicine, or other fields are bound to a culture other than that of the national language, the success of the national language in those spheres is hindered.

Lambert's motives for second-language learning (instrumental or integrative) may also be tied in to the concept of ethnic process. Integrative motives for language learning facilitate the ethnic process, whereas instrumental motives impede it. But in general, outside of Lambert's analyses there exists for the most part an apparent lack of knowledge on the part of sociolinguists about the work of psychologists in the field of language attitudes. Likewise, psychologists are generally ignorant of advances being made by sociolinguists in ways to measure language attitude (Webber 1979:219).

Cooper and Fishman (1974) see attitude studies as important to planners interested in the social psychology of language contact in anticipation that such studies will be able to answer questions about the circumstances that lead speakers to evaluate their language negatively and about the factors that contribute to positive language attitudes (such factors as ideology or demography, for instance). In the next chapter, we will point out some of the ways that have been suggested for measuring language attitudes.

Attitudes of both a psychological and sociological nature surround the usual contact situations of di- and triglossia, and multi- and bilingualism. People who use more than one language necessarily express their attitudes about their respective languages as they participate in ethnic interaction. Inherent in the concepts of di- and triglossia are the attitudes or values attached to the various speech varieties described as *high* or *low*. For diglossia, Ferguson (1959) noted that the high variety is superior to the low in a number of ways, often even to the extent that "H alone is regarded as real and L is reported 'not to exist'" (7). H is thought more beautiful, logical, better able to express important thought. Concomitantly, speakers of H are thought to be of a better class.

It comes as a shock to discover that many speakers of a language involved in diglossia characteristically prefer to hear a political speech or an expository lecture or a recitation of poetry in H even though it may be less intelligible to them than it would be in L (Ferguson 1959:7).

Diglossia becomes a language problem when trends toward more widespread literacy, regional and social intercommunication, and a standard language for nationalism appear as goals. In such a case, linguistic unification is aspired to, and proponents of H and proponents of L take sides. Advocates of H and L make the following claims, respectively (Ferguson 1959:19):

H	L
• connects the community with its past and the outside world	• is close to the "real thinking and feelings of the people."
• is superior	• people already know it

One possible change is that either H or L becomes the standard. Ferguson asserts that

> H can succeed in establishing itself as a standard only if it is already serving as a standard language in some other community and the diglossia community . . . tends to merge with the other community. Otherwise H fades away and becomes a learned or liturgical language studied only by scholars or specialists and not used actively in the community. Some form of L or a mixed variety becomes standard (Ferguson 1959:20).

Gumperz (1969) sees language distance as "a function of social interaction and social context"; he suggests that "language is not necessarily a serious barrier to communication" (247). So the question is: Why do language differences in multilingual societies persist?

> What is it within the system of roles and statuses or in the norms of social interaction that favors the retention of such overt symbols of distinctness? Under what conditions do such symbols disappear? (1969:247).

In a statement by Fishman (1960:327) that "what is easily expressable in one language is not necessarily easily or accurately expressable in another," we may see that language as an expression of world view is important in planning. Language differences are easily relatable to group differences. As Fishman notes (1960), groups of Eskimos are more interested in snow and Arabs in horses, for example. Generally, one's ethnicity finds most of its expression in the lexicon (culture-loaded versus culture-free vocabulary); it is also the area that evokes language attitudes toward *us* on the part of *them*.

In Kenya, some non-Swahili hold the stereotypical view that the Swahili (a group generally defined as nontribal) are "secretive." As Akong'a (1979) points out, it is possible to trace this stereotype as a derivation of language attitude. In Swahili culture, privacy is a strong value and is expressed in the concept *stara*, which translates variously in English as "cover," "concealment," "place of refuge," or "asylum" and figuratively includes the meanings "modesty," "reticence," "reserve," "proper covering." *Stara* is reflected in much of the shared cultural behavior of the Swahili. Each home has an area that is off limits to outsiders, for example. The *stara* concept may be that which leads outsiders to view an attitude that is considered a value *inside* the culture as being a behavior directed against others *outside* that culture (such as keeping things from others).

We have already seen the importance of language attitudes in understanding how to plan language change. First, we saw what group features might determine the likelihood of maintenance or shift. Two typologies were described: Schermerhorn's (1964) for contact situations and Fishman's (1968a) three-way classification of type of settlement in an area. Depending on the circumstances under which it settles in an area, a group will be regarded in certain ways, which in turn will affect its retention or abandonment of its language.

We then looked at language attitudes in light of the ethnic process as defined by Jessel and tied this concept into ideas discussed earlier, such as world view, primordial ethnicity, culture-loaded vocabulary, and motives for second-language learning. Building on ideas such as these, we will conclude our chapter on developing LP theory with a look at one attempt to propose a theory of language in ethnic-group relations.

5.61   The Role of Language in Ethnic Interaction

Two scholars, a sociologist (Tajfel) and a social psychologist (Giles), working with others, have attempted to come up with a theory of language in ethnic-group relations (Giles, Bourhis, and Taylor 1977). This theory has three parts: (1) a taxonomy of ethnolinguistic vitality, showing the structural factors that affect the relative liveliness of the groups in contact; (2) a theory of intergroup relations (developed by Tajfel); and (3) a theory of speech accommodation (developed by Giles) (Giles et al. 1977:324).

By combining these three components, the developers of this theory of language use intended it as a framework within which it will be possible to understand the role language plays in ethnicity and in intergroup relations. To see what part language plays in ethnic interaction, the role of language behavior in each conceptual realm of intergroup relations should be described. Conceptual realms include the social categories used and the social identities employed by groups in contact. That is, when groups interact they employ social CATEGORIZATION as a basis for their linguistic and cultural attitudes and behaviors toward others. They also classify themselves by self-IDENTIFICATION in contrast to others; a part of self-identity, just as social categorization, includes feelings and attitudes about one's own speech style vis-à-vis that of others. People not only categorize and identify each other when they come in contact, they also engage in a COMPARISON of their social identity and their attitudes toward other groups since "one's identity only acquires meaning in relation to other existing or contrasting features of one's ethnic world" (Giles et al. 1977:328). In social terms, then, we use language to see who *we* are, to see how we see who *they* are, and to see how we see ourselves stacking up in relation to *them*. The role language plays in doing this needs to be described.

An ethnic group also uses language to maintain a psychological as well as sociological distinction from others. Giles et al. (1977:330) report Parkin's (1977) finding that "members of adolescent societies and gangs in Nairobi felt a need to make themselves distinct from each other by a claimed use of English and Swahili respectively—even though their language behavior appeared objectively very similar." Generally, psychological distinctiveness is asserted by such means as varying accent, dialect differences, or the maintenance or shifting of a code or speech variety in the presence of others.

Finally, groups in contact use language as a way to perceive cognitive alternatives to use in interaction with others. By COGNITIVE ALTERNATIVE is meant the definition of a group's position as stable or unstable, as higher or lower than that of another group. If a group sees no alternative "to the existing intergroup situation, some individuals may . . . consider the position of their own group vis-à-vis the outgroup as stable and legitimate, and will attribute the blame for their low position in society internally to themselves as a group because of its inferior characteristics. Thus, they will attempt to pass into the dominant group" (Giles et al. 1977:332). To pass from what we think is a low group to a high one, it is possible "to upwardly converge" our speech patterns. An example of this may be seen in "certain Mexican Americans who turn away from Spanish to English [and] also attempt to rid themselves of all traces of a Spanish accent in their English speech" (332).

Likewise, members of a dominant group, for one reason or another, may choose to use its "superior" language to prevent slippage from its high status.

The more vitality the subordinate group is perceived to possess (and hence the more threat it holds for the dominant group), the more likely it will be that the dominant group will wish to differentiate linguistically from an outgroup speaker (Giles et al. 1977:334).

Thus, each of the five conceptual realms of intergroup behavior can be associated with given speech strategies. The theory of language in ethnic-group relations that Giles and colleagues suggest links these speech-strategy/group-behavior realms to the situational variables that operate in intergroup contexts. Ethnolinguistic groups that interact (using speech strategies in the different conceptual realms discussed above) differ from each other in terms of VITALITY. People want to belong to vital groups, and they strive for this goal in their intergroup behavior by using speech strategies.

ETHNOLINGUISTIC VITALITY is structured by STATUS, DEMOGRAPHIC, and INSTITUTIONAL-support features. That is, a group and its language have ethnolinguistic vitality to the extent that they have prestige (status), have numbers (demography), and are organized (institutionalized).

Status variables have to do with the prestige a group has in an intergroup context. The more status a group has, the more vital it is. Demographic variables have to do with the size of a group and its distribution throughout the area. The more people in a group, the more vital it is. Institutional-support variables have to do with a group's representation in the nation, region, or community. The more a group is visible and the more its language is used in high places—in "institutions of the government, church, business, and so forth" (Giles et al. 1977:309), the more vital the group is.

Status, demography, and institutional-support features interact. By looking at their point of interaction, we may reach an understanding of ethnolinguistic interaction and determine the degree of vitality that the given ethnolinguistic groups have.

A group with many people, a large amount of national visibility, much public representation, and great prestige is vital. It is healthy and likely to be around awhile. This theory of ethnic-group relations, which rests on measuring ethnolinguistic vitality by looking at group liveliness, is a comprehensive approach to studying language in context. Group vitality or liveliness is determined by comparing the social and ethnic categories that come in contact when the groups interact and the socially and psychologically distinct vocabulary used in those situations. This theory seeks to provide a broader approach than, for example, Schermerhorn's typology. It seeks to come up with a comprehensive analysis of the likelihood of language maintenance or shift.

Such a theory, by showing how the different groups conceive of themselves socially, psychologically, and cognitively, is useful for LP. Planners seeking to foster development and acceptance of a national language, for example, would need to be sure that ethnolinguistic vitality is associated with their plan and that the sociopsychological aspects of the group the language is associated with lend themselves to keeping the language and its culture alive. For instance, to plan to implement as a national language a minority-group language that has negative vitality characteristics and whose speakers use strategies designed to move them to another group is a plan doomed to failure. Planners may successfully use ethnolinguistic vitality factors, group-behavioral data, and knowledge of speech strategies to manipulate language and ethnic identity.

5.7 SUMMARY

In the preceding pages, we have seen that language-planning theory falls roughly in three broad areas related to decision-making, modernization, and intergroup behavior models in other social sciences. So far, LP decision-making theory has looked primarily to economics as a model, stressing the importance of choosing the best plan. The best plan would be one that changes a language while incurring the least costs but providing the most benefits. Another economic-based theoretical model is one seeking to use the concept of spread decisions. In such a framework, efforts are made to go beyond evaluating potentially "best" decisions with respect to each other. Spread decisions include (1) judgments about the likely effects of the decision once implemented and (2) assurances that the decisions will produce the desired effects.

Modernization models of LP look to fields such as economic and social development in other-than-language areas. The language changes proposed in language planning usually recommend language shift or language maintenance in one form or another. However, entire languages in different communities, speech varieties within linguistic communities, or parts of entire languages within single communities are variously maintained, shifted, changed, or even lost naturally as well as deliberately. To conceptualize language change in a naturalistic setting, LP scholars use the idea of domain of language behavior and see how language-behavior patterns form and vary within the many domains of a speech community.

LP theorists also see language change, like social change, to be tied to attitude as well as to actual behavior. To implement a planned change it is necessary to see how the change is likely to be accepted by the target population. To reinforce the attitude a plan seeks to foster, the planners need to codify the loyalties and values associated with the change, and the change needs to (1) be generalizable and uncomplicated so it can be widely accepted, (2) be applicable throughout the sociopolitical entity in which it is to have an effect, (3) be able to be maintained as a change, and (4) be subject to evaluation so it can be amended if need be.

Some theorists also conceive of planned language change as being analogous to planned development in an area that is becoming a nation or state. In such a framework certain factors seem to favor "development" (or, in the case of language, "change"), while others work against it. For example, in a developing area international trade fosters the development process; so, too, does an international language. If we can empirically validate such language/state evolutionary pairs, LP and development planning may well be able to cooperate in fruitful ways.

Political theories about attachment to national systems and ideas of language loyalty have also been found mutually reinforcing from a theoretical point of view. Language-planning theory also needs to make use of the concept of political integration. In integrated states or nations, language can be used to bring about social change. Politically integrated or united states are associated with a strong degree of sentimental attachment to them. But such united polities also make use of instrumental motives of loyalty.

People need to love their country, but they also need to use it to structure their lives the way they want them to be. Such theories about attachment to national systems and motives underlying loyalty find conceptual use in the language-planning sphere when we are considering ways to further particular language attitudes or manipulate language loyalties.

LP theory was also seen to be emerging from some categories used in a number of taxonomic approaches in describing language in developing nations and in classifying language change in socially stratified societies.

Standardization theories abound as conceptual frameworks for technological language planning. There are rigorous ("cultivation") as opposed to lower-level ("policy") treatments, and much theory is based on the idea that standardization *means* improvement. Efforts to standardize languages occur in modernizing, developing, or westernizing contexts and need to be sensitive to subtle contextual differences in each sphere.

Whereas most modernization theory used so far by language planners has derived from politics and economics, it may be that a change is in the wind as LP scholars begin to look at ideas in the sphere of social planning. When we consider LP theory, it is wise to remember that LP is to a great extent linguistics (albeit anthropologically oriented sociolinguistics) as well as planning. John Lyons reminds us that

> The linguist's first task is to *describe* the way people actually speak (and write) their language, not to *prescribe* how they ought to speak and write. In other words, linguistics (in the first instance at least) is *descriptive* not *prescriptive* (or normative) (1968:43).

Beyond asserting that LP as linguistics need not dictate but instead should facilitate and recommend, it is also fitting to close this chapter on LP theory with Lyons' further reminder that inevitable linguistic change in natural settings is not (as Tauli would have us believe) necessarily corrupt. All languages are created equal. They are all efficient and capable systems of communication that meet the needs of those who use them. As needs change, languages change. If new terms are needed, they are borrowed, or formed from elements internal to the system. What place does LP have, then, if language change is acceptable and inevitable? Why bother to plan? Again, Lyons:

> It should be stressed that in distinguishing between description and prescription, the linguist is not saying that there is no place for prescriptive studies of language. It is not being denied that there might be valid cultural, social, or political reasons for promoting the wider acceptance of some particular language or dialect at the expense of others. In particular, there are obvious administrative and educational advantages in having a unified literary standard. (1969:43).

LP exists to promote the "wider acceptance of some particular language or dialect at the expense of others" for "valid cultural, social, or political reasons." Language planning as a field is based on the idea that planning is to be done descriptively and in consideration of social and psychological, political and economic, as well as contextual factors.

As we surveyed the emergence of LP theory, we saw that a number of working assumptions could be identified. We will summarize them now as a synopsis of what could be called the language-planning theoretic "givens." The fourteen assumptions described in the chapter may be topically summarized as six:

1. LP seeks to provide conscious alternative language decisions and their consequences, making use of given resources in solving language problems that involve a change in the language behavior of a group of people.

2. Multilingual (and multidialectal) speakers vary with respect to the number and overlap of the domains in which they habitually employ each of their languages.

3. In developing areas,

   a. people with language skills are favored over those without.

   b. population increases correspondingly affect the relative strength of language varieties.

   c. economic growth requires the expansion of knowledge in language use (such as lexical and varietal elaboration).

   d. people need to be able to shift language varieties (to use different social dialects and special-purpose languages).

   e. people need to know LWCs to participate in international trade.

   f. social and economic mobility is easier if there is linguistic unity (homogeneity).

   g. as economic growth is cumulative, so, too, is vocabulary development; thus "borrowing" aids growth by eliminating the need to wait for vocabulary to "evolve."

4. Instrumental attachments to a language can lead to sentimental attachments.

   a. a common language strengthens both sentimental and instrumental attachments and reinforces their continued development.

5. LP should begin with the concept of standard language as a point of reference.

6. The development processes undergone by "developed" languages and nations (societies) can clarify the future development possibilities of "underdeveloped" ones.

   a. less developed languages and nations (societies), as they go through the development process, provide evidence for the reconstruction of the developmental history of other languages or nations (societies).

It is likely that most LP theory will incorporate these ideas in one way or another. We will now turn to a survey of some of the most common methods employed so far in LP research, many of which provide empirical data in support of these and other tentative assumptions.

Chapter Six

LANGUAGE-PLANNING METHOD

6.0 INTRODUCTION

Along with each broad theoretical area associated with language planning, there are various methods used by scholars to amass and analyze the data upon which plans couched in theoretical terms may be formulated and successfully implemented. Much of language planning is based on the results of:

1. Surveys and questionnaires

2. Ethnographic observations

3. Attitude analyses and measurements

4. Measurements of language distance

5. Evaluation procedures

6. Comparative and quantitative methods (including cost-benefit analysis, multiple regression analysis, and so forth)

6.1 ATTEMPTS TO FORMULATE METHOD

Many of the approaches to LP mentioned throughout this book require that the planner be familiar with certain methods and techniques of data gathering and analysis. Many of these are general methods used in the other disciplines used by LP. In this section, we will describe some of the more frequently used *tools* of planners. Our discussion will not go into detail, since to do so would require that we discuss all the methods used by scientists in the many disciplines that make up the emerging field of LP study.

Specifically, we will look at the following methods: cost-benefit analysis, multiple regression analysis, quantification of planning variables (such as degree of bilingualism), measurement of attitudes, use of questionnaires, measurement of language distance, contrastive analysis (see also Chapter Three above), and dominance configuration. We will also talk about the importance of the comparative method for LP and see how certain techniques such as the analysis of variance are useful. We will point out the need for evaluative methods in LP and talk about survey methods that have been used. We will also see which approaches to language-change study are applicable to planning and how, in some instances, LP involves descriptive linguistic methods.

Such a vast array of methods in language planning does not imply that the planner be a master or mistress of all trades. The interdisciplinary nature of LP is one of its strengths. It is hoped that economists, political scientists, sociologists, linguists, anthropologists, educators, and others will continue to use their own special approaches to planning in years to come. Our purpose here is only to give an idea of what types of tools planning may employ.

The present chapter will repeat, to some extent, what was said in earlier chapters in discussions of LP as it relates to various disciplines, for those disciplines gave rise to the particular methods used in LP. For example, in the previous chapter we looked at the theory behind cost-benefit analysis. In the present chapter we again bring up cost-benefit analysis, but this time to explain what such analysis entails.

The fact that more pages in this book will have been devoted to theory than to method creates a false impression. In actuality, more methods are available for LP than there are theories to back them up. Only now is theory beginning to emerge to account for the deliberate change of language and the evaluation of change as a way to solve language problems. Because the methods used so far are general ones borrowed from social science, they will be referred to here only as they apply. Once LP theory has developed beyond its present stage, it may well be that specific LP methods derived from that theory will emerge. At the end of this chapter, we will discuss some methodological innovations in survey research brought about by work in LP.

6.10   Tools of the Trade

6.100   Cost-Benefit Analysis

To use economic analysis in LP, planners should

1. estimate costs and benefits that can be attributed to specific goals and consequences of actual language planning (Jernudd 1971:302)

2. determine the costs of the language-planning process

3. figure out alternatives to every decision made in the planning process, from the most general to the most specific

4. make suggestions about what components of language planning are found to recur and be typical (303).

If we can determine what the "best" planned language change can accomplish for a specific price and how that "best" change resembles all other types of language change, we are in an improved position to make a language plan work. The economic planner also needs to know what alternative is "best" for a smaller expenditure and what typifies an economic change. Just as cost-benefit analysis serves the economist seeking wise change, so also some adaptation of such analysis should be useful to the language planner.

Cost-benefit analysis in language planning is a way to forecast the different results that may be obtained from alternative plans. In proposing that LP adopt cost-benefit analysis, Björn Jernudd has asserted that to study the effectiveness of a proposed language change, ideally *all* consequences the change would have in society should be defined. Those consequences that can be quantified must be quantified, and all consequences need to be compared. The consequences need to be related to the preferences of the people who will be affected by the change. "This group of people will perceive some of the consequences as *costs*, other consequences as *benefits*. Some consequences are *intangible*, some *tangible*" (1971:264). Only the tangible consequences of a plan can be quantified.

It is often more difficult for language planners to locate and identify benefits of language change than it is for economists to find benefits of economic change, because language change benefits "are *intangible* or because they affect individuals' performance with considerable *time lag* between learning and use" (Jernudd 1971:267). Language planners who want to use cost-benefit analysis need to be aware of the fact that benefits are difficult to identify, quantify, and attach a money value to. Thias and Carnoy's (1972) cost-benefit analysis of rate of return on investments in education in Kenya as compared to rates of return on investments in other sectors of the economy is an effort to consider intangibles by showing that one can analyze certain factors such as years of schooling, teacher education, and the like. The Thias and Carnoy study found differential rates of return in relation to the number of years in school, size of class, and teacher-training level. However, the correlation did *not* indicate that the more schooling, the smaller the classroom, or that the better-trained the teacher, the better the return! More efforts toward such quantification of LP variables and of LP evaluation in general would seem to be a direction more language planning studies in the future might take (Reese 1981).

Despite a preponderance of intangible consequences in LP as compared to economic planning, we still need to identify, quantify, and monetize (that is, specify in dollar-and-cents terms) the costs and benefits of a plan as far as possible. Then the costs and benefits may be analyzed by comparing:

1. monetized costs to monetized benefits to find out what the *profit maximization* is

2. quantified costs to monetized benefits to find out what the *benefit maximization* is

3. monetized costs to quantified benefits to see what the *cost minimization* is

Monetized costs and benefits are those for which cash expenditures can be calculated. In LP, monetized benefits are, for all practical purposes, always intangible. Quantified costs and benefits, however, can be measured; for example, we can count how many people do not know a language before a planned changed and then count how many do know it after the change. We can then compare this figure to the results of other changes with regard to factors such as wage earnings.

A cost-benefit analysis, then, in any sphere, is a comparison of profit and benefit maximization in the interest of cost minimization. In LP, where monetized benefits are hard to figure out but quantified benefits are relatively easy, it is most productive—at present—to focus on cost minimization. That is, given the intangible nature of LP benefits, it appears that Item 3 is most useful. To analyze the cost minimization of alternative language plans is possible because we can consider those benefits that can be measured vis-à-vis the actual costs that can be monetarily determined. At this stage of LP neither profit nor benefit maximization of language change can reliably be determined.

6.101 Glottoeconomics

An interesting economically based approach to "language as a type of human capital useful in consumption or production activity" (Vaillancourt 1979:1) has emerged in the past ten years. The economics of language or GLOTTOECONOMICS seeks to understand language choice in relation to the socioeconomic power of a language group, it is a way to see language choice within a framework of economic choice. Glottoeconomics sees language use in relationship to profit maximization as a way to explain language choice; in other words, people use a language because they get something from it, not because it is theirs. This view, then, counters the view that ethnicity is a way to explain language choice. From a glottoeconomic viewpoint, language utility rather than language-associated ethnicity provides a better explanation of language choice.

> This does not mean, however, that ethnic preferences are not present and active in real world situations. Indeed an interesting line of enquiry would be to combine both ethnic preferences and traditional economic motives to analyze in a dynamic framework the forces that make for the retention or loss of its language by individuals or groups in various socioeconomic contexts (Vaillancourt 1979:11).

This approach assumes that people's choice of labor income (employment) and leisure time involves language, "if the wage rate of individuals is a function of their productivity and if the language they work in determines in part their productivity" (Vaillancourt 1979:7). If it is safe to assume that people are more fluent in their first language than in a second language, then it can be assumed that they will take less time to carry out a given task using the first language rather than the second language, and that they will earn more in a given time period using the first language than in a similar period using the second language. Along with these background assumptions, glottoeconomics also takes as given the fact that the goal of employers is to maximize profits. The choice of language for work is influenced by

1. the desire of employers to use their own first language

2. the availability of workers who speak a given language

3. the language of the technology involved in the particular form of employment at issue

From these background assumptions, François Vaillancourt (1979), a glottoeconomics advocate, derived some general hypotheses about language and economics in bilingual Quebec. For example, he hypothesized that: people who know English earn more than those who don't; monolingual English speakers earn more than bilingual Francophones; bilingual Anglophones earn more than monolingual English speakers.

In order to test these hypotheses about the impact of language on the earnings of individuals, Vaillancourt used a form of multiple regression analysis. In general terms, sufficient for our purposes here, multiple regression analysis is a statistical technique applied to a data base where there is one dependent variable and a number of independent ones. Vaillancourt used earnings as the dependent variable, with language, experience, weeks worked, and region of residence as independent variables. Then REGRESSION EQUATIONS were formulated and coefficients for each variable interpreted. By such techniques as correlation and regression analysis, changes in language diversity can be related to other variables. Multiple regression analysis, as cumulative prediction, is a way to strongly relate predictor (independent) variables to criterion (dependent) variables that are weakly related to each other (Cooper 1975:32).

In his study, Vaillancourt found that knowing English does increase the earnings of Québecois and that English speakers do earn more than bilingual Francophones. These findings support his first two hypotheses. However, bilingualism was found not to increase the earnings of Anglophones in Quebec, a contradiction of the third hypothesis.

By using the assumptions of glottoeconomic theory and applying multiple regression analysis to a data base with earnings as a dependent variable and language (plus other work-related variables) as independent, we can determine the net returns to various language skills in terms of the independent economic variable (here, earnings). In this example, glottoeconomics has indicated that English is more valuable than French in Quebec (at least at the time of Vaillancourt's study), a finding that studies of language and ethnic interaction might not necessarily confirm. Thus, a many-faceted methodological approach to planning would seem to be useful in multilingual societies if planners want to be sure that the plan will be accepted.

6.102   Ethnic Decision-Making

An approach that applies to decision-making on the part of multilinguals is Jonathan Pool's (1979a) idea of ETHNIC DECISION-MAKING with respect to language. Ethnic decision-making is concerned with who uses what language when, where, and with what gain. Pool suggests a formal model of language diversity, again using economic analysis, that will allow planners to evaluate language policies with respect to the elimination of linguistic diversity. His model is essentially a *rational* one, whereby he urges policy makers to:

1. define the language function the policy hopes to maximize

2. calculate the pertinent costs and benefits of the policy

3. determine how much communication (language use) will yield the greatest benefit under the various alternatives

Pool's approach assumes that the object of language planning is to facilitate communication through language and that the amount of communication that takes place by way of language can be calculated. His approach also assumes that the "benefit derived by one actor from communication with the other" (1979:6) is a function of the amount of communication between them and that this amount can also be calculated. Communication costs are related to whatever "language-learning and/or translation" has to be done for communication to take place.

Pool's approach can be seen to be a social-welfare model of ethnic decision-making. It assumes that policy decisions are made by authorities and that those authorities wish to take the actors' preferences into consideration. The decision involves eliminating inferior alternatives, such as "those to which both actors prefer the same other alternative" (1979:27).

By way of example, Pool suggests how the model would work if the planning authority needed to make a policy decision between two actors—one language group rich and one poor with respect to resources. First, the relative costs of translation from the poor to rich and rich to poor group's language would need to be standardized.

> it will be more costly for the rich actor to learn a language than for the poor actor to learn the same language, because the opportunity cost in monetary terms for a given expenditure of time rises with wealth (1979:29).

Then, particular attitudes about communicating from one group to the other need to be considered. In general, "the poor actor perceives greater value in communication with the rich one than vice versa" (30). Since learning a language costs the rich person more but the poor person benefits from learning the rich one's language, a number of alternatives can be eliminated. Pool provides a formula for computing the SOCIAL WELFARE FUNCTIONS that are available language choices. In his example, he concludes that there are two alternatives that "equally maximize the social welfare function" (32): (1) the rich language group *and* the poor one can each learn a different language, or (2) the poor language group can learn the rich one's language. "These alternatives eliminate the need to translate, and therefore no decision on allocating translation costs is necessary" (32). Both alternatives are economically reasonable.

There still remains what Pool describes as the "problem of compensation." The decision-making authority needs to exact from the poor party and transfer to the rich one "a communications tax" that makes up for what the rich party would lose and the poor party would gain in benefits. Considering such payments of an "ethnicity tax" helps in deciding among the main alternatives (in this case, between his alternatives 1 and 2). According to Pool, rich actors (groups, nations, and so forth) prefer that the poor learn their language. This alternative benefits the poor more than had both rich and poor learned a third language. In contrast, poor actors feel that if both they and the rich learn a third language, the poor would be better served; they would gain more new benefits than the rich get and more than they would get had they learned the rich group's language.

The planning agency needs to decide whether it wants to minimize the discrepancy in benefits between the rich and the poor. If the discrepancy is to be minimized, the poor should learn the language of the rich. But if the planning agency wants the choice that transfers most resources from the rich to the poor, having both groups learn a third language is the answer.

These considerations of benefit and resource transfer are part of a planning agency's social welfare function. The social welfare model of ethnic (linguistic) decision-making allows choices to be made that need not and should not necessarily maximize the combined sum of the rich actors' and the poor actors' benefits (Pool 1979:33).

Where policy decisions are not made by an authority or planning agency that can coordinate the actors' behavior as the social welfare model can, it is possible to have similar forms of decision-making that still provide rational solutions . . . for the problem of linguistic diversity" (Pool 1979:34). An INDIVIDUAL-DECISION MODEL applies when one actor reacts after the other's decision is known; a GAME MODEL applies when both actors make decisions without knowing each other's choices. The individual-decision and game models seek to ensure that the implementation of changes already put into effect operate in the interest of social welfare, despite the fact that such considerations were not involved in the decision-making process.

Each model of ethnic decision-making about language requires that the function to be maximized is equitable. Whether we use an individual, game, or social welfare model, the costs and benefits are calculated, and the amount of communication that will produce the most benefits for each alternative is determined. Adjustments are made so that no group will be shortchanged.

6.103 Quantifying the Degree of Bilingualism

For many LP purposes, it is desirable to quantify habitual language use. Fishman (1968a) calls for a combination of interrelated measures:

> Linguists have been most concerned with the analysis of bilingualism from the point of view of *switching* or *interference*. The measures that they have proposed from their disciplinary point of departure distinguish between phonetic, lexical, and grammatical proficiency and intactness. At the other extreme stand educators who are concerned with bilingualism in terms of *total performance contrasts* in very complex contexts (the school, even the society). Psychologists have usually studied degrees of bilingualism in terms of speed, automaticity, or habit strength. Sociologists have relied upon relative frequencies of use in different settings (77).

Many different measures are needed if we want to understand the "social realities of multilingual settings," and these measures should consider different types of variance; that is, maintenance and shift from language to language in different MEDIA (writing, reading, speaking) and in different OVERTNESS SITUATIONS (where differences exist between INNER SPEECH, COMPREHENSION, and PRODUCTION) should be measured.

> Where language shift is unconscious or resisted, inner speech [the language in which we think] may be most resistant to interference, switching and disuse of

the mother tongue. Where language shift is conscious and desired, this may less frequently be the case (79).

We also should measure domain variance when we want to determine the degree of bilingualism in a given situation (see Chapter Five). It is important to know how situational bilingualism operates, that is, to know what language is used in what contexts. By recognizing that domains exist, we can contrast the language used by particular subgroups for certain topics with the language of larger populations in other language-use contexts. One way to measure domain variance is by dominance configurations. In Chapter Five we outlined the conceptual framework underlying dominance-configuration analysis; now we will see how such an analysis is accomplished.

6.104 Dominance Configuration

To measure domain variance we first need to construct "instruments that are based upon a careful consideration of the various domains of language behavior . . . mentioned in a scattered international literature" (Fishman 1968a:89). We can then see how the components of variants in degree of bilingualism interrelate. The dominance-configuration concept was introduced by Weinreich (1953) and consists of a set of measurable characteristics of language behavior that can be compared for each language a bilingual speaks. If we refer back to the diagram of a partial dominance configuration (Figure 2) in Chapter Five, we will notice that it is possible to represent all three sources of language variance on a tree and that an analysis of the values for each variable within each variance source leads to an analysis of one language's areas of use per domain vis-à-vis another's. From such analysis we may see that bilingualism is located differently in individuals in different situations, despite surface appearances that one language is dominant over another in the society. Weinreich's idea behind using the concept of dominance configuration (whatever the characteristics actually used in a configuration) was to overcome what he felt to be an unsatisfactory practice of "tagging two languages in contact as respectively 'upper' and 'lower' at any cost" (1953:98). This approach of using ANALYSIS OF VARIANCE in LP complements the use of the COMPARATIVE METHOD as applied to analyzing language maintenance and language shift. If we can see what factors influence shift or maintenance through time as well as in synchronic contact situations, we should be able to anticipate the language trends that will impinge upon planned change.

6.105 The Comparative Method

In order to find out what cross-cultural and diachronic (historical) regularities might influence a plan to bring about language change, the comparative method can be quite useful. Some situations of comparison that might be particularly important to consider in planning are:

1. where speakers of one language live in different speech communities that have similar social stratification

2. where speakers of one language live in different speech communities that have dissimilar social stratification

3. where speakers of different languages live in different speech communities that have similar social stratification.

A situation of the first type would be one in which two groups of German immigrants have settled in separate rural areas of Poland. A situation of the second type would be that of two Swiss-German groups, one that has settled in the region of Raetia (in the Tyrolean mountains) in contact with Swiss Raetoromans, and the other with Americans in Cincinnati, Ohio. The third type of situation of comparison would be one in which both rural Poles and rural Slovaks have settled in different neighborhoods in Cincinnati (Fishman 1968a:103).

The purpose of comparing such language and community situations is to find out what happens to each group's language vis-à-vis the other. Such comparative studies and the results they yield about circumstances of maintenance and shift will provide material for cross-cultural language-use files that can be used for planning. Gathering such files would be similar to the amassing of cross-cultural ethnographic material for storage in the Human Relations Area Files (HRAF) located at various libraries associated with American universities. In the case of maintenance-and-shift files, the stored information would be the result of the comparative method being applied to situations to provide data for later comparisons with other similar situations.

> Thus by judiciously contrasting groups, sociocultural processes, and types of contact situations . . . it should become possible to more meaningfully apportion the variance in language maintenance or language shift outcomes (103).

6.106 Measuring Language Distance

In order to make sensible language plans in a multilingual setting, it is often useful not only to know what the plan means in cost-benefit terms and what the relative dominance configuration is for each domain in which each language is used, but it is also useful to see how much the various languages influence each other. Then the planner can consider what interferences exist from one to the other language.

INTERFERENCE occurs when elements from one language are used when a person is speaking or writing another (Mackey 1965). In measuring interference, the researcher generally notes what pronunciation features, grammar peculiarities, and lexical items not naturally present in the first language are appearing in it and can therefore be attributed to influence from the second language. Measuring interference in this way is useful when speakers of the second language are speakers of a uniform standard and when the first-language speakers are earnestly trying to acquire the standard form of the second. In such cases, divergence from the standard form of the second language being learned can be seen as first-language interference.

However, in other multilingual situations, such as in stable bilingual communities where each language is highly valued in its own right and where bilinguals speak to other bilinguals, it is not necessarily the case that one language is more prestigious than another and deserving of imitation. At present, no measure exists for this type of multilingual influence, although some idea of what happens may be arrived at by means of analyzing dominance configurations as described above.

An extreme version of interference may be called UNSTABLE BILINGUALISM, a situation in which both languages interfere with each other to the extent that communication in either is difficult. To measure such interference when neither language approximates a standard is very difficult indeed. Even dominance configurations would be of little use, since domains or topical situations for either language may not be clearly drawn. An example of unstable bilingualism may be seen in certain Japanese-Americans who learned English as their first language and were then interned during World War II or returned to Japan to go to school. After such exposure to Japanese as a second language, these people were brought back into American society. As a result, they speak a language that is neither fluent English nor fluent Japanese. They have thus become communicationally disadvantaged in both the national culture (American) and in their ethnic subculture (Japanese-American). As yet, no measures are available to determine the exact nature of the interference in such a case. Unstable bilinguals can almost be thought of as having a second native language, one without a literate tradition or prestige. To study English or Japanese as a second language is often an inadequate remedy for these people, since second-language teaching generally requires a first language to which the second can be contrasted. The hybrid language of the unstable bilingual is not an adequate standard for contrast.

CONTRASTIVE ANALYSIS, as we saw in Chapter Three, is a technique useful in the teaching of a second language—as long as the structures of both it and the first language are known. Essentially, as in the case of interference analysis, contrastive analysis is a technique of interlanguage comparison. According to John Gumperz, who has described most of these attempts to measure bilingualism, contrastive analysis is a point-by-point comparison of two linguistic systems at each component of structure.

Differences are evaluated according to their place within the respective system (whether they are phonetic, phonemic, syntactic, and so forth). They are then counted under the assumption that "what the student has to learn equals the sum of the difference established by this comparison" (Banathy, Trager, and Waddle 1966, quoted in Gumperz 1969:233).

By using contrastive analysis, language teachers can find out what is likely to be most difficult for a speaker of one particular language to learn in another language. Again, as Gumperz notes, contrastive analysis is most useful in communities that have a standard and a nonstandard language, or where foreign-language speakers, rather than second-language learners, are trying to learn the local tongue. Contrastive analysis does not do much to show the differences that exist in the speech of bilinguals, particularly since in such speech there is little basis for assuming that the two languages bilinguals use are actually two distinct languages (Gumperz 1969:234), as we will see below.

LINGUISTIC REPERTOIRE ANALYSIS is useful if we abandon the assumption that the two or more languages of multilinguals are distinct. Instead, if we assume that multilingual communities are "wholes," it is possible to see what linguistic features of commonality might be helpful in planning. Once we assume linguistic communities to be wholes, we can then begin to see what linguistic behavior is appropriate in those communities. With such study, we have entered the area of sociolinguistics; the goal of our analysis is, then, the goal of that field—the description of communicative competence as the knowledge people have about how to communicate appropriately in a culturally significant setting. Gumperz refers to the shared communicative competence of the members of a multilingual but uniform speech community as a LINGUISTIC REPERTOIRE.

We then assume that bilingual behavior reflects both an underlying set of general rules which apply to the entire linguistic repertoire and lower-order nonshared language-specific rules (1969:235).

To find out how much the respective linguistic systems overlap, we should see what grammatical categories allow us to translate from one language into the other(s). Translation is easiest among languages with the greatest grammatical overlap; thus, where translation (especially machine or mechanical translation) is easiest, the languages are closest. Languages that are in the same family can be translated with greater ease. We can go from French to Spanish and back with greater ease than we can go from French to Swahili, for instance. As Gumperz also points out, "Language distance can then be measured as a function of the number of nonshared rules" (235). French and Spanish share a far greater number of grammatical rules than do French and Swahili. Such TRANSLATABILITY MEASURES are particularly useful in planning that needs to take interspeaker variation into account. By measuring translatability as a way to gauge language distance in linguistic repertoires, we should be able to determine the social significance of language behavior within a repertoire. Gumperz suggests that conversations between multilinguals in natural settings be collected. In the case of bilinguals, the next step is to have conversation texts in Language A, for example, translated into Language B, and those in B to A by a second group of bilinguals. Then a third group of bilinguals should check each translated text to see if it is acceptable.

A repertoire analysis of Hindi-Punjabi bilingual college students in Delhi, India, revealed that the languages differ only in the rules that account for the phonetic shape of certain words and affixes. Both languages have common grammatical categories and syntactic structures. However, despite such similarity, the nature of Hindi-Punjabi differences makes these differences particularly noticeable. The differences affect the sound of affixes and function words that occur frequently. Although, from a linguistic viewpoint, the differences are slight, they do make the languages sound as if they were very different.

> In spite of the underlying grammatical similarities, therefore, the shift between codes has a quality of abruptness which to some extent accounts for the speaker's view of them as distinct languages (Gumperz 1969:246).

Measuring language distance by means of repertoire analysis may show, as in the Hindi-Punjabi case, that where there is an appearance of great distance among the many languages in a multilingual society, language may after all not impede communication. The ability of Hindi and Punjabi speakers to understand one another is greatly enhanced once the pronunciation and affix differences are pointed out. The planner, then, needs to find out the role of persistent linguistic differences despite intercommunicability, to find out what factors contribute to the maintenance or disappearance of such differences where actual language distance is low. Why do Hindi and Punjabi maintain their distinctiveness? Could the reasons be social?

6.107 Interlanguage and LP Method

Related to language-distance measurement are the methods for finding out the social significance of language-variety differences, particularly in the context of ethnic interaction. INTERLANGUAGE is a psycholinguistic term that refers to an in-between language that learners of a second language may learn and then never move beyond, due to certain attitudinal or motivational factors. In learning a second language, the learner passes through a period when he or she speaks something that is neither the first nor the second language but can be referred to as interlanguage (see Selinker 1972). Jacobson (1979) urges that the concept of interlanguage be broadened to incorporate a sociological dimension so that we can see it "not as the learner's inability to reach a higher plateau of language performance because of certain attitudinal or motivational limitations, but as a deliberate fossilization in order to emphasize ethnic group membership" (2). He suggests that an important LP procedure is to find, instead of the extent of first-language interference or second-language interference, "the extent to which certain deviations from the mainstream language are suggestive of a stable ethnic dialect" (2). This approach might also be useful in attempting to define the language of unstable bilinguals in an effort to see that such speakers do gain access to one viable communication form. In the case of unstable bilinguals, we need to find out what the deviations are from both languages and offer suggestions to make the acquisition of both languages possible.

It is also advisable to use the sociologically oriented concept of interlanguage to determine the extent of deviations from standard English in the speech of English monolinguals, for example. There are many Chicanos in the United States who speak *no* Spanish yet speak a "Chicano Vernacular English" rather than "Anglo Standard English." Jacobson claims that cultural loyalty and acculturation often determine the presence or absence of interlanguage features as much as language attitude and motivation do.

Interlanguage data may be collected much in the same way data are gathered for repertoire analysis. In fact, Jacobson's idea, essentially, is to expand the concept of repertoire to include bi- and multidialects as well as bi- and multilanguages and, in the process, to focus on interlanguage. The study of both intra- and interlanguage repertoires, then, suggests that interference is not as major a factor of language distance (in linguistically complex speech communities seen as wholes) as had been thought. Dominance configurations and contrastive analysis, in particular, are in some cases better measurements of distance *between* rather than *within* linguistic communities. Intra- and interlanguage repertoire analysis, on the other hand, is a technique of measuring language distance that is sensitive to the community-based sociocultural distinctions that affect planning.

6.11   Measurements of Language Attitude

Richard Webber (1979) provides a useful survey of language-attitude studies and the scholarly literature on such studies so far. Of course, not all studies of language attitude are of direct relevance to LP, but most methods used in such studies are, in one way or another, potential tools for the planner. Webber classifies language-attitude studies as falling into categories according to whether they deal with acceptability criteria; the history of

attitudes; the relationship of language to, for instance, employment or to other languages or dialects; and the attitudes teachers have toward a language or languages.
Much of the research in this field is from an experimental social psychological perspective. A common tool used is the ATTITUDE RATING SCALE. Webber cites studies of employer language attitudes that influence their reactions to prospective employees in interviews using such a technique. For example, Hopper and associates (1972, 1973, 1977) asked employers to rate the recorded speech of Black, Mexican-American, White Southern, and Standard American speakers answering such questions as, "How do you go about solving a problem at work?" The rating scale the employers were asked to fill out was composed of oppositions such as:

THE SPEAKER SOUNDS:

educated_____:_____:_____:_____:_____:_____:_____:uneducated.
(Webber 1979:219)

After rating the speech samples, the employers were asked to "register on a five-point scale, the probability that they would hire the person being interviewed for each of seven job categories—executive, public relations, foreman, skilled technician, sales, clerical, and manual labor" (219). The results of this particular study of language attitude using an attitude rating scale indicated that employer judgments about ethnicity of speech did *not* cloud their judgments about range of employee abilities, except that standard speakers were favored in respect to white-collar jobs (219–20).
The attitude rating scale is a useful tool for planners who want to correlate the likelihood that a planned language change will be accepted in a wide-ranging sphere of use within a community that is highly stratified socially.
Another tool useful in measuring attitudes is the MATCHED-GUISE TECHNIQUE developed by Wallace Lambert and colleagues in 1960. Listeners who are referred to as "judges" are asked to react to tapes of "perfect" bilinguals or bidialectals reading, first, a passage in one of their languages (for example, French) and then reading a translation of the same passage in their other language (for example, English). The judges are asked to evaluate the personality of the speakers from their voices without being told that the speakers of both languages are one and the same person. In fact, the judges are specifically kept unaware of this fact. This technique of matching GUISES (such as a French rendering and an English rendering of the same passage by the same speaker) allows all the variables to be kept constant (Webber 1979:220), and it is especially useful for measuring "*group* biases in evaluative reactions" (Lambert 1967:215), since the same

personality traits have been found to be ascribed to a group by different judges.

In studying French/English bilinguals in Canada, Lambert et al. (1960) found that French-Canadian college-age judges, asked to react to passages concerning philosophy in both languages and to rank the speakers according to traits such as intelligence, sociability, height, and so forth, would not only "generally downgrade representatives of their own linguistic group" but also rated French-Canadian guises more negatively than English-Canadians rated them (Lambert 1967:216). Later use of the matched-guise technique with younger judges allowed Lambert and his associates to show that, at the age of ten, French-Canadian children are not yet biased against their own group but that "definite preferences for EC [English-Canadian] guises appeared at about age twelve and were maintained through the late teen years" (221). Particularly biased were upper-middle-class females after the age of twelve.

The matched-guise technique for measuring language attitudes is an effective way to find out what stereotypes one ethnolinguistic group has about another. For language planning, measuring attitudes this way lets the planner see what impact such stereotypical impressions have on "people who are either forced to learn the other group's language or who choose to do so" (Lambert 1967:223). The technique also provides for the planner, as for the bilingual or bidialectal individual, a way to find out the likely reactions to the adoption of different guises in different settings. Matched guises are useful ways to find out what the social effects of language or dialect shift would be. Given the political and linguistic changes in Quebec since Lambert's 1967 work, it would be interesting to see if French-Canadian teenage females today still prefer English.

The ratings used in the matched-guise technique are typically based on "semantic differential scales" with the basis for judgment being voice cues only. Semantic differential scales (devised by Osgood, Suci, and Tannenbaum 1957) measure attitudes in opposition on a continuum ranging, for example, from "hesitant" to "enthusiastic" about certain qualities, or from "intelligent" to "unintelligent" or "educated" to "uneducated" (as in our example above). The attitudes measured have to do with the listener's opinion of voice quality, and each attitude is rated along a seven-point scale. Respondents are asked to place a mark at the point that indicates their feeling about the quality or person or other feature being measured. Such scales measure qualifiable reactions to social phenomena and allow researchers to discover the nature of the major opposing features in particular attitude formation and stereotyping.

6.110 Sociolinguistic Surveys

In Chapter Three we discussed the work of William Labov in studying language change from a language-internal sociolinguistic viewpoint, correlating various linguistic features with different social strata. The techniques used by Labov are for the most part social survey-type techniques, which are considered to involve surveys at a "microsociolinguistic level of observation." His concern is to survey particular features of language:

> With respect to the variants of a phonological, lexical, or syntactic variable, for example, a survey might describe which variants different groups of speakers can use (proficiency), which they learned first (acquisition), and which they typically use in different types of speech situation or communication context (Cooper 1975:30).

There are also "*macro*sociolinguistic" surveys that

> describe what languages or language varieties different groups of speakers know (proficiency), the order in which they learned them (acquisition), and the contexts in which they use them (usage) (30).

Sociolinguistic surveys, at whatever level, assess three types of language behavior—PROFICIENCY, ACQUISITION, and USAGE. Sociolinguistic surveys also assess two types of behavior toward language—ATTITUDINAL and INSTRUMENTAL. The measurement of attitudes, as discussed above, is the only way known thus far in which they may be surveyed, due to the fact that "attitudes are unobservable constructs whose characteristics must be inferred on the basis of observable behavior" (Cooper 1975:30).

Implementational behavior toward language, on the other hand, is observable and may be surveyed and described:

> People act overtly toward language. For example, they may voluntarily enroll their children in schools in which the language of instruction differs from that used in the majority of community's schools; they may participate in organizations whose purpose it is to accomplish spelling reform; they may struggle to maintain or to change the status of their mother tongue by participating in organizations devoted to such purposes or by lobbying or petitioning legislators; they may correct another speaker's use of forms which they consider to be nonstandard or improper; they may work in language planning agencies or participate in activities sponsored by such agencies; or they may be actively involved in language policy decisions (Cooper 1975:30–31).

Sociolinguistic surveys may measure some or all of these behaviors which may be summarized diagrammatically as shown in Figure 4.

The International Research Project on Language Planning Processes (IRPLPP) (Das Gupta et al. 1972; Fishman 1975) measured behaviors at both levels (micro/macro), of both categories, and of all five types. This survey gathered information from high school and university students and teachers in India, Indonesia, and Israel. The information had to do with

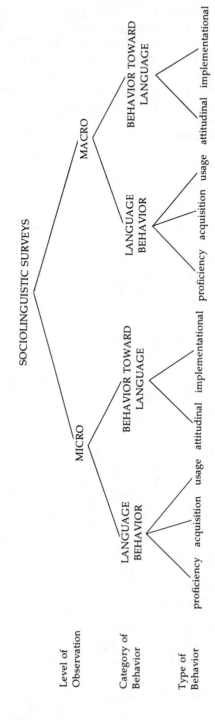

Figure 4. Measurement of Behaviors toward Language by Sociolinguistic Surveys (adapted from Cooper 1975:31)

"the languages the respondent could speak and read (macro-proficiency), the languages they used for various specified contexts (macro-usage)" (Cooper 1975:31). People were also tested as to what technical terms they knew in the standard (planned) language (micro-proficiency) and whether they knew alternative terms and, if they did, *when* they learned them (micro-acquisition). People were given word-naming tasks, and the results were tallied to see what proportion of language-academy-approved terms they used (micro-usage).

The survey also measured behaviors toward language: people were asked what they thought about a sample of words made up by the language academy in the fields of chemistry, civics, language, and literature (micro-attitudinal). They were also asked what they thought about various languages and about language planning (macro-attitudinal):

and they were asked about their participation in language-planning organizations (particularly corpus-planning agencies) or in the activities sponsored by these organizations (macro-implementational). In addition, textbook writers were asked about the source and degree of control to which they were subjected with respect to their use of technical terminology (micro-implementational) (Cooper 1975:31–32).

Most sociolinguistic surveys reported in the scholarly literature have been carried out since the mid-1960s. Although the technology of such surveys "derives from social science surveys, more generally they have features which justify their separate consideration" (Cooper 1975:28). In the present study, we will highlight the features of sociolinguistic surveys that are of particular importance when survey results are geared to planning. For our discussion, we will continue to rely heavily on Robert L. Cooper's (1975) state-of-the-art paper on sociolinguistic surveys, which was put together at the recommendation of the International Conference on the Methodology of Sociolinguistic Surveys (May 1975).

The term SURVEY RESEARCH in a sociolinguistic context refers to "research carried out with respect to an entire population," the results of which are intended to be generalizable to that population. The survey research is characterized as "sociolinguistic" because information is gathered about the social organization of language behavior and behavior toward language in specified populations (see Figure 4).

6.111   *SIL Mutual Intelligibility Studies*

Sociolinguistic surveys are motivated by many LP considerations, including the desire to assist in making language-policy decisions. An example is provided by the experience of the Summer Institute of Linguistics (SIL) in Mexico (Casad 1974):

The SIL was faced with the problem of choosing among various vernaculars for Bible translations and literacy campaigns. The extent to which various language varieties can be understood by speakers of related varieties is one factor which can appropriately be considered when deciding what variety should be used so as to reach the largest number of people at a given cost (Cooper 1975:33).

Such MUTUAL INTELLIGIBILITY SURVEYS have since then been carried out by SIL in other areas of the world as well. Ronald Sim (1979) produced *A Sociolinguistic Profile of the Mt. Kenya Bantu Languages* with the stated purpose being "to provide adequate information as a basis for language planning for the group of languages around Mt. Kenya" (Sim 1979:6). Sim sought to extend Casad's method used in Mexico to apply to dialects such as Kikuyu and Kimeru in Kenya; these dialects "have a significant degree of contact through proximity, travel, and through the use of Kikuyu and Kimeru written materials over a wide area for the last 40–50 years" (30).

Mutual intelligibility tests measure "intelligibility of the spoken word across dialects" and consist of tapes of a local dialect first tested in the home area (with 100% intelligibility expected). The tapes are then played "to people in other dialects to see how much they understand. The tapes in the SIL studies are usually passages from the Bible being read in a particular dialect. At the end of the testing, the various scores show which dialects understand each other easily, and which dialects have difficulties" (Sim 1979:49-50). SIL people use mutual intelligibility testing in order to make policy with regard to what dialects to use in Bible translations to reach the most people. Sim's survey found that a Kimeru Bible "common language" translation "would be intelligible to all Meru dialects, although Tharaka and Chuka are borderline" (51). A "common language" translation refers to one which uses only grammar and vocabulary common to all dialects of the prospective readers for whom the translation is being done.

6.112   Implementation and Evaluation Surveys

Sociolinguistic surveys are also useful at the policy-implementing stage of LP, for "implementation often requires basic information about the language situation among the people with whom the policy is to be carried out" (Cooper 1975:33). An example of the use of survey research to implement policy is the Ethiopian Work-Oriented Adult Literacy Project. This project was designed "to determine what proportion of the population in these areas to be served by the campaign would be likely to enroll in literacy classes" (33). The main task of the project was to find out how effective a vocationally oriented adult literacy campaign could be and to set up trial campaigns. The planners needed to find out how many people were illiterate and, of those, who would be likely to take literacy classes given convenient times and places. They also had to find out how much time prospective literacy trainees would be likely to spend in class per week as well as how much time they could put into getting to and from class. Also, since the medium of literacy instruction would be Amharic, planners also had to find out how many of the potential literacy learners understood Amharic (Cooper 1975:33-34).

There is an additional related form of survey research geared not so much to evaluating or implementing a plan as to promoting a particular language. In 1964-1965, a sociolinguistic survey was performed in Barcelona, Spain, to find out the status of Catalan in that city and to stimulate public interest in it. At the time of the survey (conducted by Antoni Badia i Margarit), Catalan was not used in public life in Barcelona, but since then, and largely as a result of the survey, public use of the language has increased (Cooper 1975:36).

Survey research is also a useful tool in the relatively uncharted area of LP evaluation. Surveys can help determine how effective a language policy is. An example of a survey used to evaluate policy may be seen in an evaluation done of a study of Irish children's achievement in school. John Macnamara (1966) found that the Irish policy of promoting the Irish language by seeing that it is used and studied in schools was too expensive from the point of view of education achievement. Macnamara's survey found that students' ability to do arithmetic problems suffered when that subject was taught in Irish. Native English speakers who had to use Irish in the schools suffered a decrease in their ability to write English, and their attainments in written Irish did not come up to the standard achieved by native Irish speakers. Clearly, the Irish policy in the schools was not accomplishing its goal of spreading the use of Irish effectively. Subsequently, most likely due to the evaluative survey of the policy, the policy was weakened.

The analysis of Thias and Carnoy (1972; referred to earlier), which looked at how investment in education in Kenya compared to investments in other economic areas there with respect to rate of return, also involved survey research with an evaluative goal. When we discussed the paucity of evaluative approaches in LP theory so far (Chapter Five), we mentioned that this kind of cost-benefit approach might be adapted to looking at "investments" in language. Survey research would then be the means by which relative rates of return due to language versus other types of investments could be determined.

The results of sociolinguistic surveys to evaluate plans or measure effectiveness can be used to help set up language policies or to alter existing ones. Information gathered by surveys in order to set up language policies can also often be used for implementing policies. In turn, information gathered by surveys to implement policies can frequently be used to alter policies if the information indicates that changes are needed for the policies to work or be economically feasible (Cooper 1975:35).

6.113   Microsociolinguistic Surveys

MICROSOCIOLINGUISTIC SURVEYS often focus on particular areas of the interrelationship between language use and social structure. Vaillancourt's glotteconomic study (see Chapter Five) to test hypotheses about employment choices and language use demonstrates such a use of a survey of this type. Likewise, Labov's work on pronunciation differences in New York City English showed that what appeared to be random differences correlated with factors of social status and degree of formality of the context of use. Labov made use of social survey techniques in order to attempt to correlate phonological variables (such as the differential use of *r* coloring in the speech of New Yorkers) with the different social statuses of the speakers. He hypothesized that a higher degree of *r* coloring would be associated with higher social status. He tested this hypothesis by asking shop attendants at stores, who he believed represented three levels of social status, for the location of a certain department which he knew to be on the fourth floor. His microsociolinguistic survey was a survey of the different ways people would say "fourth floor," that is, whether they would use *r* in one of the two words, in both, or in neither. People of high social status used *r* in both *fourth* and *floor*. The more careful Labov's informants were trying to be in their speech, the more they tended to use *r*. People high on the social-status scale would tend to say "fourth floor." Others, perceiving the use of *r* as prestigious, would try to emulate it in contrast to the lesser rendering, "fowath flowah," thought to mark people as being from a lower social class. Labov's hypothesis was confirmed.

Microsociolinguistic surveys, then, are "micro" in the sense that they look at specific variables in language (such as the use of *r*) and see how they correlate with social status, economic class, sex differences, ethnic differences, and the like. Macrosociolinguistic surveys, in contrast, are "macro" in that they look at more general phenomena such as the effectiveness of a particular language policy in doing what it set out to do.

6.114   Contributions of Sociolinguistics
to Survey Research Methods

Sociolinguistic surveys, in many ways, are just social surveys. However, in the area of interviewing, testing, attitude scales, and nonreactive observations, survey research in general has been enhanced by sociolinguistic approaches. This area, then, is one in which research related to language planning is beginning to contribute to other fields rather than borrow from them.

Labov introduced the SOCIOLINGUISTIC INTERVIEW. The sociolinguistic interview uses techniques specially designed to gather speech data that show variation along a continuum from, for example, careful speech to casual speech or from formal speech to informal speech. The purpose of the sociolingustic interview is to gather a more representative sample of a speaker's entire verbal repertoire than would be possible by means of traditional methods for eliciting linguistic data (Cooper 1975:37). Traditional elicitation techniques in descriptive linguistics involved asking speakers to say specific words or sentences in isolation (that is, out of context). Data gathered in this way would reveal neither the very formal, not the informal, casual, or natural aspects of speech. The material obtained could be used by the linguist to describe the linguistic system underlying speech in that language but not its use aspects. The sociolinguistic interview is geared to gathering speech data in naturalistic settings. It attempts to elicit speech data without directing speakers to concentrate on their speech. The people who answered "fourth floor" in the study by Labov thought that the questioners wanted to know where to buy shoes, not how they themselves said the words "fourth floor"!

The need to use unwitting informants in natural settings in order to get natural, not forced, data in conducting sociolinguistic interviews has the potential of causing some moral qualms. However, as long as the focus is on such harmless variables as the use of *r*, it seems counterproductive to question this technique. The danger would come from using the survey results to treat people differently depending on the linguistic/status group they fall into. Sociolinguistic interviewers should therefore be aware of a moral and ethical responsibility to informants who are unaware of the research context of their answers.

Earlier, we discussed the development of mutual intelligibility tests, attitude scales, and Lambert's matched-guise technique. In addition, Fishman has introduced the CONTEXTUALIZED PROFICIENCY TEST (1968a), which aims to reveal contextually based differences in the use of language among multilinguals. For example, blanket tests of bilingual proficiency might show that people use one language more than another; however, the test context might have skewed the result to favor one language over another. The test might have involved a topic favoring the use of one language (such as Yiddish) over another (such as English), for example. Robert Cooper (1969) administered a word-proficiency test especially contextualized for five domains to Spanish-English bilinguals in New Jersey. He wanted to find out what words they used in each language in the domains of the family, the neighborhood, in religion, education, and at work. He found that "for some domains there were more words produced in Spanish than in English, whereas the reverse was true for other domains. Such differences would have been missed if only an undifferentiated, global score had been obtained for each language" (Cooper 1975:38).

Sociolinguistic surveys such as sociolinguistic interviews and contextualized proficiency tests, then, make extensive use of NONREACTIVE PROCEDURES, that is, "techniques which gather data without the person realizing he is being observed as part of an investigation" (Cooper 1975:39). Labov's sociolinguistic interviews asking New Yorkers to say "fourth floor" were conducted in the form of a nonreactive survey technique known as the STAGED ENCOUNTER. By pretending to need to know where to locate a specific item in the store (in this case shoes), he elicited the response "fourth floor" from the salespeople.

> A customer's request for directions is such a familiar occurrence that the encounter barely enters the consciousness of the employee, who can scarcely have realized that he was a subject in an investigation (39).

To reiterate, such a data-elicitation technique, when innocent, is useful; but researchers must be aware of potential problems if a nonreactive observation begins to resemble spying. To avoid being caught staging an encounter, some sociolinguists advocate another nonreactive approach known as the TRANSACTION COUNT PROCEDURE which does not "require the investigator to participate in the observed interactions" (Cooper 1975:40). Such a procedure may involve recording language heard on the streets, for example, "as used by pedestrians with one another, as well as the language overheard in the shops which lined the streets, as used by customers with shopkeepers and shopkeepers with one another" (40). In this approach the surveyors simply analyze what they hear. The disadvantage is that it is difficult to correlate speech variables with social or economic variables, since all the researcher knows is where the speech took place, the sex of the speakers, and their probable age. Nonetheless, for studies that aim to see the correlation between location, sex, and approximate age with speech differences, a transaction count procedure can be quite useful.

6.2   AN APPLICATION OF LP METHOD

To conclude this chapter on LP methods, we will describe an example of their application by looking at a macrosociolinguistic survey in East Africa in the late 1960s. We will also see which effects of that survey may or may not be useful to LP. The wide-ranging Survey of Language Use and Language Teaching in Eastern Africa (SLULTEA) conducted in 1968 and financed by the Ford Foundation was a survey making use of a number of related techniques in the form of questionnaires, interviews, and various other language-use measures. The aims of this survey were:

1. to get basic information on what languages are taught and used in Ethiopia, Kenya, Tanzania, Uganda, and Zambia

2. to stimulate research in the fields of linguistics and language teaching in East Africa

3. to bolster the resources of linguistically oriented institutions in East Africa

4. to enhance communication among scholars in linguistics and related disciplines with an interest in East Africa

(Whiteley 1974:n. 1, 8).

A post-survey evaluation by the sociolinguists who participated described the survey results thus:

> The survey justified its aims and organizational principles, but . . . an important deficiency was revealed: an inadequate flow of information about the survey results, and about language in general among the countries involved (Pool 1975:2).

Another problem was that each country's team designed its own survey, with no prior agreement of common hypotheses to be tested.

Even though SLULTEA did not specifically aim to generate LP recommendations, some researchers do feel that as a by-product of such surveys techniques should be developed "for influencing policy, including the translation of quantitative findings into understandable prose" and that goals of surveys be "tempered by realistic appraisals of the available resources" (Pool 1975:12).

In all of the countries where the survey was carried out, the governments gave permission for conducting the survey; however,

> subsequent language policy statements by the governments of Kenya, Uganda, and Tanzania would not seem to have been influenced by survey activities or finding [sic]. In fact, it is doubtful if the three volumes, Language in Uganda, Language in Kenya, and Language in Ethiopia, had any appreciable circulation among the Government policy-makers or general public (Abdulaziz 1979:6–7).

Because of the great amount of linguistic diversity in the East African countries surveyed, STRUCTURED QUESTIONNAIRES were difficult to devise and administer. Other data-collecting methods such as PARTICIPANT OBSERVATION, INTERVIEWING, and UNSTRUCTURED QUESTIONNAIRES were also used.

Once the material had been gathered and the survey completed, various types of analyses were used to interpret the data, including social science statistical analyses. The statistics used frequently were of a type that "assumes a knowledge of the technical approaches to social science data-processing methods on the part of the reader" (Abdulaziz 1979:16). If survey results are supposed to be useful to planners, it would be beneficial if they could be presented in a style understandable to the nonspecialist.

> The implementation of sociolinguistic survey findings implies cooperation between the researchers, planners, policy-makers, officials charged with the implementation of policies, and the general public who are affected by the particular decisions taken (20).

It is not unusual that a long time passes before survey results are recognized by policy-makers to be policy input. LP researchers are well-advised to develop good public relations with policy-makers and to learn how to sell their ideas to them. If LP materials do not reach policy-makers, little planning can be done using the accumulated insights.

It may be said that, for the most part, the East African language survey accomplished its objectives. An evaluation report (Abdulaziz and Fox 1978) prepared for the Ford Foundation concluded that the survey had aroused interest in East Africa in language problems and had provided up-to-date information on what languages are used and taught in the countries involved. The survey also contributed to strengthening the departments of linguistics and African languages at East African universities (Abdulaziz 1979:25). The survey circulated a Bulletin to inform people of survey progress, and it launched the *Journal of the Language Association of Eastern Africa*. The survey also helped create the Language Association of Eastern Africa and provided grants for linguistic research. Given the expressed aims of the survey, as outlined above, the survey seems to have accomplished what it set out to do.

To implement sociolinguistic survey results in LP, it would help if from the outset of the survey the researcher could identify the policy-level aspects of the research that might influence linguistic change. The survey researcher could then involve everyone connected with policy-making and implementation in commenting on and making suggestions about the planned project. It is particularly important to establish early and firmly government involvement with regard to funds and personnel—if the survey findings are going to be used (Abdulaziz 1979:24). The experience of SLULTEA and the reports on it that have been appearing since the time of the survey provide a good example of how language-planning research on a large scale can be done, used, and learned from. Many of the articles on LP referred to in these pages appeared first in the various volumes produced as a result of SLULTEA.

6.3   SUMMARY

In the preceding pages, we have reviewed some of the major research and analytical tools used in the language-planning process. Throughout this book we have stressed the idea that sensible language planning is carried out with an interdisciplinary approach. And it is the case that LP theory and LP methods derive from diverse areas in social science.

In this chapter we have again seen that LP, although popularly thought of as linguistics, is in fact more an area of economic, sociological, and political orientation as far as methodology is concerned. Descriptive linguistic methods (such as phonological, morphological, and syntactic analysis) are used chiefly by people who are involved in planning to standardize languages that have previously not been described. Aside from such corpus-planning activities, some knowledge of linguistic analysis is also important in microsociolinguistic research of the Labov type, where language structural variables are correlated with social structural variables. Although it is a branch of sociolinguistics, LP is more properly the sociology of language than the linguistics of society, as Fishman has long claimed. The work of Labov on language variability and of Hymes on the ethnography of speaking, though useful in LP, represents for the most part a nonplanning form of sociolinguistic research.

In viewing various methodological approaches to LP, we saw what is involved in doing a cost-benefit analysis. We also talked about two related approaches to planning represented by Vaillancourt's GLOTTOECONOMICS and Pool's ETHNIC DECISION-MAKING.

Next, we saw how the social realities of language use are measured in multilingual settings. One tool for measuring is dominance-configuration analysis. Another approach is to use the comparative method to find out how language situations changed in the past and are likely to change again. Planners find out under what circumstances languages are maintained or are not maintained, and when influence of one on another takes place. The two techniques seen as particularly useful for planning were REPERTOIRE and INTERLANGUAGE ANALYSIS, whereby the actual use of language among multilinguals and multidialectals is analyzed without any prior assumptions about distinct systems used by the participants.

For planning to succeed, not only do planners need to understand prevailing language use where the plan will be put into effect, but they also need to know how people feel about prevailing language use and how they are likely to react to change. In this area of research, ATTITUDE SCALES are helpful, particularly in the form of the MATCHED-GUISE TECHNIQUE. Attitude measurement and other forms of sociolinguistic survey are perhaps the chief tools of the language planner. We have seen how LP-oriented research has, in fact, brought new techniques to bear on general social science research in the form of the SOCIOLINGUISTIC INTERVIEW, CONTEXTUALIZED PROFICIENCY TESTS, and NONREACTIVE PROCEDURES. Survey research in the interest of LP occurs at both "macro" and "micro" levels and looks at both language use and behaviors toward language use. Surveys assess how much of a language is used, how the language is acquired, and how the language is actually used. Surveys also reveal how people feel about the languages being used and how these feelings are shown.

In the next and final chapter we will see what has been done to put into effect the ideas about language planning developed so far. We hope to demonstrate how LP has used its theory, methodology, and interdisciplinary stance to accomplish its ends.

Chapter Seven

THE APPLICATION OF
LANGUAGE PLANNING

7.0 INTRODUCTION

Now that we have seen the need for (1) planning *what* languages should be used *where*, and (2) planning *how* languages should be standardized and writing systems devised to adequately represent languages, it is time to see some examples of the various ways in which these needs have been met.

In Chapter Two, we described Nahir's classification (1977) of language plans into five types from the point of view of the tasks faced by planning agencies. In Nahir's view, language plans are basically geared to purifying, reviving, reforming, standardizing, or modernizing languages. Further, such planning functions can be placed on given points on a continuum, depending upon shifting circumstances in the context wherein the plan is to have its impact. Thus, each type of plan is likely to involve aspects of the other types as well, even though the plan's main purpose may be focused on one of the five tasks.

In the present chapter, we will take examples from the LP literature on each type of plan and show how each makes use of the concepts developed and explained in the previous chapters. We will point out the interdisciplinary nature of each plan and show what the planning agency, authority, or academy actually accomplished.

To illustrate language purification, we will use the classic example of French and the purification efforts of the French Academy (see also Chapter One). We will also take another look at Hebrew, this time considering it as an example of how a plan for language revival was carried out. Then we will describe the case of Turkish, which is often regarded as a classic example of language reform. We will use Swahili to exemplify

language standardization. Finally, we will describe how lexical modernization is taking place in Swedish.

As we describe what each type of language plan has consisted of, note
how each element of a language plan, as we have defined LP, is realized.
Try to discern for yourself, for each type of plan, what actually constitutes
the formulation (determination), codification, elaboration, and implementation of policy. Try also to see how the language choice was made and how
evaluation of the plan has been or could be accomplished and how the
particular LP agency functions.

Language planning, to a great extent, is the decision-making done by a
speech community to carry out the intents, purposes, and goals it has for
language. Language that is planned is altered in some way (purified,
reformed, standardized, revived, modernized) to enhance communication
within and between nations *and* to encourage feelings of unity and solidarity.
To this extent, all plans may be seen to have a common goal. Also, all plans,
regardless of their function (type), involve:

1. LANGUAGE CHOICE: by selecting the language(s) to be planned

2. POLICY FORMULATION: by articulating the plan through a planning agency
   or authority
   (DETERMINATION: by deciding on the plan's purpose)

3. POLICY CODIFICATION: usually by technically preparing the formulated
   and determined policy

4. POLICY ELABORATION: by extending what has been technically prepared
   (that is, the formulated language change) to all areas where the
   change is intended to take place

5. POLICY IMPLEMENTATION: by putting into effect the planned change by
   means of an organization generally supported by the planning
   authority or agency

6. POLICY EVALUATION: by assessing the whole plan (steps 1–5) to see where
   changes might be needed to ensure that communication is enhanced
   and unity and solidarity achieved, that is, whether language planning has worked

With regard to elaboration, it is interesting that we do not know, in most
cases, what determines whether the policy's intended change has been
accepted or rejected. Planning agencies make decisions about the direction
of policy elaboration in a particular (political) context, but the factors by
which a plan takes hold, as we shall see in the sample plans discussed, are
little understood.

7.1   LANGUAGE PURIFICATION: A SAMPLE PLAN

A language plan to purify language is generally an attempt by LP agencies to prescribe "correct" usage so as to defend and preserve the purity of the language. The French Academy, the "most well-known puristic agency" (Nahir 1977:109) was established in 1635 and is still functioning. In order to see purification as a plan, we will look back in history at how the French Academy "presumed to codify French vocabulary, grammar, and spelling to perfect refined conversation and written usage" (Fishman 1971:10).

The major tasks of language purification—codification (grammar, orthography) and the elaboration of the codified change—might, at first glance, be likened to these same tasks in a standardization, modernization, and reform plan. However, purification is distinctive in that it is specifically a plan that *precedes* modernization.

In fact, one might go so far as to say that purification is *anti*-modernization. In the seventeenth century, France could not be typed as Fishman's Type A (a-modal), Type B (uni-modal), or Type C (multi-modal) nation (see Chapter One). In terms of modal-nation criteria, a Great Tradition did exist in France at that time, but no political integration was present as yet. The concept of an LWC had not yet appeared; still, one could say that situational bilingualism and biculturalism did exist. The French language could be used to enhance communication in the absence of any language of wider communication (LWC), and, because of a burgeoning Great Tradition, it could be set up as better for purposes of political integration than the other situationally used languages. Such a combination of factors would be extremely rare in today's world. The fact that they were present in seventeenth-century France contributed greatly to the success of French purification. Such accidents of history, as much as planning, will be seen to account for successful change in each sample plan we will discuss below.

The French language purified by the French Academy was a vernacular first language and a literary language in a linguistically heterogeneous region. The Academy could establish the language as "pure" and endow it with prestige, so that others would aspire to its use, thereby bringing about political integration and linguistic homogeneity. Instead of attempting to come up with technical vocabularies for business, industrial, professional, or commercial use, the Academy actually refused to have anything to do with such "uncultured" and "unrefined" concerns (Fishman 1971:10). The Academy directed its publications for over three hundred years at people who already knew French rather than at the masses who did not. As Fishman put it,

instead of appealing to anything essentially French in "spirit," in "genius," in "essence," or in "tradition," it defended its recommendations via appeals to such purportedly objective criteria as euphoria, clarity, and necessity (redundancy). More than two hundred years after its founding, when the Academy's continued lack of concern for the technical vocabulary of modernization had come to be accompanied by attacks on *anglomania* and the tendency to *angliciser*, the worst that was said about overly frequent English borrowings was that they were unnecessary rather than they were un-French (10).

In a language-purification plan, the policy-formulating body is usually some form of an academy like the French Academy or the various Arabic and Spanish academies mentioned earlier. We saw that these academies generally function to oppose changes in the orthography, grammar, and vocabulary of the languages they seek to purify. In their opposition to change, purification plans are distinct from plans to reform language. A "pure" language is "perfect" as it is; it would make no sense to seek to reform it. Purification plans are *prescriptive*, being implemented by academies that decide what is or is not proper in the language. Modernization plans, as we will see later, are *adaptive*, whereas reform plans can be seen as *transformative*.

In the modern world and in the world of LP scholarship, strict language purification is now quite controversial. It is increasingly the case that language-purification plans have relatively moderate policies. Evidence of this may be seen in Fishman's observation that the French Academy now sees English borrowings as unnecessary rather than un-French! In Chapter Two we saw that the academies that began with the purpose of keeping Classical Arabic pure now seek to renovate and unify the language for all Arabic speakers in the modern world. Thus, language purification per se is becoming a type of language plan that is beginning to take a more moderate stance with regard to modernization, although it is still distinguished by the aim of setting up an ideal to which the language users should aspire. Thus, prescription is being modified in the direction of adaptation.

The Spanish Academy of today is bound together with sister academies in Latin America for the purpose of implementing Academy decisions and, significantly, through its Permanent Commission, also for keeping "watch over the development of the life of the language" (Guitarte and Quintero 1974:329). Language-purification plans today recognize that language change is not necessarily all bad or polluting. The Spanish Academy is even beginning to allow some of the sister academies to adopt indigenous vocabulary!

The French Academy is particularly interesting in that it has been a language-planning agency forming purification policy for three hundred years. It has thus elaborated and implemented a language-purification plan long enough for history to have had time to evaluate it. The French Academy is something many people have heard of yet about which very little is known. Even the person on the street can tell us that we better not say it if it hasn't been approved by the Academy! D. MacLaren Robertson's *A History of the French Academy* (1910) remains the only broad-based published discussion of the linguistic efforts of the Academy, even though there are a number of other books on the history of the French Academy. However, as a group these other publications have been called "naively laudatory" (Hall 1974:192). Only one work, by Henry Bellamy (1939), stands out as a "critical over-all survey" (192).

As we discuss the different types of plans in this chapter, we will also see that the planning agencies' work may not always, as in the case of the French Academy, be judged as "good" by specialists and experts. Often the evaluators of the plan are lay people with little linguistic or planning knowledge. However, high-quality codification is not required for a plan to be successfully implemented. It is sufficient, for example, that French people *think* that the Academy is keeping the language pure! Since the people think the language is pure, French is seen as unified and prestigious, and the speakers keep it pure regardless and in spite of actual Academy dictums.

For the planner, the French Academy is a classic example of language planning in a situation where a state becomes a nation. The Academy began in France at a time when the language was by no means generally understood everywhere within the French political context. In 1635,

> no more than two hundred thousand participated in the intellectual life of the country, and many of these considered Italian, Spanish, and Occitan far more fitting vehicles of cultured conversation whereas for publications Latin, too, was a common rival (Fishman 1971:9-10).

The purification plan of the French Academy had (and still has) a policy of dealing only with cultured and refined areas of language. It elaborated this policy by having "studiously aimed its publications (at least for three centuries, if not longer) at those already learned in the French language" (Fishman 1971:10). The goal of the French Academy's language-purification plan has always been "to fashion and reinforce French nationality" (10) by keeping the language free from outside influence. Language-purification plans, then, generally precede nationalism and often exist to provide a catalyst for it. Thus, purification plans are unable to use nationality as a tool of implementation. In the interest of sparking nationalism, both a rejection of international vocabulary (even for rather technical scientific or government work) and a limiting of influences from vernaculars are typical ways to keep purification policies, once codified and elaborated, in effect.

By the end of the seventeenth century in France, the French Academy's language-purification plan stood behind "everything that was most noble,

polished, and reasonable in human speech" (Hall 1974:177). It was believed that "Whatever is not clear is not French"! The French Academy, like
the earlier Italian and later Spanish academies, had the goal

> of furnishing men of letters an opportunity to discuss problems connected with
> the use of the literary languages. Their common ideal was the neoclassical belief
> that for each language and its literary manifestations there was an ideal fixed for
> all time, already reached by the classical writers of Greece and Rome, and which
> could be attained in modern days only by setting up similar models of perfec-
> tion. They viewed language itself as something unruly and unserviceable for the
> lofty purposes of culture and literature unless tamed and "reduced to rule" like a
> highstrung but wayward colt (Hall 1974:178-79).

The Academy ideal and their idea of language purification coincide to a
great extent with the ideas of Valter Tauli (see Chapter Five). Tauli, being a
language "idealist," would like purification to be the one goal of all
language planning. He would like standardization (as carried out by the
academies and other LP agencies) to take on a more purificational aspect.
Tauli would like to formulate principles to guide language change in such a
way that language becomes beautiful, clear, elastic, and economical. The
problem with this seemingly wonderful idea is that it assumes that some
languages are better and others worse. Further, in Tauli's view, the job of
the linguist is to determine which is the best language. However, linguists have no way of deciding what is "good" in a language and what is
"bad"—or even what is "efficient." As Björn Jernudd puts it (criticizing
Tauli's idealism):

> We know very little about the structure and use of language; and we know very
> little about people's thoughts, likes or dislikes, about language. The conflict
> between a linguistically based "ideal" language planning and an empirically
> based problems-of-speech-communities language planning demonstrates that a
> linguist's view of language and his vision of the beauty of language constitute but
> one aspect of social and linguistic reality (1973:14).

Throughout the pages of this book we have emphasized that the only
sensible approach to LP is one in which the problems of speech communities are considered. LP is evolving as an applied field where the "ideal"
approach to language, with the language isolated from its cultural context,
is, for most purposes, impractical. The fact that the language academies
promoting purification plans (such as the French and Spanish Academies)
are beginning to soften their approaches in an adaptive vein indicates that
the practical is beginning to make inroads on the ideal.
Language academies often begin as small discussion groups that gather

in private houses to take up various problems connected with literary creation and scientific investigation. Gradually such groups assume a more important role in the intellectual development of each country and eventually are granted official status and converted into academies. At that point the academies have special rooms or separate buildings in which they operate; they have a formal organizational structure and hold regular meetings (Hall 1974:178).

The French Academy began as a group of forty men—the "forty Immortals"—made into an official body by Cardinal Richelieu "to exert absolute power, under his close supervision, over literature and language" (Hall 1974:180). The composition of the Academy throughout its history has been interesting from a planning perspective:

> At any given time, not over fifty percent of its members have been even professional writers. The rest of its membership has consisted of such types as nobles, military men, and clergy. It has never admitted women. Only two men with competence in philology or lexicography have ever been members of the Academy: Antoine Furetière, whom it expelled . . . and Gaston Paris (1839–1903) (192).

Interestingly, since the above was written in 1974, the Academy elected its first woman member, Marguerite Yourcenar, in 1980. As reported in the magazine *Newsweek* (March 17, 1980:48), the "Immortals" "meet every Thursday to revise the official French dictionary; on special occasions, they dress in gold-braided green frock coats and carry ceremonial swords." The appointment of a woman to this formidable body was not without opposition. One member complained, "A woman, as a woman, simply has no place in the Academy." He continued, "Of course, I have a great deal of admiration for her work. But it is like putting a dove in the rabbit hutch. The Academy has survived 300 years without them."

In order to keep a language pure, a language academy sets itself up as the arbiter of linguistic good taste. It helps if the agency charged with purification is an arm of the government, so that its pronouncements have clout. (We will see later that government support also helps other LP agencies to implement different language plans.) The French Academy has excelled in this regard:

> Ever since Richelieu's time, the Académie Française has been above all a state institution, enjoying a veneration, at all levels of French society, far out of all proportion to its merits. There have been, beginning in the seventeenth century, a number of attacks on the Academy, none of which [has] been really successful in deflating its pretensions or diminishing its prestige, which has been maintained down to the present day through the French school system (Hall 1974:180).

The French Academy, shown here as an example of an agency putting forth a purification plan, can be illustrative not only of purification but also of what a planning agency is. We will now look at a situation in which an agency is being contemplated as a body to unify a number of organizations involved in implementing an implicit language policy.

In present-day Kenya, as part of the government's nine-year plan, the University of Nairobi is being asked to set up some form of language agency to coordinate the dozen or so bodies now in existence that contribute to implementing Swahili as the national language. Being contemplated is an Institute of Swahili Research modeled after the University's Institute of African Studies and Institute for Development Studies. Despite the fact that the University's Chancellor is also the President of the country, the relegation of language planning to a university institute rather than a government office means that the institute's suggestions will have little real authority behind them.

Interestingly, at the same time the government of Kenya is urging the University of Nairobi to develop an Institute of Swahili Research, a body called the Kenya National Culture Council has been set up (1980) by an Act of Parliament to advise the government on matters of developing both a Kenyan national culture and regional cultures within the country. This council is a high-powered body headed by the Minister of Social Services. It includes politicians, civil servants, *and* university scholars (in fields such as literature, language, and sociology). Kenya also has a new Directorate of Culture with a permanent staff. It would seem that for any future cultural and linguistic planning activities the Kenya National Culture Council might be the body through which ideas could be channeled to the government. These ideas could then be implemented as policy under the Directorate of Culture.

What the "officials" appear to want for a Kenyan language policy from an institute, council, or directorate is a modified purification plan for Kenyan Swahili as distinct from the East African regional standard and the Tanzanian national standard. The Government of Kenya is seeking an "authority" at the University of Nairobi to which it can turn when it needs teaching materials, specialized vocabularies, teacher training, and research on the relative strengths of Standard Swahili, English, various Swahili dialects, and the vernaculars.

It would seem that Kenya is looking for a language academy in the French sense, although the facts of history in twentieth-century Kenya are somewhat different than those in seventeenth-century France. Kenya is already a modern industrializing nation, and Swahili does exist in a standardized form (see below), albeit as a national language in Tanzania, not Kenya, and as a regional language in East Africa. In Tanzania, the National Swahili Council and the Institute for Swahili Research fill the role of an academy or an LP agency. This Council with the Institute associated with it is the descendant of the Interterritorial Language Committee that standardized Swahili for all East Africa in the 1930s and 1940s. Today, the institute in Tanzania is an academic body set up to implement official government language policy specified through the National Swahili Council. When Tanzania became independent, the Institute was used for nation-building ends, abandoning its regional agency role.

Kenya, despite or because of having a different Swahili history than Tanzania, appears to be seeking a similar body of its own now—a university-based institute likely to be under the Kenya National Cultural Council and likely to serve as a kind of language academy.

In seventeenth-century France,

> The Academy was entrusted with the tasks of preparing an official dictionary, grammar, and treatise on rhetoric. It was given a legal monopoly on its dictionary, which took sixty years to prepare, and did not appear until 1694 (Hall 1974:180).

In Dar es Salaam (Tanzania), the Institute for Swahili Research (since 1967 under the auspices of the National Swahili Council) has been working on an official Swahili dictionary since the 1960s and saw it published in 1981—a relatively quick accomplishment from the perspective of the French Academy model! *The Dictionary of Standard Swahili* (*Kamusi ya KiSwahili Sanifu*) is claimed by the Institute of Swahili Research that published it to encompass the present state of the language. To keep up with new coinages, future versions will be published as well. Thus, the current product, which took "only" twenty years to produce, is a work in progress. Along the same lines, the Philological Society of Great Britain took eighty years to produce the *OED* (*Oxford English Dictionary*), which came to be accepted as the final authority on the English language.

The role of language academies is as much symbolic as it is practical. Academies, as we have seen, serve as the markers of linguistic taste, as courts of appeal where people may turn with language questions. The goal of keeping language pure is, for all practical purposes, unattainable. Whether an academy's prescriptions are followed, though, is irrelevant to the goals of a purification plan. It is more important that the Academy exists as a body willing to prescribe. For prenational, premodern societies, a language academy may provide the people with their language in a pristine state; they can then use the language to form political solidarity and promote centralization. In nation-building contexts such as Kenya and Tanzania, plans mixing the academy role of purification with standardization practices (see below) may be the ideal direction for language policy to take.

By prescribing "good" Swahili and standardizing national forms of the language, yet simultaneously allowing the language to be adaptive to modern ideas and sensitive to each country's vernaculars in accepting new vocabulary, Swahili academies could well be effective planning agencies in both Kenya and Tanzania. It cannot be overstated that an academy's pronouncements have psychological power in making people feel that they have a language and that it is a "proper" one. Whether the criteria for a "proper" language could be realistically determined is beside the point.

In France, when the Academy finally brought out its dictionary, the book itself "was, even on its first appearance, manifestly an inferior job"; but, says Robert Hall, this might have been expected from "a group of dilettantes with no competence or training as lexicographers" (1974:180). Nevertheless, the dictionary has gone through a number of editions and continues to be regarded "with superstitious veneration, as an infallible authority, in many quarters of France" (180).

Language-purification plans are usually formulated by some kind of an academy that sets up "a single, unified ideal for usage, which could be prescribed for official documents, legislative and judicial activities, and could be taught in schools and used as a touch-stone in judging literature" (Hall 1974:181). What an academy does, then, by way of purification often resembles standardization except that, at the implementation stage, standardization involves putting the language to work in various spheres (such as school, government, industry). In contrast, to implement language purification is primarily to let people know that an academy exists and that it has the last word on language matters. Academy publications have, as it were, the imprimatur of the language authority; publications without the academy stamp of approval are somehow less pure. Purification strives to keep the language as it is, not let it be tainted by borrowings or modernization, or be taken into uncharted domains. Pure languages are put forward as "good" languages, hallmarks "of learning and social acceptability." They observe "all the grammatical niceties prescribed by academies or other 'authorities' and [avoid] any features of grammar or vocabularies that might be considered inelegant" (182).

When political centralization is the goal, purification is a language-planning function. A language-purification plan, as exemplified by the work of the French Academy for the past three hundred years, fills the bill as a plan as follows:

1. LANGUAGE CHOICE: French

2. POLICY FORMULATION: By the French Academy, which seeks to fashion and reinforce French nationality
   (DETERMINATION: The need for a plan to keep French "pure")

3. POLICY CODIFICATION: The Academy prepares a dictionary, grammar, and treatise on rhetoric.

4. POLICY ELABORATION: The Academy approves official publications and decides what is good French.

5. POLICY IMPLEMENTATION: The Academy is a state institution, and its policy is enforced through the use of Academy materials (such as publications and grammars) in the school system. The Academy has a physical location and a formal membership.

6. POLICY EVALUATION: The Academy keeps its publications current, updating vocabulary yet keeping borrowings to a minimum. Over three centuries, the Academy's role has been accepted. It *does* decide what is French. The fact that it now sees borrowings as unnecessary rather than un-French shows that it is evolving a modified purification stance. The plan has worked insofar as language purification has been the major language plan for French since the seventeenth century. Purification has been supplemented only recently by adaptive strategies of lexical modernization (also carried out under Academy sanction), so that "pure" French could keep up with the times.

As a planning agency, the French Academy may change from a purification-type plan. However, it seems likely that the implementation of purification will remain a major function, supplemented by modernization.

7.2   LANGUAGE REVIVAL: A SAMPLE PLAN

A language plan to revive language is generally an attempt to reestablish a language that once was but no longer is "a normal means of conversation and communication" among people (Nahir 1977:110). Language revival is currently being attempted with Irish in Ireland and with Cornish in Cornwall, England. Another example of revival is that of Hebrew, which we will use for our sample plan.

The authority in charge of the Hebrew revival was the Committee of the Hebrew Language (originally The Language Council; today, The Hebrew Language Academy). In 1911, the Committee of the Hebrew Language set the development and codification of Hebrew as one of its main objectives. The Committee wanted to ensure that Hebrew could be spoken everywhere—in the home; in school; in public life; in commerce, business, and industry; in the arts; and in science (Nahir 1977:111). The fact that this objective was met and that the Hebrew language was revived is thought to be an outstanding phenomenon of modern sociolinguistics. The success of the Hebrew revival, which was initiated at the beginning of the twentieth-century, was partially due to the fact that at the time the revival was begun Hebrew was not yet a dead language. Fellman (1974:428) tells us that the speaking of Hebrew among European Jews who came to Palestine "*once begun*, was *almost* natural." The idea behind the revival was to see that all people who lived in the Jewish state would have access to the language in all aspects of life. Hebrew revival is associated with the name Eliezer Ben Yehuda of Jerusalem. Ben Yehuda proposed seven initiatives designed to restore Hebrew, which along with supportive factors in the world around him, led to the success of the revival.

However, because Ben Yehuda lived in Jerusalem and not near many of the centers of innovation where the revived language would be commonly spoken, a paradox arose. His own Hebrew speech played a very minor role and was quite distinct from the actual Hebrew speech that was revived. Revival took place largely in the agricultural colonies, which Ben Yehuda was able to visit only at infrequent intervals. The result was that the language revived and the language of the reviver were very different (Nahir 1977:430)! In fact, some claim that Ben Yehuda's Hebrew was not particularly good! However, as in the case of the French Academy's attempts at purification, success in language revival is not so much the result of an authority promulgating a plan *in the appropriate context*. As the agent of Hebrew revival, Ben Yehuda's seven steps functioned success-fully even though his "personal brand of Hebrew played but a minor role in the revival" (431).

Ben Yehuda backed up his fight for a Hebrew linguistic and national revival by founding two societies to foster and further Hebrew speech. The *Tehiat Yisrael* ("Revival of Israel") Society was founded in 1882, and the *Safa Berura* ("Clear Language") Society was founded in 1889. Yet these societies did little to actually revive Hebrew. However, after its demise, the Safa Berura was seen to have laid the foundation for many other Safa Berura societies throughout the diaspora in the 1890s and 1900s. These societies adopted the same goals and ideologies of the "parent-model in Jerusalem" and were directly involved in the revival that took place (432). The desire for revival gradually extended to agricultural areas and to all Jewish settlements outside Palestine.

The seven steps taken by Ben Yehuda to revive Hebrew were:

1. He set up his own home as a model Hebrew-speaking household for others to follow.

2. He sought assistance from the diaspora and the local population.

3. He created Hebrew-speaking societies.

4. He set up Hebrew classes in the schools.

5. He published a modern Hebrew newspaper.

6. He compiled a dictionary of ancient and modern Hebrew.

7. He formed a Language Council.

The Language Council (*Waad Na-Lashon*) was set up by Ben Yehuda in 1890 in order to extend the idea of revival throughout the countryside. That is, the Council came into being for the express purpose of elaborating Steps 1 through 6. This official agency of revival was begun with just five members and got off to a slow start. The Council became an instrument of Hebrew revival only after 1904, when the Hebrew teachers and their teachers' union jointly gave it their support. After the state of Israel was established, the Council was renamed the Hebrew Language Academy in 1953.

In its revival effort, the Council set out to create:

1. a unified Hebrew terminology

2. a unified system of pronunciation

3. a unified spelling system

4. a fixed set of grammatical forms

Thus, in LP terms, the Council aimed to codify the revival plan. In its first years, the Council's Vice-President, David Yellin, took upon himself the tasks of unifying spelling and pronunciation, while the work of dealing with grammar and terminology fell to Ben Yehuda. From the outset, the Council's views and those of Ben Yehuda differed with regard to the exact language that was to be revived as "Hebrew." Ben Yehuda saw Hebrew "as one continuously developing language with no phase intrinsically preferable to any other," whereas Yellin and the Council "viewed Hebrew in its entire historical development, [and] particularly hallowed the Hebrew of the Bible" (Nahir 1977:452).

Whereas the French Academy sought to keep French pure and failed, but still succeeded in unifying French and making people think it was pure, the Language Council sought to revive Biblical Hebrew and failed, but still succeeded in reviving the spoken language. The success of the Hebrew revival was due in part to effectively unifying terminology by means of word coining. The Council felt, as do most lay people, that "language could be defined as a collection of words pronounced, spelled, defined, and inflected in a certain predetermined fashion" (Nahir 1977:453). That is, it thought language change could be prescribed or legislated—done by fiat!

Luckily, by the time the Council got going, its aim of language revival had already been largely accomplished. The very fact that the Council was founded is good evidence that revival had occurred! The existence of the Language Council presupposed

> that Hebrew was *already* being spoken by a sizeable number of persons and that the language merely needed regulating and expanding rather than actual reviving. Indeed, in many if not most cases the Council merely noted its acceptance of material already in use which had been coined by the public (teachers, farmers, tradesmen and so on) (454).

Even though Ben Yehuda (with his seven steps, the Council, and the societies) was the force behind all the projects designed to revive Hebrew, the schools ultimately were the most important fact in the revival. Particularly instrumental in the success of the revival were the schools in the agricultural colonies. These schools used the "Hebrew through Hebrew" approach, a direct Berlitz-like approach of language teaching that used Hebrew speakers who taught by example. This approach, supplemented by some use of other modern teaching methods as well and an educational structure based on Hebrew, brought about the revival of the language.

A language-revival plan is practicable where a need exists for a language as a means of communication. In Chapter Three, we introduced a similar notion, language RESURRECTION (or reintroduction), which can be brought about in areas where a need exists for language to function as an aspect of culture rather than as a means of communication. Resurrection works where a group that once had a common language has lost the language due to its suppression through contact with other languages that moved into the area. Language revival works where the events of history have put people with different language backgrounds in contact with one another in an area that had once shared a common language. Revival may occur when a need for a common spoken language for communicational purposes arises once again, as in Israel. Resurrection is a feasible plan when the key purpose is to establish common ethnic identification or association. When a group does not have a common language, out of necessity it

> will select one as a vehicle for communication. Then, if it [that is, the common language] is unsuitable for modern needs, the group, usually under some authority (i.e., a language-planning agency), will codify it and concurrently make all its members use it rather than various languages they have been using to communicate (Nahir 1977:111).

Hebrew was revived so that Jews in and outside of Palestine and in urban as well as agricultural areas could communicate. Today, Hebrew is the national language of Israel, although many people there continue to use more than one language. A large number of the present immigrant population came to Israel knowing no Hebrew—after the state was formed in 1948, which was well after the language revival had occurred.

As Hebrew has become more firmly established as the language of Jews in Israel, protagonists of that language have tended to treat with greater leniency the use of foreign tongues by immigrants who cannot be expected to have mastered Hebrew. The erstwhile negative attitude towards the publication of newspapers in foreign languages has also been modified. The faulty use of Hebrew is widely tolerated, and old-timers will frequently help out an immigrant speaking a halting Hebrew by suggesting the proper word or phrase or even correcting his mistakes (Herman 1968:500).

A language-revival plan, as exemplified by the development of teaching "Hebrew through Hebrew" in Palestinian schools, conforms to the components of a plan as follows:

1. LANGUAGE CHOICE: Hebrew

2. POLICY FORMULATION: By the Language Council (Committee of the Hebrew Language, Hebrew Language Academy)
    (DETERMINATION: The need for a plan to provide a common vehicle of communication)

3. POLICY CODIFICATION: The policy is codified through Berlitz-type teaching of "Hebrew through Hebrew"; by development of official terminologies and word coinings; and through Safa Berura societies.

4. POLICY ELABORATION: The schools teach the language and the official terminology.

5. POLICY IMPLEMENTATION: Revival succeeds largely through the schools, which are seen as the best places to acquire new vocabulary. The school is perhaps the place where most revival expenditure should be made in the form of textbooks and modern glossaries (Alloni-Fainberg 1974:504).

6. POLICY EVALUATION: Modern Hebrew's revival is continuing up to the present time, in that the schools are continuing to teach the language and to update official terminologies. Since immigration is continuing, language teaching as policy implementation is likely to go on.

Hebrew revival is the only successful language revival so far. We saw earlier that efforts to bring back Irish are continuing, but in Ireland the plan involves restoration of Irish as a second language alongside English. Likewise, the emerging Cornish revival plan is seeking to see that the language is used only in certain domains while English will continue to predominate in the county. Nahir believes that "no other attempt at language reviving has succeeded because this rare combination of conditions—a need for a means of communication resulting from the 'right' historical circumstances, and an old revivable language—has nowhere prevailed as yet" (1977:112). The plan to revive Hebrew has worked insofar as language revival has been the major language plan for Hebrew since 1890. The Hebrew Academy today keeps the language revived by continuous teaching modified by minor concurrent plans of purification, reform, and lexical modernization chiefly devoted to spelling reform and the updating of terminologies.

As a planning agency, the Hebrew Academy today no longer is actively in the process of reviving Hebrew. Instead, the schools are implementing the now-revived language and using Academy-approved tools (such as spellings and terminologies) to do so. In recent years, the Hebrew Language Academy has been seeking to improve its communication with the general public, and it has even hired a spokesperson who finds as many opportunies as possible to publicize the decisions made by the Academy. This person is thus a public-relations official for the Academy, seeing that Academy pronouncements get press and media coverage. The speaker also "reacts to the appearance of terms in the press that conflict with those established by the Academy" (Rabin 1971:121). The Academy publishes "A well-printed regular news-sheet, made specially to be exhibited on walls of schools, offices, and factories," giving sets of new terms and grammatical information (121).

Once a language is revived, it can be re-revived. Where a language is found to be unsuitable for modern needs, the group who uses the language

usually under some authority (i.e., a language-planning agency), will codify it and concurrently make all its members use it rather than the various languages they have been using to communicate. The process involves first codification (i.e., linguistic adaptation to current communicative needs) and then standardization. The latter involves all activities, including codification, aimed at popularizing a language in a community. In terms of language-planning functions it could be formulated as follows:

revival = codification + standardization (+ reform) (Nahir 1977:111).

We will now look at a situation wherein a language, though not "dead" or "dying," became unwieldy and needed reform.

7.3 LANGUAGE REFORM: A SAMPLE PLAN

One characteristic of reform as a type of language plan is that it is generally done while the planning agency is simultaneously carrying out other functions as well (such as purification or revival). The classic case of language reform is that of Turkish, beginning in 1922 under the auspices of Kemal Atatürk. The goal of language reform in Turkey was to establish a simple Turkish (*sade türkçe*) that could lead to a pure Turkish (*öz türkçe*). This was meant to be achieved through "the processes of detraditionalization, de-Arabization, de-Persification, secularization, and modernization" (Gallagher 1971:161). Again, as we saw with purification and revival, the success of a particular language plan has as much to do with history as with the planning authority's conception and execution of a plan. Turkey, even in the days of the Ottoman Empire, was open to European influence and ideas, and it was viewed by Europe as "an equal and a participant in the European and international power system" (Gallagher 1971:160). The reform of Turkish in the 1920s was conditioned by a number of historical factors:

1. the existence of reformist writers in the nineteenth century and of Turkish people in foreign embassies who perceived the need for the language to be useful in the broader world

2. the need of the early twentieth-century Young Turks in the government to have their policies understood

3. the need of World War I army officers to use the language for military purposes

These literary, political, and military factors culminated in a perceived need in Turkey to see that the Turkish language keep up with Europe. The object of reform was the official written language known as *Osmanlicá,*

> a synthetic amalgam of Arabic, Persian, and Turkish, with grammatical and syntactical features of each. As a literary language it was unintelligible to the peasantry, even to the ordinary townsmen, and inaccessible without prolonged special study. It was contrasted with disdain to the crude Turkish (*kaba türkçe*) of the illiterate masses. In sum, it was the language of a religion, Islam; of its culture and its Caliphate; and of the Ottoman political institution, which had been the defender of the faith since the fifteenth century (161).

The need to reform Osmanlicá was catalyzed by the need to cope with new administrative, legal, educational, and military terminology. It was considered not fitting to express modern ideas with Persian and Arabic loanwords.

The call for reform began in the mid-nineteenth century and was issued by political writers urging both a simplification of the language and the elimination of Arabic and Persian loans. By the beginning of the twentieth century, a perceptible narrowing of the gap between written *Osmanlicá* and spoken Türkçe had appeared. Reform was further hastened by the feelings of Turkish nationalism that came to a head in 1908 during the Young Turk

Revolution. These political happenings led to increased journalistic activity and a resulting simplification of the language used in the newspapers in the interest of getting the ideas expressed. At this time, a group of writers and journalists, the *Genç Kalemler* (Young Pens), was formed in Salonike. The group goal was to simplify the language and to avoid foreign influences. That is, the Young Pens took it upon themselves to answer the nineteenth-century political writers' call for reform. By 1918, a more simple and flexible language was beginning to emerge. This language was based largely on the speech of educated urban Turks.

> In the desperate, hectic era of defeat, redressment, and refocusing of national purpose between 1918 and 1923, the multirooted *Osmanlicâ* was dying, along with the multilingual empire whose tongue it had been for five centuries (Gallagher 1971:163).

The reform carried out in the twenties by Atatürk as the authority figure applied to the more pure and simple language that was already emerging. Atatürk's reform dealt with both planned (script and vocabulary) and unplanned (borrowings, evolution of style) changes. As President of the Turkish Republic, Kemal Atatürk stressed language reform as important for social development. Since reform had been begun decades earlier with simplification and purification of educated speech, Atatürk focused first on script reform. This step was to be followed by language reform, the "Turkization" of the language to eliminate all remaining Arabic and Persian influence and to make the language generally understandable to the people. "On the primary initiative of the state and Kamal Atatürk, linguistics assumed the role of 'the first branch of science' in Turkish scientific life for a long time" (Hazai 1974:128).

A major aspect of planned reform of Turkish was the move from Arabic to Latin script. This change was instituted in 1927 and stemmed from "Atatürk's desire to cut the new Turkey off from what he held was the dead weight of the Islamic past" (Gallagher 1971:164). Script reform was possible largely because only 10 percent of the population was literate in any language at that time and had no attachment to speak of to the Great Tradition embodied in "the Perso-Arabic literary heritage of Ottoman civilization" (164). The other major area where reform was successful was in emphasizing that all kinds of affixes could be used in forming new Turkish words but that a limited set of fixed suffixes would mark those Arabic or Persian words still thought to be necessary.

As we already have seen, the leaders or instigators of a language plan (Richelieu, Ben Yehuda, and now Atatürk) eventually need an agency or academy to push the plan forward. In fact, these authoritative bodies, more than the individuals (who happened to be at the right place at the right time), are the most influential forces in getting the deliberate language change accomplished. A planner needs to realize this fact, as well as understand that implementation is generally best accomplished through the school system if he or she is to knowledgeably participate in the planning process. Atatürk's academy, the Turkish Linguistic Society (*Türk Dili Tetkik Cemiyeti;* now the *Türk Dil Kurumu,* or *TDK*) was formed at his instigation in 1932. The Society's Central Committee set out

> to collect Turkish words from the popular language and from old Turkish texts; to define the principles of word formation and to create words from Turkish roots; and to encourage the use of true Turkish words in replacement of foreign words used in the written language (Gallagher 1971:165).

As was the case in the other two sample plans discussed above, in order to be effective, the LP agency needs to have official government sanction. The quality of the academy's production is not as important as the fact that it is producing materials and ideas geared to the plan's function. Thus, it is fitting that "the zealousness of the first years [of the Turkish Linguistic Society] was supported by all the authority of the state, but because the work was carried out in many instances by volunteers and local amateurs, the initial results threatened to lead to linguistic anarchy" (Gallagher 1971:165).

From 1936 to 1941, reform seemed to slow down; in fact, it met with some opposition to the weeding out of foreign words. Nonetheless, during that time lists of Turkish scientific and mathematical terms began to appear and started to be used in official textbooks after being tested by scholarly commissions. In 1942, the reform was intensified by a set of Turkization changes proposed by the Turkish Linguistic Society in order to develop national terminologies. Academicians opposed such Turkish chauvinism, however, and wanted "greater internationalization in scientific and learned terminology, both to insure accuracy of translation and to preserve ties between Turkey and the advanced countries" (Gallagher 1971:167). This national versus international struggle over terminology is still going on. The present LP function being carried out in Turkey as a part of continuing reform appears to be the specific standardization of technical terminology and some efforts to standardize the reformed language as a whole.

As reform moves toward standardization as Turkey's major LP activity, academicians are replacing the former members of the Turkish Linguistic Society as the agents of change. The Society is thus losing its former "official" status. The TDK now has

> had its semi-official status removed and lost its government subsidy, while a wide range of moderate scholars was elected to the Executive Committee. On the whole, it can be said that since 1950 the TDK has worked in a more sober and scholarly way. It has tried to continue the simplification and modernization,

without undue nationalist fervor, suggesting and counseling more often without than with success. The TDK now lacks the authority to impose decisions, and it is looked upon by many Turks as an exotic group of specialists whose endeavors and pronouncements have little relation to their own problems or those of the nation today (167–68).

During the 1940s and 1950s the TDK made substantial contributions to Turkish lexicography and thereby successfully enabled both script and word-formation reforms to proceed, even when the Society's efforts had "not been adequately supported by the state in the fields of education and publishing" (Hazai 1974:142).

A language-reform plan as exemplified by the work of the TDK (Turkish Linguistic Society) to reform script and regularize new and loanword formation by means of concentrated lexicographic work conforms to the components of a plan as follows:

1. LANGUAGE CHOICE: Turkish

2. POLICY FORMULATION: By the TDK (Turkish Linguistic Society)
   (DETERMINATION: The need for a plan to reconcile the written *Osmanlicà* with the spoken *Türkçe* and to eliminate Arabo-Persian influence in the language

3. POLICY CODIFICATION: The TDK produces numerous dictionaries, including a four-volume historical dictionary (1943–1957) and a six-volume dictionary of Turkish dialects. Codification takes the form of a *neological movement* ("new word" movement) focusing on the history of vocabulary and on etymology as a basis for suggesting new Turkish words.

4. POLICY ELABORATION: Language reform is extended largely through simultaneously political, social, and economic structures in Turkey.

5. POLICY IMPLEMENTATION: Reform is brought about rapidly, thoroughly, and without resistance by the Ministry of Education through the schools. As an example, "The new letters were first taught in November 1928; Arabic writing was abolished from the beginning of 1929; and Arabic and Persian were no longer taught as foreign languages from September of 1929" (Gallagher 1971:164–65).

6. POLICY EVALUATION: The planned reform of Turkish is moving toward a planned approach to standardization of the language; yet, the reform plan as a whole, "despite excesses and occasionally ridiculous pomposities," has had considerable success in its major aims. Modern Turkish is simpler and freer of loans from Persian and Arabic than its predecessor. Atatürk's reform brought about the forebear of

Turkey's current national language. The reform spurred research in the history of the language. It sponsored the compilation and publishing of specialized vocabularies. It generated debate about language issues. Now that reform is accomplished, the "genius of the language community" can be seen to be developing on its own (Gallagher 1971:168).

The introduction of the new script in 1928 was the major factor in cutting Turkey off from the Middle East. Script reform allowed the country to focus on itself and then turn away from a Perso-Arabic world toward increased contact with the West.

The current focus on standardization is to ensure that the newly reformed Turkish language can be held in common by all Turkish people. The TDK has lost much of its power and influence. Modern Turkey is gradually becoming socioeconomically linked to Europe; still, the country is about 50 percent illiterate (Gallagher 1971:175). Academicians are now seeking to take over the LP agency role by urging modernization and standardization along with, and as part of, programs to eliminate illiteracy.

7.4   LANGUAGE STANDARDIZATION: A SAMPLE PLAN

Whereas language revival and reform have had relatively few successes in the world to date, language standardization has succeeded a number of times in a number of places. In general, "language standardization may be defined as a process whereby one language or dialect spoken in a region (usually a single political region) becomes accepted as the major language of the region for general usage" (Nahir 1977:115; see also Chapter Three). The standardization plan we will look at in this section is that of Swahili. One of the distinguishing features of Swahili standardization is that it was intended for East Africa as a region, rather than for a particular nation or nations, since the process of standardization took place before the East African nations achieved independence.

In 1925, at an education conference in Dar es Salaam (in what was then called Tanganyika but is now Tanzania), Swahili was chosen as the most suitable language to serve as a lingua franca for use in as large a number of schools as possible. It was chosen because of its predominance over a large area and the participants in the conference believed that the best language of education is a common vernacular.

However, in order for Swahili to be used as the language of education in East Africa, there needed to be "a common orthography and dialectal form for the written language, ... whatever variations in spoken language occurred" (Whiteley 1969:79). In 1930, all four countries of East Africa (Kenya, Tanganyika, Zanzibar, and Uganda) agreed to work together in an organization to be known as the Inter-Territorial Language (Swahili) Committee. This Committee was later referred to simply as the East African Swahili Committee.

Between choosing Swahili as the language of education and the setting up of the East African Swahili Committee five years later, a number of proposals about a possible standard language were made to the various education departments of the different countries. Later the various proposals served as the basis for the standard written language. The proposals were considered by the Committee and

> were criticized in points of detail over the years, but as a result of their adoption and implementation in the preparation and publication of school textbooks a standard written form of the language was largely achieved during the thirties and forties (Whiteley 1969:80).

A Central Publishing Committee was set up and was to be informed of all publication plans for secular textbooks so as to avoid duplication of effort. In the "Plan of Standardization for Education in East Africa," it was decided to adopt the Zanzibar dialect (known as the KiUnguja dialect) as the standard. The choice of dialect boiled down to a selection between the dialect proposed by the Universities Mission to Central Africa and the one proposed by the Church Missionary Society (the KiMvita dialect of Mombasa, Kenya).

By choosing KiUnguja, some people argued, language planners were cutting East Africa off from an important part of its heritage. A standard based on KiUnguja would bypass linguistic influence from the centuries-old literary tradition of the northern dialects of Kenya. This argument had little effect, however. The literary tradition of the North was one in which poetry excelled, particularly Islamic poetry, rich in inspired heroic epics of a religious nature. The language planners, in contrast, were Christian missionaries or educators steeped in Western culture "and not sympathetic with Islamic traditions" (Hinnebusch 1979:268).

The East African Swahili Committee was formed to supervise the establishment of KiUnguja-based standard. The Committee was approved and sanctioned by the colonial governors of the four territories. The Committee, originally composed of seventeen members, had no African members until 1946! The aims of the Committee were to

1. standardize orthography throughout the territory

2. control the publication of dictionaries and standard grammars

3. secure uniformity in word usage and syntax

4. encourage Swahili authors, answer their questions about Swahili lan-

guage and literature, supply them with advice, and keep them informed of territorial teaching methods and practices

5. revise, when necessary, general books and textbooks already in print and keep an up-to-date list of such books in the language

6. translate selected books and commission others for direct authorship in Swahili, editing these before publication (Whiteley 1969:82–83).

An interesting feature of Swahili standardization is that it was done to a nonliterary dialect which, in the process, was transformed into a literary language by non-native speakers. From 1930 to 1947, the East African Swahili Committee functioned under the aegis of the Conference of East African Governors. From 1948 to 1952 it was based at Makerere College in Kampala, Uganda. Then, in 1962, it moved to the University College at Dar es Salaam, where it eventually became a sort of Tanzanian national language academy, known today as the Institute of Swahili Research. This is the Institute we discussed earlier in this chapter as a language academy working in concert with the Tanzania National Swahili Council.

Today, largely because of the history of this Committee, it is beginning to be believed that Standard Swahili is particularly Tanzanian and that Kenya, for example, might again investigate the possibilities of standardizing the Mombasa dialect as its national language.

Swahili standardization, as it concerns our investigation, was carried out during the years 1930 to 1947 under the East African Swahili Committee authorized by the Conference of East African Governors. The main task in standardizing the Zanzibar dialect was the production of a two-volume Swahili/English and English/Swahili dictionary by the Committee's Secretary, Frederick Johnson. These dictionaries are still the main source of the Swahili standard, although the Institute for Swahili Research in Dar es Salaam, as part of its academy role, has just brought out its *Dictionary of Standard Swahili* (1981), as we mentioned earlier.

Another task of standardization was to see that textbooks used the proposed forms. This objective was accomplished by giving the Committee imprimatur (sanction or approval) rights:

All suggestions regarding new books and manuscripts came to the committee from the Directors of Education, to whom copies of the work in question were sent for consideration. The Secretary of the Committee was then informed . . . whether the book . . . was approved for use in schools. . . . Those books that were written or translated into Swahili, together with those that were sent to the committee for revision of the language, were forwarded to two of the Committee's Readers for perusal, comment, and suggestions, thus ensuring the uniform standard orthography as decided on by the Committee as a whole. The Imprimatur of the Committee was granted when the Secretary was satisfied that the recommendations approved by the Committee had been incorporated in the author's text (Whiteley 1969:84-85).

The standard grammar for Swahili was written by E. O. Ashton and published in London in 1944. It remains to this day one of the main reference works for Swahili grammar.

One result of the standardization of Swahili by the Inter-Territorial Language Committee was that, in practice, there appeared to be an "over-rigid application of the standard forms" (Whiteley 1969:87). Consequently, books written in the standard had an artificial, stilted style. In fact, many Swahili speakers perceived the standard language more as a *KiZungu* or *KiSerikali* ("European" or "government-type") dialect than as a codified form of the spoken language on the island of Zanzibar.

After standardization was accomplished, the Committee and its role changed. The LP function for East Africa has since become more one of modernization. In fact, after World War II, educational policies in the four territories—despite the availability and existence of standard Swahili—had for the most part shifted to allow English to gradually replace Swahili. At that point, the Committee "left the stage and moved into a back room" (Whiteley 1969:88)! It remained the authority on matters of Swahili research and orthography but no longer scrutinized Swahili manuscripts for final approval. By the 1960s, when the Institute for Swahili Research in Dar es Salaam came into being (emerging from what was left of the Committee), the focus of Swahili language policy had moved from education and standardization (and linguistic research) across all of East Africa toward the fostering of Tanzanian literary and historical studies in Swahili and the preparation and collection of up-to-date vocabulary to be used in nation-building (93). That is, standardization began to be supplemented by purification and modernization tasks in the interest of nation-building within one country.

In this standardization sample plan, we see that originally Swahili was largely standardized by expatriates as a regional language for all of East Africa. It is now the national language of both Kenya and Tanzania. Each of these places, as nations, is today evolving distinct language policies and requiring distinct plans. Since LP functions shift through time, it may well be that new sub-plans to accompany Swahili standardization may emerge such as reform, modernization, or purification) sensitive to the particular needs of each country. Recently there has been a call in Kenya for the "liberation" of Kenyan Swahili from outside influences (Khalid 1977). In Tanzania, it is likely that "with the greatly increased use of Swahili . . . during the past few years, coupled with the increasing production of books, some new efforts in the field of standardization may be required" (Whiteley 1969:93).

New standardization efforts in either place are likely to be undertaken by local scholars rather than expatriates, in the interest of current national goals. There appears to be a feeling today in Tanzania that Swahili needs to be updated as a national, instead of a regional, standard incorporating scientific and technical vocabulary without relying on loanwords. "Newspaper Swahili" (as well as the Swahili of literature and textbooks) also needs to be restandardized to eliminate its stilted quality.

The sentiment also prevails that the language needs to be extended as the language of instruction to *all* areas of education. The then Tanzanian language academy (the Institute for Swahili Research, or *Chama cha Uchunguzi wa KiSwahili*) was already being encouraged in 1965 by the Ministry of Community Development and National Culture to develop a plan "to rid the language of bad influences and to guide it along the proper road." In the words of the Ministry spokesperson, "We want to standardize its orthography and usage and to encourage all our people to learn to speak and write properly grammatical Swahili" (Whiteley 1969:104).

In Kenya, as we noted earlier, the government is looking to academicians to set up some form of organization for that country analogous to the Tanzanian National Swahili Council and its Institute for Swahili Research to serve as a language-planning agency now that an interterritorial or regional structure is no longer practical. Although Swahili is Kenya's national language, the only current academy for Swahili is the National Swahili Council and the Institute for Swahili Research in Tanzania. Kenya needs its own LP authority to guide its national language policy with regard to Swahili, whether it be standardized or reformed, modernized, revived, or purified!

In Nairobi, Kenya's capital, people from a number of different language backgrounds live and work together. As a result, people have begun to communicate in a pidginized form of Swahili that differs from the prescribed Zanzibar-derived standard. The pidgin, as any pidgin, has a small vocabulary and little grammatical complexity. Although these characteristics limit the range of creative expression for pidgin speakers, the language is easier to learn by non-native speakers than the standard or than the Mombasa dialect. However, "pidgin speakers are not fully accepted in areas where the language is spoken natively, or in up-country areas where standard Swahili is the norm as a national language as in Tanzania" (Hinnebusch 1979:257). Currently, Nairobi Swahili is changing in the direction of gaining more regularities and complexities than a pidgin, yet becoming quite different from Tanzanian Swahili. Simultaneously, outside the city, speakers of other languages are beginning to learn the standardized dialect as a result of having been taught the standard in the schools. An LP authority is being sought to guide these changes and bring about a standardized form of Swahili for the whole of Kenya.

A language-standardization plan, as exemplified by the work of the Inter-Territorial Language Committee in East Africa in the 1930s and 1940s to ensure that schools in the whole region had a common language of instruction, conforms to the components of a plan as follows:

1. LANGUAGE CHOICE: Swahili (KiUnguja, or the Zanzibar dialect)

2. POLICY FORMULATION: By the Inter-Territorial Language Committee (East African Swahili Committee)
   (DETERMINATION: The need for a plan to provide a common school language throughout the territory)

3. POLICY CODIFICATION: The publication of Ashton's *Swahili Grammar* and the *Standard Swahili/English* and *English/Swahili* Dictionaries establishes the standard to be promulgated.

4. POLICY ELABORATION: Language standardization is accomplished largely through the educational system of the colonial administration (the Conference of East African Governors).

5. POLICY IMPLEMENTATION: Standardization takes place through the East African Swahili Committee's power to put its stamp of approval on the textbooks and literary publications that use the codified standard grammar and orthography.

6. POLICY EVALUATION: When the territories were no longer centralized and Tanzania (the union of Tanganyika and Zanzibar), Uganda, and Kenya became separate nations, the regional standard was no longer as useful, and the need for distinct LP functions in each country developed. These distinct policies are beginning to be pursued today.

The Inter-Territorial Swahili Committee evolved to become today's Tanzanian Institute for Swahili Research and the National Swahili Council of Tanzania. These bodies are being encouraged by the Ministry of Development and National Culture to purify and modernize Swahili as Tanzania's national language. The National Swahili Council was formed in 1967 by an Act of Parliament as the main Swahili language-planning body and charged with elaborating the standard and modernizing the language. The Institute of Swahili Research is the National Swahili Council's operational arm, preparing dictionaries and word lists, promoting literature, and so forth.

Kenya, deprived by history of a historically evolved LP agency, is now seeking to develop one so that it may pursue a plan to implement the current government policy of Swahili as the national language.

As of now, Swahili is *the* designated national and *a* designated official language in Kenya. Understandably, the government wants to extend the use of Swahili in the country as a way to detribalize it and build a nation. The Kenyan government wants to use Swahili to "Kenyanize" the country and seeks a language-planning body to decide on what constitutes "good" Kenyan Swahili, that is, to decide what constitutes a "good" Kenyan national language.

Current language-policy agencies in Kenya include:

1. The Kenya Institute of Education (which has a curriculum-development section with a Swahili panel)

2. The University of Nairobi's Department of Linguistics and African Languages

3. Kenyatta University College's Department of Literature and Linguistics

4. The Kenya Institute of Administration

5. The Kenya Institute for Adult Studies

6. The Adult Education Section and Research Division of the Ministry of Housing and Social Services

7. The Inspectorate of KiSwahili (headed by a Swahili inspector)

8. More than ten teacher-training colleges

9. The *Chama cha KiSwahili,* a Swahili "club/party" (*chama*) started by interested citizens and registered with and backed by the government (this group has an avowed purification goal and may be seen as an incipient academy)

10. The Voice of Kenya (VOK) newsroom which promulgates VOK English, chooses the form of Swahili broadcasts, and decides on which vernaculars to use in programming and how much time should be allotted to the different languages

11. The Kenya Association of Swahili Teachers, a professional organization that holds conventions, elects officers, and presents scholarly papers

The national plan calling for the setting up of an Institute for Swahili Research sees such an Institute as extending or replacing these language-policy boards in a unified way.

In addition to the plethora of organizations dealing with language in Kenya, publishing houses are now actively preparing instructional materials at various levels and encouraging written Kenyan literature in Swahili. This emergent activity by publishers—after many years of not helping to implement a Swahili policy—should lead to a way for the university Institute of Swahili Research to interpret and elaborate government policy, once the institute is set up and has consolidated the other organizations. If more and more material is published in Swahili, it will begin to appear to be a feasible national language, and government policy will be credible.

In Uganda, it is not clear what role Swahili will eventually play in language policy, nor can we yet see what type of language plan will develop, given the absence of a specific government language-planning authority. Kawoya (1982) discusses Swahili during the recent politically turbulent times in Uganda, bringing to light the interesting fact that one of the first actions of the military government of Idi Amin in 1971 was the introduction of Swahili on radio and television. Today Swahili remains a Ugandan media language along with English and Luganda. Amin brought Swahili, formerly the language of the police, prisons, and armed forces, out of the barracks to the public (10). After Amin, the language was given another boost in 1979 with the arrival of the Tanzanian army in Uganda. This Tanzanian troop Swahili, known as *Bakombozi* (the Ugandan Swahili word for "liberators"), initially "had an aesthetic appeal for the people" (10) and would have boded well for improving people's attitudes toward Swahili had the "liberators" not lost much of their appeal. Currently Ugandan political authorities are not putting in any effort to formulate Swahili language policy and the university (Makerere) and the schools are in no position to provide systematic training in the language. Without serious government backing, the spread of a standard form of Swahili in Uganda is not likely to be favored, although Swahili is likely to continue as a language of the streets.

In 1975, the Ugandan *National Curriculum Development Centre* made a set of proposals for promoting Swahili as "a language of communication at all levels" and "eventually a medium of instruction in the primary classes" (Kawoya 1982:19), but since then nothing has been done toward their implementation.

In the East African region as a whole, we may say that the externally standardized Swahili of colonial days is giving way to a consciously planned national Swahili based on policy decisions of the separate countries. It is possible that a new standardized plan would be useful in one country, purification or reform in another. Whereas Swahili is likely to be the planned language in Tanzania, in Kenya the emergent policy will need to also address the functional allocation of English as well as some of the other local vernaculars.

7.5   LEXICAL MODERNIZATION: A SAMPLE PLAN

A language plan to modernize a language's lexicon generally deals with efforts to update vocabulary and special terminologies. Lexical modernization through the creation of terms is thought to be of two types: (1) part of the codification aspect of planning, when new words are devised to revive, reform, or standardize a language, or (2) part of the implementation aspect of planning, when new words are devised to adjust already revived, reformed, or standardized languages to new scientific and technological ideas (Nahir 1977:117).

We will use Type 2 lexical modernization to exemplify a lexical modernization plan, using the Swedish language as our example. In technologically advanced countries, lexical modernization plans use "very detailed definitions and foreign language equivalents and emphasize 'systematicity of terminology' "; in developing countries, however, word lists are used simply to "enumerate a series of terms without definitions" (Nahir 1977:117). As a technologically advanced country, Sweden carries out lexical modernization in the first, more elaborate sense. The aims of Swedish systematic terminological work as lexical modernization are "to create and maintain semantic order in already available terminology and to implement or suggest new terms in relation thereto" (Jernudd 1973:20). To create and maintain semantic order where terms already exist means that relationships need to be set up between concepts and that the meanings of concepts need to be made explicit. This specificity is necessary so that words have clear and unambiguous meanings regardless of their context of use. Where this clarification cannot be made, new terms are suggested to ensure understanding.

The LP agency for lexical modernization in Sweden is the Swedish Center of Technical Terminology (*Tekniska Nomenklatur Centralen,* or TNC). One feature of the Swedish language that augurs well for lexical modernization is that the Swedes have long been interested in remedying word shortages in their language by liberally borrowing and adapting words from other languages (Austen 1970:21). In the other language plans discussed so far the opposite has generally been the case. Purification, revival, and reform plans, especially, seek to keep borrowings to a minimum. In the seventeenth, eighteenth, and nineteenth centuries some efforts were made to keep Swedish pure, but today,

> Swedish purism for purism's own sake has little value, and a radical purge of the foreign element would result not merely in trimming the hedge but in veritable devastation of the resources of the language (Bergman 1973:85–86).

In Sweden, both the written language and the spoken language are standardized. Lexical modernization is being made possible by increasing literacy and popular education. In addition, radio (after 1925) and television (after 1954) have supported an increased breadth of language. Also, as time goes by, in the press and in literature more is being written originally in Swedish rather than being translated from other languages. Planning is now needed to keep meaning clear in writing and to ensure that what people need to say can be said.

As we saw to be the case with the French Academy, the Swedish Academy, founded in 1786 by Gustav III, saw its " 'modest and most urgent' task [to be] to work for the 'purity, strength, and sublimity' of the Swedish language" (Bergman 1973:31). However, the agency that carries out lexical modernization in Sweden today is not the Swedish Academy but rather a different authority, the Swedish Center for Technical Terminology. The Swedish Academy is still in existence and is still, as seems typical of academies, working on a historical dictionary—this one begun in 1890 and still "in progress"! By 1972, twenty-six volumes of the Swedish Academy's dictionary had appeared, and at that time it was reported that "the letter S has been reached" (38).

Meanwhile, in twentieth-century Swedish—almost despite the dictionary scholars—a marked increase was seen in the amount of international vocabulary in the language. This increase was clearly related to an increase in international communications. In particular, "since World War II the influence of British and American English upon Swedish has become even more obvious" (Bergman 1973:38). The Swedish Center for Technical Terminology, under the management of its director, Einar Selander, is a type of special commission designed to provide equivalents for new terms. In the Language Planning Newsletter of May, 1981 (7/2:1–2), Anna-Lena Bucher, an officer and member of the management collective of the Center for Technical Terminology, contributed an article entitled "The Swedish Center for Technical Terminology—40 Years Old." The article offered information about the organization to the rest of the world. TNC was founded in order to "elaborate technical terminology well-suited to the Swedish condition." Terminology refers to the kind of words used in special purpose languages known as fackspråk in Swedish. TNC is supported by the Swedish government, private enterprise, and various other organizations and institutions. The Center publishes a series of publications entitled Teknishe Nomenklaturens Publikationer ("Technical Terminology Publications"). In 1970, as publication #44 of this series, for example, a study of the language of technology appeared. The Center also produces glossaries of technical terms geared to particular areas of technology and science. For example, in 1971, as publication #46, a Glossary of Concrete Terms (that is, words used to talk about concrete) was produced. It was compiled in consultation with a former director of the Swedish Cement Association. The Glossary of Concrete Terms, as are other specialized vocabularies being produced by the Center in the process of lexical modernization, is intended "as a comprehensive and authoritative collection of terms," in this case, "related to cement and concrete" (TNC 46:9). The reason for the Glossary of Concrete Terms, in particular, is to serve "as a link in current efforts to establish a systematic terminology for building in Sweden" (9).

The Swedish Center (Centre) of Technical Terminology reviews the terms and definitions put forth by consulted experts by having them gone over by a number of organizations and individual specialists in the field. The glossaries contain the terms, their definitions, and their equivalents in other languages (for example, terms for concrete in English, French, Danish, German, Finnish, and Norwegian). The terms are also grouped together, at least in the case of the words associated with concrete, according to the order in which the various aspects of concrete production and use occur. Thus, terms (and their definitions) are given the constituents of concrete; then for aspects of concrete production; for items and procedures involved with concrete during transport; for machines and tools for treating and reinforcing concrete; and so forth.

The LP function of lexical modernization in Sweden carried out by the Swedish Center for Technical Terminology has largely usurped the authoritative position of the Swedish Academy, which sought to establish a pure language. The extant Swedish Academy is visible to the general public today mainly by means of a normative word list called the *Svenska Akademien Ord Lista* (SAOL; literally, "The Swedish Academy's Word List"), which the Academy issues from time to time (Haugen and Markey 1972:1487). As of 1972, the latest list was the ninth, and came out in 1950. The first official list appeared in 1889. For the most part, though, despite the official nature of the Swedish Academy's publications, its lists are mere enumerations and do not fulfill a modernization function in the sense of Type 2 above.

Thus, the Swedish Academy of today, although it has undisputed authority with respect to linguistic questions, does not exercise it. The Academy continues as a conservative force, having been placed "on the back burner," so to speak, the same as the East African Swahili Committee (discussed earlier).

The transition of active linguistic authority in Sweden from the Academy to the Center may have been mediated by the setting up of the Institute for Swedish Language Cultivation in Stockholm in 1953. The Stockholm office was intended to answer questions about language usage and to publish popular guides to "correct" grammar and "good" spelling and pronunciation, and to explain dialect differences and linguistic history. The Institute found that

> one of the most sensitive areas of language cultivation in our time has been the rendering into Swedish of modern technical terminology, which tends to overflow in undigested form from English. To solve this problem the *Tekniska Nomenklatur Centralen* (Centre for Technical Terminology), first established in 1941, evolved as an instrument "for the purely technical fields" of coordinating modern scientific usage and publishing handbooks for the guidance of government and industry (Haugen and Markey 1972:1493).

A lexical modernization plan, as exemplified by the work of the Swedish Center, for the past twenty years, to coordinate technical language usage for government and industry in Sweden, conforms to the components of a plan as follows:

1. LANGUAGE CHOICE: Swedish (creation of terms and adaptation of foreign loanwords)

2. POLICY FORMULATION: By the Swedish Center for Technical Terminology (DETERMINATION: The need to coordinate technical terms for government and industry)

3. POLICY CODIFICATION: The Center publishes specialized glossaries and reports that define the terms and provide their equivalents in other languages.

4. POLICY ELABORATION: Lexical elaboration is accomplished by using the new and adapted terms both in the standard written *and* spoken languages in newspapers and other publications and on radio and television, that is, in the popular media as well as in specialized communications of business and industry.

5. POLICY IMPLEMENTATION: Lexical modernization takes place through the Center's policy of compiling glossaries with the help of specialists in the fields to which the specialized terminologies apply.

6. POLICY EVALUATION: Lexical modernization in Sweden is currently going on, as evidenced by the Center's continued publication of their series on technical vocabulary. It is too soon to know if the lexicon changes will be accepted and used in all spheres where they are intended to be used. One area of success that seems assured with respect to the Center's work is in seeing that Swedish becomes "the equal of other developed languages as a medium of communication" (Ferguson 1968:32). This success is apparently assured by the Center's efforts to go beyond a mere listing of terms to compile glossaries that take into account intertranslatability of terms, underlying concepts, and the relationship of processes. The Center's glossaries act in the interest of helping Swedish and Sweden join "the world community of increasingly intertranslatable languages recognized as appropriate vehicles of modern forms of discourse" (Ferguson 1968:32).

For Swahili, like Swedish, the development of a modern vocabulary has also long been a concern of planners, but for Swahili modernization is a subsidiary interest to the major emphasis on standardization. In the case of Swahili, lexical modernization is of the Type 1 variety—a part of codification related to standardization. As noted earlier, the journal *KiSwahili* (put out by the Institute of Swahili Research) contains a regular feature that presents suggested new words, including, for example, terms for stars and constellations, religious vocabulary, and mathematical terms. Thomas Hinnebusch (1979:288) reports that the March, 1966, issue of the journal lists some terms that children are expected to know before entering school, as well as lists of terms in the fields of math, geography, history, and other fields of science and art.

With regard to lexical modernization, we have to be sure that planning and usage interact. A good illustration is the way astronomical terms were adjusted for Swahili astrology by astrologers:

> For example, in the list of astronomical terms, *mchota maji* (literally 'water-bearer' from *-chota* 'dip up' and *maji* 'water') is suggested for "Aquarius" but a very popular astrologer in East Africa today uses *ndoo* (literally 'bucket, pail') for that sign; for "Saggitarius" he uses *mshale* (literally 'arrow'), while the suggested list gives *mpiga shabaha* 'shooter of the target': in some cases, however, the astrologer's terms agree with the planners' list, whether by coincidence or design is not clear: *mapacha* 'twins' for "Gemini," *simba* 'lion' for "Leo," *mizani* 'scales' for "Libra," *nge* 'scorpion' for "Scorpio," and *samaki* 'fish' for Pisces (Hinnebusch 1979:288).

If lexical modernization is to succeed, planners need to consider and reflect the actual usage by the people for whom the vocabulary is intended, as well as come up with semantically appropriate vocabulary.

7.6 SUMMARY

In each of the five sample plans looked at in this chapter we saw that some form of official planning agency is in charge. In each case, a language choice was made, then policy was formulated as a result of the determination of the specific problem to be addressed. The nuts-and-bolts work of technologically getting the problem solved was the next task which, as codification, generally entails the production of dictionaries, lists of words, or grammars reflecting the change being advocated. Next, the codified change was extended throughout the area where the change was to occur, and then the change was put into effect.

The last stage of planning is an evaluative check to determine if the change occurred and the plan worked. In those cases where evaluation shows lack of success or lack of acceptance of the change, the need for a new LP function or a modification of the plan may be indicated.

All language-plan types occur in a political and socioeconomic context. French is now a national language in a linguistically homogeneous polity. It is an endoglossic, mature standard language with official juridical status. It is a monocentric endonormative language; that is, it has an ideal form of correct usage based on the language's own history in the region where it is now used. It has a high degree of autonomy in that it has sociolinguistic and genetic distinctiveness in France and a tradition behind it (historicity), and it is used in all spheres of cultural and social activity (vitality). For French, language purification was successful. The situation of Swedish in Sweden, though much like that of France politically and socioeconomically, is different in that in Sweden the language is a fully established standard but not an LWC. In France, the "natural development of the language" may be seen to have supplied the necessary terminolgoy for "technological and scientific innovations" (Nahir 1977:117), whereas in Sweden it did not. Thus, in the former case, purification is and was feasible; in the latter, it gave way to lexical modernization.

Hebrew is now a national language in a linguistically heterogeneous polity, and, like French and Swedish, it is an endoglossic, mature standard with official juridical status. The language, now revived, is moving in the direction of standardization—a common planning function in areas where linguistic heterogeneity still exists. Though Hebrew has official juridical status in Israel, its evolving form is exoglossic, yet the *standard* will be endonormative.

The situation in Turkey today is such that it does not conform to any of the three modal types of nation proposed by Fishman (Chapter One). In fact, it is a problem "whether contemporary Turkey should be regarded all in all as a developing country or as a non-Western nation or both" (Gallagher 1971:176, n. 2).

The nations where Swahili is the national language are in a somewhat similar position to Turkey. Both Swahili and Turkish had a previous literary tradition (both owing a great deal to Persian-Arabic influence); however, this tradition was unintelligible to a large proportion of the population. In the case of Turkey, the planned language was reformed; in Tanzania it was standardized; and in Kenya it is being considered for standardization as a language separate from the regional standard. In the case of both Swahili and Turkish, the selection of the language to be planned was made in the interest of solving the problem of linguistic heterogeneity and at the same time unifying the constituency it was to serve. Neither Swahili nor Turkish, however, is currently in a position for strict purification or for Type 2 modernization.

The five sample plans discussed in this chapter are compared from the point of view of their respective components in Table 3.

From Table 3 we see, as Nahir (1977:120) did, that "Language Planning agencies may, in the course of time, shift from one function class to another, abandon functions, or adopt new ones, when a change in needs, circumstances, or ideology in a society or speech community takes place." This conclusion is particularly clear when we evaluate the five sample plans. The French purification policy is bending toward lexical modernization with Academy approval. Hebrew language policy has shifted from revival to standardization and modernization. Turkish reform has proceeded far enough so that standardization of the reformed language is now feasible. In

Table 3. A Comparison of Language-Planning Types
and Components of Language Plans

	Plan Type				
	Purification	*Revival*	*Reform*	*Standardization*	*Lexical Modernization*
Lexical Choice	French	Hebrew	Turkish	Swahili (Zanzibar)	Swedish
Agency	French Academy	Language Council	Turkish Linguistic Society (TDK)	Inter-Territorial Language Committee	Center for Technical Terminology
Formulation/ Determination	To keep French pure, form French nationality	To have a common vehicle of commu-nication	To recon-cile *Türkçe* and *Osmanlicâ;* eliminate Arab-Persian influences	To have a common terri-torial school language	To coordinate technical terms for government and industry
Codification	In-progress dictionary, grammar, rhetoric treatise	Teaching "Hebrew through Hebrew"	Historical dictionary and neolo-gist move-ment; new script	Standard grammar and dictionaries	Standard written *and* spoken language in media, government, industry
Implemen-tation	Academy has physical form, members; materials are "official" and are used in schools.	Teaching with direct address, up-to-date texts, glossaries	Coopera-tion between Ministry of Infor-mation and schools; new script	East African Swahili Committee's imprimatur	Use of specialists in technical fields
Evaluation	Purification is changing to lexical moderniza-tion.	Revival is becoming standard-ization and moderniza-tion.	Reform is moving to standard-ization.	New nations are develop-ing their own agency functions.	Moderniza-tion is continuing.

Tanzania, the standardization policy is becoming that of Type 1 lexical modernization, while in Kenya a new agency and possible plans are being contemplated to accompany the political and socioeconomic changes that country has gone through. In Sweden, the current function of the Center for Technical Terminology appears viable for the moment, having taken over much of the power of the Swedish Academy as the LP agency in that country.

Appendix

GUIDE TO INFORMATION RESOURCES IN LANGUAGE PLANNING [1]

Thomas Reese and Jonathan Pool [2]

INTRODUCTION

An increasing number of scholars and other professionals consider "language planning" to be one of their fields of interest. The typical concerns of this field are to identify, understand, and in some conscious, systematic way deal with social problems related to language. This brief guide is intended to help those who are looking for information about language planning.

Though the term "language planning" was coined only in the 1960s, language problems and conflict have existed for millenia. The work of theorists, planners, agencies, foundations, social movements, and others to solve or alleviate these problems has left a rich legacy of ideas and experiences. Scholarship and documentation of interest to language planning continues today in many of the social sciences and humanities, and in some branches of engineering; indeed, language planning is an interdisciplinary subject par excellence.

All this makes it especially difficult to locate studies and data relevant to

[1]Reprinted with revisions from *Language Planning Newsletter*, Joan Rubin (ed.), published by East-West Culture Learning Institute, East-West Center, Honolulu, Hawaii, 5/2, pp. 1–3, 10–12; 5/3, p. 3.

[2]c/o Jonathan Pool, Department of Political Science, University of Washington, Seattle, Washington 98195, U.S.A.

language planning. But the resources for information retrieval are expanding rapidly, not only in volume but also in efficiency. People who work on language planning, too, can be beneficiaries of this revolution in information technology, as we shall make clear below.

EXPLANATORY NOTES

This guide presupposes that you have access to a public or research library. Information that is readily available there, e.g., the addresses of major publishers, will not be given here.

The literature of language planning naturally appears in a multiplicity of languages. Only a few languages, however, are regularly used to index and abstract current publications from different countries (Charles A. Ferguson has called these "W3 languages"). This is why you will find a preponderance of English and French sources here. Information resources in one language often cover materials in other languages.

Corrections and supplementary information will be welcomed from readers and will be incorporated into subsequent editions. Please send comments to the authors at the address on the preceding page, footnote 2.

A.   SERIAL PUBLICATIONS AND RELATED RESOURCES

1.   Newsletters

Newsletters provide information about a field, including its forthcoming and recent conferences, organizations, new publications, and work in progress. The three most generally useful ones for language planning are the quarterly *Language Planning Newsletter* (1975–), edited by Joan Rubin and available free from the publisher, East-West Culture Learning Institute, East-West Center, Honolulu, Hawaii 96848, U.S.A.; *The Linguistic Reporter* (1959–), published nine times a year for $18 ($15 in the U.S.A.) by the Center for Applied Linguistics, 3520 Prospect St., N.W., Washington, D.C. 20007, U.S.A.; and *Sociolinguistics Newsletter* (1969–), published three to four times a year by the Research Committee on Sociolinguistics of the International Sociological Association and available for $12 per year ($22 for institutions) from Scholars Press, 101 Salem St., Chico, California 95927, U.S.A.

2.   Journals

Articles on language planning appear in a wide variety of journals. The only international journal that concentrates specifically on that field is

Language Problems and Language Planning (1977–), published three times a year for $15 for individuals and $24 for institutions by the University of Texas Press (Austin). In addition, articles on language planning appear frequently in the Mouton-published periodical, the *International Journal of the Sociology of Language* (1974–), $27; (about $67 for institutions) for four issues a year; and in *Language in Society* (1972–), published three times a year by Cambridge University Press (London and New York) for $28.50 ($56 for institutions); and in *Multilingua* (1982–), published by Mouton four times a year for 50 DM (110 DM for institutions).

More or less related fields, such as translation, language teaching, terminology, ethnicity, and the promotion or reform of particular languages, have their own journals. To discover what journals exist in a given subject area, consult *Ulrich's International Periodicals Directory* (annual), which has "language" as one of its headings; or *Liste mondiale des périodiques spécialisés: linguistique/World List of Specialized Periodicals: Linguistics* (Mouton, 1971), where there are such headings as sociolinguistics, linguistic minorities, and bilingualism.

3. Bibliographies

Several bibliographies of language planning and related topics have been published that include references not only to books but also to chapters within multi-authored books and to articles in periodicals. The utility of such bibliographies is crucially dependent on their methods of subject indexing and classification. Unfortunately, some information sources contain many references to literature on language planning but make them hard to find because of poor indexing. In this guide we de-emphasize those.

The major bibliography dedicated exclusively to this field is *References for Students of Language Planning* (1979), compiled by Joan Rubin and Björn H. Jernudd (University Press of Hawaii). Its approximately 300 citations almost exclusively in English) are organized systematically by subtopics as well as listed alphabetically by author. Most are extensively abstracted, something that makes this bibliography unique in the field.

The most comprehensive bibliography with a heavy emphasis on language planning is *Bibliographie internationale sur le bilinguisme/International Bibliography on Bilingualism* (1972), edited by William F. Mackey (Québec: Les Presses de l'Université Laval). It contains about 11,000 unannotated entries, in alphabetical order by author, and topic-subtopic subject indexes in French and English. Useful subject headings include (among others):

administration	assimilation
applied linguistics	auxiliary language
artificial language	bibliography

bilingual education
bilingual school
bilingual state
census data
civil service
colonial language
disadvantages
discrimination
economics
education
education of bilinguals
educational law
effect of bilingualism
ethnic school
experimental teaching
foreign language education
government
human rights
international language
international law
international relations
language choice
language conflict
language development
language dominance
language education
language imposition
language instruction
language law
language loyalty
language maintenance
language of instruction
language planning
language policy
language reform
language rights
language standardization
language statistics
language status

language teaching
language test
law
lingua franca
linguistic barrier
linguistic nationalism
mass media
methodology
minority language
minority rights
multilingual state
national determination
national development
national language
nationalism
nationality
official language
political attitudes
political party
political science
politicolinguistics
politics
press
school
schools
script
segregation
self-determination
social stratification
standard language
statistics
teachers
technology
television
translation
university
working language
writing
written language

No other source on language behavior or applied linguistics has nearly as comprehensive an index (still, some important headings, like "terminology," are omitted). Specific countries, languages, and combinations of languages are also indexed. The articles that are referenced span a wide range of (sometimes obscure) sources, decades, and languages. A second volume, updating the original edition, is in preparation.

Meanwhile, another comprehensive bibliography has been published: *Langues et sociétés: bibliographie analytique informatisée*, compiled by Conrad Sabourin and Normand Petit. It was published by Office de la langue française, C.P. 316, Tour de la Bourse, Montréal, Québec H4Z 1G8, Canada, in 1979, and may be purchased from Éditeur officiel du Québec, 1283, boul. Charest, ouest, Québec G1N 2C9, Canada. The bibliography contains over 5200 unannotated entries, arranged alphabetically. It is indexed by languages, countries, fields, and pairs of topic words.

Another helpful publication is *Bibliographie zur Soziolinguistik* (197), compiled by Gerd Simon et al. (Tübingen: Max Niemayer Verlag). It contains almost 3,000 (mostly unannotated) references, principally about social-class differences in language. Chapters II and V, however, deal with language planning more generally. The publications cited are largely Western European and North American; they are listed alphabetically within a few subject divisions and are not indexed.

There are many bibliographies in related fields that contain some references useful in language planning. One that is organized to facilitate retrieval of such references is *Nationalism and National Development: An Interdisciplinary Bibliography* (1970), compiled by K. W. Deutsch and Richard L. Merritt (Cambridge, Mass.: M.I.T. Press).

4. Article Abstracting and Indexing Services

There are several regularly published sources for information about articles in language planning. They can be distinguished chiefly by their frequency (from once a year to once a week), coverage (the kind and number of journals whose articles are included), systematicity (whether they cover a journal fully, i.e., citing every article in it, or selectively), content (abstracts and indexes, or just indexes), and organization (how they are indexed). Here we list the most useful ones, with a summary of these features for each.

LLBA (Language and Language Behavior Abstracts, 1967–, quarterly) may be the most fruitful place to begin. Every issue alphabetically lists articles within subjects, and one of these subjects is "language planning." Since about 1,000 periodicals in about twenty languages are selectively covered, scanning *LLBA* can be profitable. If you want to search for articles on specific topics, however, you will probably find the quarterly, annual, and multi-year indexes somewhat coarse. Only a few specific index headings (e.g., national language, international language, synthetic language, languages in contact) are related directly to language planning, and headings like language planning, and language policy have been added to the index only recently. The general headings that include language planning (e.g., sociolinguistics, applied linguistics) have literally hundreds of citations under them, each consisting of just a citation number, making those headings nearly useless. Recently, however, *LLBA* undertook a thorough reorganization of its indexing system. Each issue's index has now been made a complete index of topics and subtopics, making retrieval of desired articles much easier than before.

The *MLA International Bibliography of Books and Articles on the Modern Languages and Literatures,* Volume III, *Linguistics* (1884–, annual) lacks abstracts but does include language policy in its classification system. Citations are alphabetical by author within each category. The bibliography covers about 2,000 periodicals published throughout the world in many languages.

Journals dealing primarily with such subjects as planning, policy, politics, and law are not covered by the above services, but these journals occasionally do contain articles dealing with language planning. Only a few of the services that abstract and index them are organized so as to make it easy to find the fairly small number of language-planning-related articles that appear in these journals.

The *Social Sciences Citation Index* (1973–) appears three times a year and covers fully or selectively about 4,000 periodicals in many languages from throughout the world. Its indexes (issue and annual) contain all pairs of key title words. Thus, for example, "Language Conflict in Ruritania" could be found under "language: conflict," "language: Ruritania," "conflict: language," etc. Articles are also indexed by the names of all the other authors that they cite.

International Political Science Abstracts/Documentation politique internationale (1951–) appears six times a year. It fully covers about 600 periodicals and treats several hundred others selectively, published in many languages throughout the world. Issue index headings beginning with language or linguistics, e.g., "linguistic minorities" and "language policy," are useful in finding relevant articles.

Sociological Abstracts (1952–) appears five times a year and covers about 1,600 periodicals from throughout the world in many languages. Although its indexing categories are overly broad (language, linguistics), its annual index presents a list of several key topic words in each cited article (e.g., "Sweden, immigrant children, bilingual, bicultural education; purpose, Finnish groups, preschool, project design, models, results"), making discovery of language-planning-related articles fairly quick.

The monthly *Current Index to Journals in Education* (1969–) covers approximately 700 (mostly English) journals. Its monthly and semiannual indexes are based on the *Thesaurus of ERIC Descriptors*. This means that it is possible to look for articles under such headings as language planning, language of instruction, language standardization, romanization, language programs, official language, bilingual education, and written language.

Articles in about 250 major social science journals published in English, mainly in the United States, Britain, and Canada, are indexed by the *Social Sciences Index* (1907–), which appears quarterly and is cumulated annually. Articles are listed alphabetically by title under subject headings, which are well cross-referenced and include "language and languages—political aspects," as well as bilingualism, sociolinguistics, and artificial languages.

Other services which at least offer "language" or "languages" as an indexing term, or which are well indexed but quite restricted in their coverage, include *Abstracts in Anthropology, Advance Bibliography of Contents: Political Science and Government, Bibliographic Index, Bibliographie linguistique de l'année/Linguistic Bibliography for Year, Current Contents/Social and Behavioral Sciences, Index to Legal Periodicals, Index to Foreign Legal Periodicals, Public Affairs Information Service Bulletin, Public Affairs Information Service Foreign Language Index* (there is a cumulative index from 1915 to 1974 for these two publications), *United States Political Science Documents,* and *Universal Reference System Political Science Series* with its *Annual Supplement.*

5. Periodical-Article Data Bases

Several of the services mentioned above have recorded the entire contents of their indexes and/or abstracts on a computer-readable medium and continually update these "data bases" for public use. This permits the user to specify any combination of subject headings, author names, publication years, title words, abstract words, etc., and receive a custom-made bibliography citing every item that meets the criteria laid down by the user. During this process, the user can ask how many items meet the criteria: if the number is too large, the user can impose additional conditions until a reasonable number of citations remain, before the bibliography is actually printed (or displayed on the screen of one's computer terminal).

Computer-based searching can make an indexing or abstracting service useful even if, in printed form, it is ruined by a poor index. With well-indexed services, computer searching can still save time and (if carefully performed) yield citations that would otherwise be missed. Computer searching does, however, cost money (generally about U.S. $5 to $50 per search).

There are generally two ways to conduct computer searches. One is to do this together with a specialist at one's library. Many libraries in North America and Western Europe, and an increasing number in Japan, South America, and elsewhere, have terminals which can communicate with computer search services. The other procedure is to correspond with a computer search service that has access to the data base that one wants to search. Typically, searching is considerably (as much as ten times) more expensive, and also less precise, by mail than at one's library.

Of the services mentioned above, *LLBA, MLA International Bibliography, Social Sciences Citation Index, Sociological Abstracts, Public Affairs Information Service* (both services), and *Current Index to Journals in Education* are recorded in computer-readable form and are widely available for public access through major libraries. If you do not have access in this way, you may write for information about searching by mail. For Public Affairs Information Service data bases, write to PAIS, 11 West 40th Street, New York, New York 10018, U.S.A. For other data bases, write to Lingua Franca, P.O. Box 22206, San Diego, California 92122, U.S.A.

Some of the bibliographies described in section A-3 have also been recorded in computer-readable form, but public access to these data bases has not been provided for, at least not on a regular basis. These include the *Bibliographie internationale sur le bilinguisme, Langues et sociétés,* and *Nationalism and National Development.* Readers willing to pay for the opportunity to consult these data bases by computer are advised to contact the respective publishers.

B.   MONOGRAPHIC PUBLICATIONS AND RELATED RESOURCES

1.   Publishers' Book Catalogues

Catalogues of book publishers are usually an inefficient source of information about new books related to language planning, since the literature is spread thinly across the publishing market, and since book catalogues are almost never well indexed. A handful of publishers, however, issue books dealing with language planning so frequently that just perusing their catalogues may be worthwhile. Among these are Mouton Publishers (sold by Walter de Gruyter, West Berlin and New York), Newbury House Publishers (Rowley, Massachusetts), Издательство "Наука" (Izdatel'stvo "Nauka") (Moscow), and two major institutions: the Center for Applied Linguistics (3520 Prospect St., Washington, D.C. 20007, U.S.A.) and the Centre international de recherches sur le bilinguisme (Université Laval, Cité universitaire, Québec, Québec G1K 7P4, Canada).

2.   Monograph Abstracting and Indexing Services

For the best introduction to the accumulated monographic literature in language planning, see the bibliographies described in section A-3 above. New books on language planning can be located on a continuing basis with the *Subject Guide to Books in Print* (annual), which includes "languages—political aspects" as well as more general headings in its subject index. For books not yet published, see *Subject Guide to Forthcoming Books* (bimonthly). To discover entire series of books related to language planning, look under "linguistics" in *Irregular Series and Annuals* (biennial), which is international in coverage, or under "language" in a publication titled *Books in Series in the United States, 1966–1975* (annual supplement).

3. Library Card Catalogues

The subject catalogue of one's library is an obvious place to look for information on locally available monographic publications. Knowing what subjects to look under is not so obvious, but here are some language-planning-related headings used by the United States Library of Congress cataloguing system:

Bilingualism	Languages in Conflict
Language—International	Language in Contact
Language—Universal	Linguistic Change
Language—World	Multilingualism
Language Planning (plus subheadings)	Planned Language Change
Language—Political aspects	Sociolinguistics
Language—Revival	Standard Language

In addition, "reform" is a subheading under the names of specific languages, e.g., "Chinese language—reform."

4. Published Library Catalogues

Some libraries publish their catalogues so they may be consulted in other libraries. We have found only one such catalogue that is of much use for finding books on language planning: the *Library of Congress Catalogs Subject Catalogs*. It relies on the subject headings described in the preceding section, and it is updated four times a year.

5. Monograph Data Bases

As computer technology is extended, files of information on books will become increasingly available for automated searching. In some libraries it is already possible to conduct such searches. The most extensive monographic data base with which we are familiar is *Machine Readable Cataloging (Books)*, produced by the United States Library of Congress (but accessible through computer search services in other countries also). It contains records of all books collected by that library in English since 1968, in

French since 1973, and in German since 1975, and it is being extended to include all languages. It uses the subject heading system described above. A companion data base indexes serials (not the articles in them) in all languages with the same system.

Because "language planning" has recently been added as a subject heading, few publications are catalogued under it yet. We did a computer search of this data base under "language planning" and generated a five-item bibliography, while a search under "sociolinguistics" printed out more than 200 items. *Language Planning: Current Issues and Research* (1973) was indexed under language planning, but *Advances in Language Planning* (1974) could be found only under sociolinguistics. With time, one hopes, such discrepancies will be reduced.

C. PROFESSIONAL CONFERENCES AND RELATED RESOURCES

1. Conferences

The major international conferences at which information about language planning is regularly exchanged are the triennial World Congress of Applied Linguistics (to be held in Brussels in 1984) and the quadrennial World Congress of Sociology (to be held in 1986). The former contains sessions on language planning, and the latter contains a program on sociolinguistics. To learn about more specialized meetings, consult *World Meetings: Social and Behavioral Sciences, Human Services, and Management* (quarterly), which provides extensive information about meetings up to two years ahead. Meetings related to language are listed under "Anthropology and Linguistics." Meetings in the USSR and Eastern Europe, however, are better covered in *Biulleten' mezhdunarodnykh nauchnykh s'ezdov, konferentsii, kongressov, vystavok,* which appears six times a year. Relevant meetings can be found in the subject index under язык (iazyk) or лингвистика (lingvistika) — "language" or "linguistics."

2. Conference Proceedings

Some conferences publish their papers or (like the World Congress of Sociology since 1982) sell them individually after the conference ends. Others do not do this, so one must write to the author to obtain a copy of the paper. To request a paper one must know that it exists, which brings us to the next topic.

3. Conference Proceedings Abstracting and Indexing Services

Discovering papers that have been delivered at conferences is almost always difficult. Beginning in 1979, however, there is an *Index to Social*

Sciences and Humanities Proceedings, published quarterly and cumulated annually by the Institute for Scientific Information. Its subject index is based on titles of about 1,000 proceedings and 20,000 papers per year. Every pair of significant title words is listed alphabetically, so titles related to language planning should be relatively easy to find.

In addition, abstracts of papers presented at the World Congresses of Sociology are published in supplements of *Sociological Abstracts*, and abstracts presented at the International Congresses of Applied Linguistics are published in supplements to *LLBA*.

4. Conference Proceedings Data Bases

As mentioned in A-5 above, *LLBA* and *Sociological Abstracts* are both searchable by computer. Otherwise, we are not aware of any data base of conference proceedings that is currently available for automated searchings.

D. RESEARCH PROJECTS AND RELATED RESOURCES

1. Organizations, Institutes, and Committees

There are many institutes in many countries that are engaged in pure and applied research on language planning or particular aspects thereof. We shall make no attempt to list them here. The *Directory of Language Planning Organizations*, compiled by Joan Rubin (University Press of Hawaii, 1979), describes about 150 such entities in about 50 countries, giving the personnel, publications, and research of each organization in some detail.

For a wider range of organizations on the peripheries of language planning, one useful source is the *Yearbook of International Organizations*, which has English and French subject indexes with such headings as language, linguistics, bilingual, and the names of particular languages and language families. Research institutes in the United States and Canada can be efficiently discovered with the *Research Centers Directory*, published about every three years with supplements between editions. It has linguistics, languages (with qualifiers), sign language, and bilingualism among its subject headings.

Two of the best-known research institutes concerned with language planning have already been mentioned (see B-1). The two major international research committees active in this field are the Commission on Language Planning of the International Association of Applied Linguistics (chaired by Joan Rubin, National Center for Bilingual Research, 4665 Lampson Ave., Los Alamitos, California 90720, U.S.A.), and the Research Committee on Sociolinguistics of the International Sociological Association, whose membership chairman is Charles Kaplan, FB Gesellschaftswissenschaften, Universität, Frankfurt Senkenberganlage, 13–17, 6000 Frankfurt, Federal Republic of Germany.

The best information on language planning programs in universities is found in the *Sociolinguistics Newsletter,* which often reprints syllabi and lists of sociolinguistics courses.

2. Research Project Reporting Services

We are not aware of any *printed* reporting services that would keep one informed about new research projects in language planning. The newsletters described in A-1 are the best regular source of this kind of information. See also D-3 below.

Many ongoing projects, however, issue reports that are available to interested scholars long before they appear in published form. Discovering such reports often depends on being a member of an appropriate informal network, but there are some public sources of regular information about unpublished documents. The most comprehensive is *Resources in Education* (1966–), which is issued monthly. It uses the *Thesaurus of ERIC Descriptors,* discussed in A-4 above. *Sociological Abstracts* also accepts unpublished papers for abstracting.

3. Research Project Data Bases

The two services just mentioned are available for computer searching. *Resources in Education* is, in fact, part of the same data base as *Current Index to Journals in Education,* and it is called the ERIC data base. If you want to know what research is going on even before any results are presented at meetings or published, you can make use of the data base that is maintained by the Smithsonian Science Information Exchange. SSIE collects data on more than 100,000 research projects every year from governmental and private institutions in the United States and other countries, indexes these projects by subject, and makes the entire data base available for searching. Four types of searches are possible: (1) a custom search performed by SSIE (write to SSIE, Room 300, 1730 M Street, N.W., Washington, D.C. 20036, U.S.A.); (2) a search by the scholar from a computer terminal; (3) a periodic automatic search of the data base for new projects meeting the scholar's interest "profile" (write to SSIE); and (4) the latest edition of one of SSIE's regular searches of common subjects (revised four or more times a year). Several of these regular search topics are related to language planning, including "bilingual bicultural education" and "bilingualism and behavioral and social problems of speaking a dialect or nonstandard English." These two "packages" currently cost U.S. $45.00 each.

CONCLUSION

The purpose of this guide has been to point interested scholars in the direction of periodicals, books, conferences, and organizations that can provide yet *further* guidance in the search for information about language planning. This guide is, then, not one but two steps removed from the actual literature of language planning itself. The explosion of information, and of tools for processing that information, has hit language planning like other fields, making a guide to the guides a necessity. Some of the information contained here may unintentionally be erroneous, and some will certainly be out of date. As we struggle to keep it accurate, we shall be most grateful for feedback from readers.

This paper was prepared in response to a proposal made at the Language Planning Commission meeting at the Fifth International Meeting of AILA (Association Internationale de Linguistique Appliquée) in Montreal, Canada, August, 1978. Research for this guide was made possible by support provided to the Program in Comparative Studies in Ethnicity and Nationality by the Graduate School of the University of Washington. The authors are grateful to Alvin E. Fritz for extensive consultation on data bases.

Bibliography

Abdulaziz, M. H. (1971). "Tanzania's National Language Policy and the Rise of Swahili Political Culture," in Whiteley, ed. (1971), pp. 160–78.

_____ (Mkilifi) (1972). "Triglossia and Swahili-English Bilingualism in Tanzania," *Language and Society*, Vol. 1, pp. 197–213; also in Fishman, ed. (1978), pp. 129–49.

_____ (1975). "Methodology of Sociolinguistic Surveys—Problems of Interpretation and Implementation." Paper Presented at International Conference on the Methodology of Sociolinguistic Surveys, May 19–21, 1975, Montreal, Quebec, Canada.

_____ (1979). "Methodology of Sociolinguistic Surveys—The East African Language Survey Experience," *Journal of Eastern African Research and Development* 9/2:1–27.

_____ (1980). "The Ecology of Tanzanian National Language Policy," in Polomé and Hill, eds. (1980), pp. 139–75.

_____ and Mel Fox (1978). "Evaluative Report on Survey of Language Use and Language Teaching of Eastern Africa 1978." Ford Foundation Report.

Akong'a, Joshua J. (1979). "Social Training Strategies: The Swahili of Old Town Mombasa Kenya," University of Nairobi Institute for African Studies Paper No. 132, February 5, 1980, University of Nairobi.

Alloni-Fainberg, Yafa (1974). "Official Hebrew Terms for Parts of the Car: A Study of Knowledge, Usage and Attitudes," in Fishman, ed. (1974), pp. 493–517.

Altoma, Salih J. (1974). "Language Education in Arab Countries and the Role of the Academies," in Fishman, ed. (1974), pp. 279–314. Reprinted from *Current Trends in Linguistics* 6 (1970):690–720.

Ansre, Gilbert (1974). "Language Standardization in Sub-Saharan Africa," in Fishman, ed. (1974), pp. 369–89; also in *Current Trends in Linguistics* 7 (1971): 680–98.

Armstrong, Robert G. (1963). "Vernacular Languages and Cultures in Modern Africa," in Spencer, ed. (1963), pp. 64–72.

_____ (1968). "Language Policies and Language Practices in West Africa," in Fishman, Ferguson, and Das Gupta, eds. (1968), pp. 227–36.

255

Austen, Paul Britten (1970). *The Swedes (How They Live and Work)*. David and Charles.

Banathy, Bela, Edith Trager, and Carl D. Waddle (1966). "The Use of Contrastive Data in Foreign Language Course Development," in Valdman, ed. (1966), pp. 35–56.

Basso, Keith H. (1974). "The Ethnography of Writing," in Bauman and Scherzer, eds. (1974), pp. 425–32.

Batelle, Phyllis (1981). "Men–They're All Talk!" *King Features Syndicate, Seattle Post-Intelligencer*, Sunday May 17, 1981, p. C12.

Bauman, Richard, and Joel Scherzer, eds. (1974). *Explorations in the Ethnography of Speaking*. Cambridge University Press.

Beardsley, R. Brock, and Carol M. Eastman (1971). "Markers, Pauses, and Code Switching in Bilingual Tanzanian Speech," *General Linguistics* 11:17–27.

Bellamy, Henry (1939). *L'Académie Française*. Paris. (Crapeuillot: Numéro Spécial, Mars 1939).

Bergman, Gösta (1973). *A Short History of the Swedish Language*, translated and adapted by Francis P. Magoun, Jr., and Helge Kökeritz. Berlingska Boktryckeriet.

Bernstein, Basil B. (1971). *Class, Codes and Control*. Theoretical Studies Towards a Sociology of Language, Vol. 1. Routledge and Kegan Paul.

—————— (1973). "Social Class, Language and Socialization," in Sebeok, ed. (1974), pp. 1545–62.

Berry, J. (1968). "The Making of Alphabets," in Fishman, ed. (1968), pp. 737–53.

Bolinger, Dwight (1975). *Aspects of Language*, 2nd ed. Harcourt, Brace, Jovanovich.

Bowen, J. Donald (1971). "Organizing International Research in Sociolinguistically Oriented Language Surveys." Paper prepared for the Conference on Socio-linguistically Oriented Language Surveys, September 6–7, 1971.

Bowers, John (1968). "Language Problems and Literacy," in Fishman, Ferguson, and Das Gupta, eds. (1968), pp. 381–401.

Brass, Paul R. (1979). "Elite Groups, Symbol Manipulation and Ethnic Identity Among the Muslims of South Asia." Paper presented to the Comparative Studies in Ethnicity and Nationality Seminar (CSEN), February 20, 1979, University of Washington.

Bright, William, ed. (1966). *Sociolinguistics*. Proceedings of the UCLA Sociolinguistics Conference, 1964; Janua Linguarum Series Major 20. Mouton.

Broyard, Anatole (1981). "Money Speaks in US Fiction," *New York Times Book Review, Seattle Post-Intelligencer*, June 29, p. D6.

Brudner-White, Lilian A. (1978). "Occupational Concomitants of Language Variability in Southern Austrian Bilingual Communities," in Fishman, ed. (1978), pp. 153–84.

"By Way of Introduction," from *Slovo a Slovesnost* [Word and Verbal Art] (1935). Vol. 1, pp. 1–7, in Johnson, ed. (1978), pp. 32–46.

Casad, Eugene H. (1974). *Dialect Intelligibility Testing*. Summer Institute of Linguistics of the University of Oklahoma.

Comhairle na Gaelige (Consultative Council for the Irish Language) (1974). "Implementing a Language Policy," in Fishman, ed. (1974), pp. 527–53. Reprinted from Comhairle na Gaelige (Dublin: The Stationery Office, 1972).

Cooper, Robert L. (1969). "Two Contextualized Measures of Degree of Bilingualism," *Modern Language Journal* 53:172–78.

_____ (1975). "Sociolinguistic Surveys: State of the Art," in Pool, compiler (1975), pp. 28–41.

_____ (1978). "The Spread of Amharic in Ethiopia," in Fishman, ed. (1978), pp. 459–76.

_____ and Joshua A. Fishman (1974). "The Study of Language Attitudes," *Linguistics* 136:5–19.

Crampton, Diana (1979). "Language and Tourism in Kenya." Research Proposal and Unpublished Project for Research, Department of Linguistics and African Languages, University of Nairobi, Nairobi, Kenya.

Daily Nation, The. Nairobi, Kenya. October 30, 1979, p. 11.

Das Gupta, Jyotirindra (1968). "Language Diversity and National Development," in Fishman, Ferguson, and Das Gupta, eds. (1968), pp. 17–35.

_____ (1969). "Religious Loyalty, Language Conflict and Political Mobilization." Consultative Meeting on Language Planning Processes, EWC-IAC, Honolulu. Also in Rubin and Jernudd, eds. (1971), pp. 53–62, as "Religion, Language and Political Mobilization."

_____, Charles A. Ferguson, Joshua A. Fishman, Björn Jernudd, Joan Rubin, et al. (1972). *Draft Report of International Research Project on Language Planning Processes*. Mimeographed.

_____ and John J. Gumperz (1968). "Language, Communication and Control in North India," in Fishman, Ferguson, and Das Gupta (1968), pp. 151–66.

deSaussure, Ferdinand (1966; 1st ed. 1916). *Cours de Linguistique Générale* [Course in General Linguistics]. McGraw-Hill, The Philosophical Library.

Deutsch, Karl (1953; 2nd ed. 1966). *Nationalism and Social Communication*. MIT Press.

Dil, Anwar S., series ed. (1971–) *Language Science, and National Development* series. Pakistan Linguistic Research Group. Stanford University Press.

Diringer, David (1948; 1968). *The Alphabet: A Key to the History of Mankind*. Vols 1 and 2. Hutchinson and Co.

258   *Bibliography*

Eastman, Carol M. (1975). *Aspects of Language and Culture.* Chandler & Sharp.

——— (1978). *Linguistic Theory and Language Description.* J. B. Lippincott.

——— (1979). "Culture-Loaded Vocabularies and Language Resurrection" (Research Note), *Current Anthropology* 20/2:401–02.

——— (1979a). "Language Reintroduction: Activity and Outcome Language Planning," *General Linguistics* 19/3:99–111.

——— (1979b). "Language Resurrection: A Language Plan for Ethnic Interaction," in Howard Giles and Bernard Saint-Jacques, eds. (1980), pp. 215–22.

——— (1981). "Language Planning, Identity Planning and World View," *International Journal of the Sociology of Language* 32:45–53.

Fellman, Jack (1974). "The Role of Eliezer Ben Yehuda in the Revival of the Hebrew Language: An Assessment," in Fishman, ed. (1974), pp. 427–55.

Ferguson, Charles A. (1959). "Diglossia," in Dil, series ed. (1971), pp. 6–20, from *Word* 15 (1959):325–40.

——— (1966). "On Sociolinguistically Oriented Language Surveys," in Dil, series ed. (1971), pp. 149–56, from *The Linguistic Reporter* 8/4:1–3.

——— (1967). "National Sociolinguistic Profile Formulas," in Dil, series ed. (1971), pp. 157–84, from Bright, ed. (1966), pp. 309–24.

——— (1968). "Language Development," in Fishman, Ferguson, and Das Gupta, eds. (1968), pp. 27–35.

——— (1971). *Language Structure and Language Use.* Anwar S. Dil, series ed. Stanford University Press.

——— (1975). "Rationale of the Language Survey in Eastern Africa, 1967–70." Paper Presented at International Conference on the Methodology of Sociolinguistic Surveys, May 19–21, 1975, Montreal, Quebec, Canada.

Fishman, Joshua A. (1960). "A Systematization of the Whorfian Hypothesis," *Behavioral Science* 5:323–39.

——— (1965). "Varieties of Ethnicity and Varieties of Language Consciousness," in Fishman (1972), pp. 179–90, from *Georgetown University Monograph Series in Languages and Linguistics* 18:69–79; reprinted from Georgetown University Round Table Selected Papers in Linguistics 1961–1965, J. Alatis, ed., pp. 91–101.

——— (1965a), "Language Maintenance and Language Shift: The American Immigrant Case within a General Theoretical Perspective," *Sociological Journal for Empirical Social Psychology and Ethnic Research* 10/1:19–39.

——— (1966). *Language Loyalty in the United States.* Mouton.

——— (1968). "Some Contrasts Between Linguistically Homogeneous and Linguistically Heterogeneous Polities," in Fishman, Ferguson, and Das Gupta, eds. (1968), pp. 53–68.

_____ (1968a). "Language Maintenance and Language Shift as a Field of Inquiry Revisited," in Fishman (1972), pp. 76–134.

_____ (1968b). "The Relationship Between Micro- and Macro-Sociolinguistics in the Study of Who Speaks What Language to Whom and When," in Fishman (1972), pp. 244–67.

_____ (1968c). "Sociolinguistic Perspective on the Study of Bilingualism," *Linguistics* 39:21–50.

_____ (1968d). "Sociolinguistics and the Language Problems of the Developing Countries," in Fishman, Ferguson, and Das Gupta, eds. (1968), pp. 3–16.

_____ (1968e). "Introduction," in Fishman, ed. (1968), pp. 5–13.

_____ (1968f). "Nationality-Nationalism and Nation-Nationalism," in Fishman, Ferguson, and Das Gupta, eds. (1968), pp. 39–51.

_____ (1969), "The Sociology of Language," in Giglioli, ed. (1972), pp. 45–60.

_____ (1969a). "National Languages and Languages of Wider Communication," in Fishman (1972), pp. 191–223, from *Anthropological Linguistics* 11:111–35.

_____ (1971). "The Impact of Nationalism on Language Planning," in Rubin and Jernudd, eds. (1971), pp. 3–20.

_____ (1971a). "The Sociology of Language," in Fishman, ed. (1971), pp. 217–404.

_____ (1972). *Language in Sociocultural Change.* Anwar S. Dil, series ed. Stanford University Press.

_____, in collaboration with Erika Luders (1972a). "What Has the Sociology of Language to Say to the Teacher?—On Teaching the Standard Variety to Speakers of Dialectal or Sociolectal Varieties," in Fishman (1972), pp. 340–55.

_____ (1972b). "Author's Postscript," in Fishman (1972), pp. 356–62.

_____ (1972c). "Sociocultural Organization: Language Constraints and Language Reflections," in Fishman (1972), pp. 286–305.

_____ (1973). "Language Modernization and Planning in Comparison with other Types of National Modernization and Planning," in Fishman, ed. (1974), pp. 79–102, from *Language in Society* 2/1 (1973).

_____ (1974). "The Sociology of Language," in Sebeok, ed., Vol. 12 (1974), pp. 1626–1784.

_____ (1974a). "Language Planning and Language Planning Research: The State of the Art," in Fishman, ed. (1974), pp. 15–33.

_____ (1974b). "Language Modernization and Planning," in Fishman, ed. (1974), pp. 79–102.

_____ (1975). "Some Implications of 'The International Research Project on Language Planning Processes (IRPLPP)' for Sociolinguistic Surveys," in Ohannessian, Ferguson, and Polomé, eds. (1975), pp. 209–20.

———— (1977). "Language and Ethnicity," in Giles, ed. (1977), pp. 14–57.

———— (1978). "Foreword," in Jessel (1978), pp. 9–10.

————, ed. (1968). *Readings in the Sociology of Language.* Mouton; also Humanities Press.

————, ed. (1971). *Advances in the Sociology of Language.* Vol 1. Mouton.

————, ed. (1972). *Advances in the Sociology of Language.* Vol 2. Mouton.

————, ed. (1974). *Advances in Language Planning.* Mouton.

————, ed. (1976). *Advances in the Creation and Revision of Writing Systems.* Mouton.

————, ed. (1978). *Advances in the Study of Societal Multilingualism.* Mouton.

————, Jyotirindra Das Gupta, Björn H. Jernudd, and Joan Rubin (1971). "Research Outline for Comparative Studies of Language Planning," in Rubin and Jernudd, eds. (1971), pp. 293–305.

————, Charles A. Ferguson, and Jyotirindra Das Gupta, eds. (1968). *Language Problems of Developing Nations.* John Wiley & Sons.

Friedman, John (1967). "A Conceptual Model of the Analysis of Planned Behavior," *Administrative Science Quarterly* 12:225–52.

Gallagher, Charles F. (1971). "Language Reform and Social Modernization in Turkey," in Rubin and Jernudd, eds. (1971), pp. 159–78.

Garvin, Paul L. (1973). "Some Comments on Language Planning," from "Language Planning: Current Issues and Research," in Fishman, ed. (1974), pp. 69–79; and in Rubin and Shuy, eds. (1973), pp. 24–33.

————, trans. (1973). "Prague School 'General Principles for the Cultivation of Good Language,'" in Fishman, ed. (1974), pp. 417–26; and in Rubin and Shuy, eds. (1973), pp. 102–11.

———— and Madeline Mathiot (1968). "The Urbanization of the Guarani Language," in Fishman, ed. (1968), pp. 365–74. Reprinted from *Men and Cultures: Selected Papers of the Fifth International Congress of Anthropological and Ethnological Sciences,* A. F. C. Wallace, ed. University of Pennsylvania Press (1956), pp. 783–90.

Giglioli, Pier Paolo, ed. (1972). *Language and Social Context.* Penguin Books, Penguin Modern Sociology Readings.

Giles, Howard, ed. (1977). *Language, Ethnicity and Intergroup Relations.* Academic Press.

————, R. Y. Bourhis, and D. M. Taylor (1977). "Towards a Theory of Language in Ethnic Group Relations," in Giles, ed. (1977), pp. 307–48.

———— and Bernard Saint-Jacques, eds. (1980). *Language and Ethnic Relations.* Selected Papers from the Ninth World Congress of Sociology. Pergamon Press.

Gladwin, T., and W. C. Sturtevant, eds. (1962). *Anthropology and Human Behavior.* Anthropological Society of Washington.

Gleason, H. A. (1965). *Workbook in Descriptive Linguistics.* Holt, Rinehart, and Winston.

Goodman, Jane (1981). "Linguistic Universals in Legal Language Simplification." Unpublished Manuscript, University of Washington, Department of Anthropology.

Gorman, Thomas P. (1975). "Retrospective Notes on the Survey of Language Use and Language Teaching in Eastern Africa." Paper Presented at the International Conference on the Methodology of Sociolinguistic Surveys, May 19–21, 1975, Montreal, Quebec, Canada.

Greenberg, Joseph, Norman A. McQuown, Morris Halle, and William Labov (1970). *Linguistics in the 1970s.* Pre-publication Edition. Center for Applied Linguistics.

Gudschinsky, Sarah C. (1968). "The Relationship of Language and Linguistics to Reading," *Kivung* 1/3:146–52.

_____ (1974). "Linguistics and Literacy," in Sebeok, ed. (1974), Vol. 7, pp. 2039–55.

Guitarte, Guillermo L., and Rafael Torres Quintero (1974). "Linguistic Correctness and the Role of the Academies in Latin America," in Fishman, ed. (1974), pp. 315–68, revised from *Current Trends in Linguistics* 4 (1968):562–604.

Gumperz, John J. (1958). "Dialect Differences and Social Stratification in a North Indian Village," *American Anthropologist* 60:668–82.

_____ (1962). "Types of Linguistic Communities," *Anthropological Linguistics* 4/1: 28–40; also in Fishman, ed. (1968), pp. 460–72.

_____ (1968). "The Speech Community," in Gumperz (1971), pp. 114–28, from *International Encyclopedia of Social Sciences,* Vol. 9, pp. 381–86 (1968 ed.).

_____ (1969). "Communication in Multilingual Societies," in Gumperz (1971), pp. 231–50.

_____ (1971). *Language in Social Groups.* Anwar S. Dil, series ed. Stanford University Press.

_____ and Dell Hymes, eds. (1972). *Directions in Sociolinguistics: The Ethnography of Communication.* Holt, Rinehart and Winston.

Hall, Robert A., Jr. (1974). "External History of the Romance Languages." Elsevier.

Haugen, Einar (1938). "Language and Immigration." *NASR* (*Norwegian-American Studies and Records*) 10:1–43; and in Haugen (1972), pp. 1–36.

_____ (1959). "Planning for a Standard Language in Modern Norway," *Anthropological Linguistics* 1 (1959):8–21; and in Haugen (1972) as "Language Planning in Modern Norway," pp. 133–47, from *Scandinavian Studies* 33:68–81.

———— (1965). "Construction and Reconstruction in Language Planning: Ivar Aasen's Grammar," *Word* 21/2:188–207; and in Haugen (1972), pp. 191–214.

———— (1966). "Linguistics and Language Planning," in Bright, ed. (1966), pp. 50–71; and in Haugen (1972), pp. 159–90.

———— (1966a). "National and International Languages," in Haugen (1972), pp. 255–64.

———— (1971). "Instrumentalism in Language Planning," in Rubin and Jernudd, eds. (1971), pp. 281–89.

———— (1972). *The Ecology of Language: Essays by Einar Haugen.* Anwar S. Dil, series ed. Stanford University Press.

———— (1976). *The Scandianvian Languages: An Introduction to Their History.* Faber and Faber.

———— and Thomas L. Markey (1972). "The Scandinavian Languages: Fifty Years of Linguistic Research," in Sebeok, ed. (1972).

Hayward, Richard (1979). Personal Communication.

Hazai, Georg (1974). "Linguistics and Language Issues in Turkey," in Fishman, ed. (1974), pp. 127–61, reprinted from *Current Trends in Linguistics* 6 (1970): 183–216.

Heine, Bernd (1970). *Status and Use of African Lingua Francas.* Weltforum Verlag.

Hempel, Carl G. (1966). *Philosophy of Natural Science.* Prentice-Hall.

Henley, Nancy M. (1977). *Body Politics.* Prentice-Hall.

Herman, Simon R. (1968). "Explorations in the Social Psychology of Language Choice," in Fishman, ed. (1968), pp. 492–511.

Hinnebusch, Thomas J. (1979). "Swahili," in Shopen, ed. (1979), pp. 209–94.

Hopper, R. (1977). "Language Attitudes in Employment Interviews," *Communication Monographs* 44:346–51.

————, N. Hewitt, D. B. Smith, and C. Watkins (1972). "Speech Characteristics and Employability," *Communication Research Notes.* Center for Communication Research, University of Texas, Austin.

———— and F. Williams (1973). "Speech Characteristics and Employability," *Speech Monographs* 40:296–302.

Hymes, Dell (1962). "The Ethnography of Speaking," in T. Gladwin and W. C. Sturtevant, eds. (1962), pp. 13–53.

———— (1972). "Models of the Interaction of Language and Social Life," in Gumperz and Hymes, eds. (1972), pp. 35–71.

———— (1974). *Foundations in Sociolinguistics.* Tavistock Publications.

_____ (1974a). "Anthropology and Sociology: An Overview," in Sebeok, ed. (1974), pp. 1445–75.

Itebete, P. A. N. (1974). "Language Standardization in Western Kenya: the Luluyia Experiment," in Whiteley, ed. (1974), pp. 87–113.

Jacobson, Rodolfo (1979). "Language Competence and Incompetence as Strategies of Interethnic Behavior." Paper Presented to Comparative Studies in Ethnicity and Nationality Seminar (CSEN), University of Washington, Seattle, May 8, 1979.

Jernudd, Björn H. (1971). "Notes on Economic Analysis for Solving Language Problems," in Rubin and Jernudd (1971), pp. 263–76.

_____ (1971a). "Appendix on Economic Analysis," in Fishman, Das Gupta, Jernudd, and Rubin (1971), pp. 302–05.

_____ (1973. "Language Planning as a Type of Language Treatment," in Rubin and Shuy, eds. (1973), pp. 11–23.

_____ and Jyotirindra Das Gupta (1971). "Towards a Theory of Language Planning," in Rubin and Jernudd, eds. (1971), pp. 195–215.

_____ and Joan Rubin (1971). "Some Introductory References Pertaining to Language Planing," in Rubin and Jernudd, eds. (1971), pp. 311–23.

Jessel, Levic (1978). *The Ethnic Process: An Evolutionary Concept of Languages and Peoples.* Mouton.

Johnson, Marta K., ed. (1978). *Recycling the Prague Linguistic Circle.* Karoma Publishers.

Kachru, Braj B. (1978). "English in South Asia," in Fishman, ed. (1978), pp. 477–551.

Karam, Francis X. (1974). "Toward a Definition of Language Planning," in Fishman, ed. (1974), pp. 103–24.

Kari, James, and Bernard Spolsky (1978). "Athapaskan Language Maintenance and Bilingualism," in Fishman, ed. (1978), pp. 635–64.

Kawoya, Vin. F. K. (1982). "Kiswahili in Uganda." Paper Presented to the Conference on Swahili Language and Society, S.O.A.S. University of London, April 20–22, 1982.

Kelman, Herbert C. (1971). "Language as an Aid and Barrier to Involvement in the National System," in Rubin and Jernudd (1971), pp. 21–55.

Khalid, Abdallah (1977). *The Liberation of Swahili.* The Kenya Literature Bureau.

Kjolseth, Rolf (1978). "The Development of the Sociology of Language and its Social Implications," in Fishman, ed. (1978), pp. 799–825.

Kloss, Heinz (1967). " 'Abstand' Languages and 'Ausbau' Languages," *Anthro-*

pological Linguistics 9/7:29–41.

―――― (1968). "Notes Concerning a Language-Nation Typology," in Fishman, Ferguson, and Das Gupta, eds. (1968), pp. 69–85.

―――― (1969). *Research Possibilities on Group Bilingualism: A Report.* International Center for Research on Bilingualism, Quebec.

Kuznets, Rolf (1966). *Modern Economic Growth: Rate, Structure and Spread.* Yale University Press.

Labov, William (1970). "Applied Linguistics in a Broad Context," in Greenberg et al. (1970), pp. 15–28.

―――― (1972). *Sociolinguistic Patterns.* University of Pennsylvania Press.

Laitin, David D. (1979). *Politics, Language and Thought: The Somali Experience.* University of Chicago Press.

Lambert, Wallace E. (1967). "A Social Psychology of Bilingualism," *Journal of Social Issues* 23:91–109, in Lambert (1972), pp. 212–35.

―――― (1972). *Language, Psychology, and Culture.* Anwar S. Dil, series ed. Stanford University Press.

―――― and R. C. Gardner (1959). "Motivation Variables in Second Language Acquisition," *Canadian Journal of Psychology* 13:266–72.

――――, R. C. Hodgson, R. C. Gardner, and S. Fillenbaum (1960). "Evaluation Reactions to Spoken Languages," *Journal of Abnormal and Social Psychology* 60:44–51.

Lane, H. (1968). "Research on Second Language Learning," in Rosenberg and Koplin (1968), Chapter 3.

Lewis, E. Glyn (1974). "Linguistics and Second Language Pedagogy," in Sebeok, ed. (1974), pp. 2131–84.

―――― (1978). "Migration and the Decline of the Welsh Language," in Fishman, ed. (1978), pp. 263–351.

Lyons, John (1968). *Introduction to Theoretical Linguistics.* Cambridge University Press.

Mackey, William F. (1962). "The Description of Bilingualism," *Canadian Journal of Linguistics* 7 (1962):51–85, in Fishman, ed. (1968), pp. 554–84.

―――― (1965). "Bilingual Interference: Its Analysis and Measurement," *Journal of Communication* 15:239–49.

Macnamara, John (1966). *Bilingualism and Primary Education: A Study of Irish Experience.* Edinburgh University Press.

McQuown, Norman A. (1970). "Applied Linguistics in a Broad Context," in Greenberg et al. (1970), pp. 15–28.

Meillet, A. (1921). *Linguistique Historique et Linguistique générale.* La Société Linguistique de Paris.

Meisel, John (1978). "Values, Language, and Politics in Canada," in Fishman, ed. (1978), pp. 665–717.

Mencken, H. L. (1936). *The American Language.* 4th ed. Knopf.

Nahir, Moshe (1977). "The Five Aspects of Language Planning," *Language Problems and Language Planning* 1/2:107–24.

Neustupný, Jiri V. (1968). "Some General Aspects of 'Language' Problems and 'Language' Policy in Developing Societies," in Fishman, Ferguson, and Das Gupta, eds. (1968), pp. 285–94.

_____ (1970). "Basic Types of Treatment of Language Problems," in Fishman, ed. (1974), pp. 37–48, from *Linguistic Communications* 1 (1970):77–98.

Newsweek (1980). March 17. "First Lady of Letters." Bob Levin with Edward Behr, p. 48.

Ohannessian, Sirarpi, Charles A. Ferguson, and Edgar Polomé, eds. (1975). *Language Surveys in Developing Nations: Papers and Reports on Sociolinguistic Surveys.* Center for Applied Linguistics.

O'Neil, Wayne (1970). "Comes the Revolution," *Harvard Graduate School of Education Bulletin* 14/3:2–3.

Osgood, C. E., G. S. Suci, and P. H. Tannenbaum (1957). *The Measurement of Meaning.* University of Illinois Press.

Owens, Jonathan (1977). "Aspects of Nubi Grammar." Unpublished Ph.D. Dissertation, University of London.

Parkin, D. J. (1974). "Language Switching in Nairobi," in Whiteley, ed. (1974), pp. 189–216.

_____ (1977). "Emergent and Stabilized Multilingualism: Polyethnic Peer Groups in Urban Kenya," in Giles, ed. (1977), pp. 185–210.

Passim, Herbert (1968). "Writer and Journalist in the Traditional Society," in Fishman, Ferguson, and Das Gupta, eds. (1968), pp. 443–57.

Polomé, Edgar C. and C. P. Hill, eds. (1980). *Language in Tanzania.* Oxford University Press.

Pool, Jonathan, compiler (1975). International Conference on the Methodology of Sociolinguistic Surveys Proceedings, pp. 1–18.

_____ (1979). "Toward a Rational Calculus of Ethnic Decisionmaking: The Case of Language Policy." Paper Presented to Comparative Studies in Ethnicity and Nationality Seminar (CSEN), University of Washington, Seattle, February 27, 1979.

———— (1979a). "Language Planning and Identity Planning." *International Journal of the Sociology of Language* 20.

Prague School Manifesto. Manifesto Presented to the First Congress of Slavic Philologists in Prague, 1929, in Johnson, ed. (1978), pp. 1–31.

Prator, Clifford, ed. (1971). *Language in Uganda.* Oxford University Press.

Rabin, Chaim (1971). "Spelling Reform—Israel 1968," in Rubin and Jernudd (1971), pp. 95–121.

Ray, Punya Sloka (1962). "Language Standardization," in Fishman, ed. (1968), pp. 754–65, reprinted from F. A. Rice, ed. (9162), *Study of the Role of Second Languages in Asia, Africa and Latin America* (Center for Applied Linguistics of the Modern Language Association), pp. 91–104.

———— (1963). *Language Standardization.* Mouton.

Records of the Hebrew Language Committee (in Hebrew). Jerusalem and Hebrew Language Committee Publications (1912), p. 11. (Reproduced in its original form on the occasion of the 80th anniversary of the founding of the Committee.) The Hebrew Language Academy Publications.

Reese, Thomas (1981). "Language Planning in Kenya: The Role of Linguistic Resources in National Development." Unpublished Research Competency Paper on LP in Kenya, University of Washington, Seattle.

————, and Jonathan Pool (1979). "Guide to Information Resources in Language Planning," *Language Planning Newsletter* 5/1:1–3, 10–12; 5/3:3.

Rieger, Ladislav (1941). "Toward a Semantic Analysis of Philosophical Texts," in Johnson, ed. (1978), pp. 47–68, from *Slovo a slovesnost* VII (1941), pp. 180–91.

Robertson, D. MacLaren (1910). *A History of the French Academy 1635 (1634)–1910.* Dillingham.

Rosenberg, S., and J. H. Koplin, eds. (1968). *Developments in Applied Psycholinguistics Research.* Macmillan.

Rossi-Landi, Ferrucio (1974). "Linguistics and Economics," in Sebeok, ed. (1974), pp. 1789–2017.

Rubin, Joan (1971). "Evaluation and Language Planning," in Rubin and Jernudd, eds. (1971), pp. 217–52.

———— (1973). "Introduction," in Rubin and Shuy, eds. (1973), pp. v–x.

———— (1973a). "Language Planning: Discussion of Some Current Issues," in Rubin and Shuy, eds. (1973), pp. 1–10.

———— (1978). "The Approach to Language Planning within the United States," *Language Planning Newsletter* 4/4:1, 3, 4.

———— (1979). "The Approach to Language Planning within the United States," *Language Planning Newsletter* 4/5:1, 3–6.

_____ (1979a). "City Planning Model of LP." Presented to *Comparative Studies in Ethnicity and Nationality Seminar* (CSEN), University of Washington, Seattle, May 15, 1979.

_____ and Björn H. Jernudd, eds. (1971). *Can Language Be Planned? Sociolinguistic Theory and Practice for Developing Nations.* East-West Center Press.

_____ Björn H. Jernudd, Jyotirindra Das Gupta, Joshua A. Fishman, and Charles A. Ferguson, eds. (1977). *Language Planning Processes.* Mouton.

_____ and Roger Shuy, eds. (1973). *Language Planning: Current Issues and Research.* Georgetown University School of Languages and Linguistics.

Safire, William (1981). "At the caste party, sit on the couch, not sofa," *Seattle Post-Intelligencer,* June 24, p. A11.

Saint-Jacques, Bernard (1973). "Sex, Dependency, and Language," *La Linguistique* 9.

Samarin, William J. (1972). "Lingua Francas of the World," in Fishman, ed. (1968), pp. 660–72.

Saporta, Sol, ed. (1961). *Psycholinguistics: A Book of Readings.* Holt, Rinehart and Winston.

Schermerhorn, Richard A. (1964). "Toward a General Theory of Minority Groups," *Phylon* 25:238–46.

Schramm, Wilbur (1964). *Mass Media and National Development: The Role of Information in the Developing Countries.* Stanford University Press.

Scotton, Carol Myers (1978). "Language in East Africa: Linguistic Patterns and Political Ideologies," in Fishman, ed. (1978), pp. 719–60.

Sebeok, Thomas A., ed. (1972). *Current Trends in Linguistics 9,* "Languages in Western Europe"; Part 2, "The Study of Languages." Mouton.

_____ (1974). *Current Trends in Linguistics 12,* "Linguistics and Adjacent Arts and Sciences." Mouton.

Selinker, Larry (1972). "Interlanguage," *International Review of Applied Linguistics* 10/3:219–31.

Shils, Edward (1960). "The Intellectuals in the Political Development of the New States," *World Politics* 12/3:329–68.

_____ (1962). *Political Development in the New States.* Mouton.

Shopen, Timothy, ed. (1979). *Languages and Their Status.* Winthrop Publishers.

Sim, Ronald James (1979). *A Sociolinguistic Profile of the Mt. Kenya Bantu Languages.* Summer Institute of Linguistics, June, 1979, Nairobi.

Sjoberg, Andree F. (1966). "Socio-cultural and Linguistic Factors in the Development of Writing Systems for Preliterate Peoples," in Bright, ed. (1966), pp. 260–76.

Smith, P. M., G. R. Tucker, and D. M. Taylor (1977). "Language, Ethnic Identity and

Intergroup Relations: One Immigrant Group's Reactions to Language Planning in Quebec," in Giles, ed. (1977), pp. 285–306.

Spencer, John (1963). "Language and Independence," in Spencer, ed. (1963), pp. 25–39.

———, ed. (1963). *Language in Africa.* Cambridge University Press.

——— (1968). "Language Policies and Language Practices in West Africa," in Fishman, Ferguson, and Das Gupta, eds. (1968), pp. 227–36.

Spolsky, Bernard (1974). "Linguistics and Education: An Overview," in Sebeok, ed. (1974), pp. 2021–26.

Spradley, James P. (1970). *You Owe Yourself a Drunk: An Ethnography of Urban Nomads.* Little, Brown.

Stewart, Jon (1981). "Saving America from foreign tongues," *Pacific News Service, Seattle Post-Intelligencer,* May 31, p. B2.

Stewart, William A. (1968). "A Sociolinguistic Typology for Describing National Multilingualism," in Fishman, ed. (1968), pp. 530–53.

Swedish Center of Technical Terminology Publication No. 46 (1971). *Betongteknish Ordlista* [Glossary of Concrete Terms]. Tekniska Nomenklaturcentralen.

Tabouret-Keller, A. (1968). "Sociological Factors of Language Maintenance and Language Shift," in Fishman, Ferguson, and Das Gupta, eds. (1968), pp. 107–18.

Tanner, Nancy (1967). "Speech and Society Among the Indonesian Elites: A Case Study of a Multilingual Community," *Anthropological Linguistics* 9/3:15–40.

Tauli, Valter (1968). *Introduction to a Theory of Language Planning.* Acta Universitatis Upsaliensis, Studia Philologiae Scandinavicae Upsaliensia 6. Almquist and Wiksells.

——— (1974). "The Theory of Language Planning," in Fishman, ed. (1974), pp. 49–67, from *Las Concepciones y Problemas de la Sociolingüística,* Oscar Uribe Villegas, ed. (Mexico: Universidad).

Thias, Hans Heinrich, and Martin Carnoy (1972). "Cost-Benefit Analysis in Education." A case study of Kenya, World Bank Staff Occasional Paper 14. Johns Hopkins Press.

Thorburn, Thomas (1971). "Cost-Benefit Analysis in Language Planning," in Rubin and Jernudd, eds. (1971), pp.253–62.

Time Magazine (1981). May 18. Time/Life Inc., p. 26.

Troike, Rudolph C. (1974). "Linguistics and the Language Arts in Elementary and Secondary Education," in Sebeok, ed. (1974), pp. 2117–30.

UNESCO (1951). "The Use of Vernacular Languages in Education: The Report of the

UNESCO Meeting of Specialists, 1951" (Paris), in Fishman, ed. (1968), pp. 688–716; also in *Monographs on Fundamental Education* 8.

Vaillancourt, François (1979). "The Economics of Language and Earnings: A Case Study of Quebec Males in 1970 for Specific Industries and Occupations." Paper presented to *Comparative Studies in Ethnicity and Nationality Seminar* (CSEN), University of Washington, Seattle, May 22, 1979.

Valdman, A., ed. (1966). *Trends in Language Teaching.* McGraw-Hill.

van der Plank, Pieter H. (1970). "The Assimilation and Non-Assimilation of European Linguistic Minorities," in Fishman, ed. (1978), pp. 424–56.

von Glasenapp, Bernt W. (No Date). "Caterpillar Fundamental English." Caterpillar Tractor Co., Smart Communications Inc., N.Y.

Wallace, Irving, David Wallechinsky, and Amy Wallace (1982). "Significa," *Parade,* May 30.

Webber, Richard (1979). "An Overview of Language Attitude Studies with Special Reference to Teachers' Language Attitudes," *Educational Review* 31/3:217–32.

Weinreich, Uriel (1953). *Language in Contact: Findings and Problems.* Publications of the Linguistic Circle of New York, No. 1. Reprinted 1963. Mouton.

_____ (1953a). "Languages in Contact," in Weinreich (1953), pp. 1–6; and in Sol Saporta, ed. (1961), pp. 376–81.

West, Michael (1926). *Bilingualism.* Calcutta.

Whatmough, Joshua (1957). *Language: A Modern Synthesis.* A Mentor Book, The New American Library.

Whiteley, Wilfred (1969). *Swahili: The Rise of a National Language.* Methuen and Co.

_____ (1974). "Introduction," in Whiteley, ed. (1974), pp. 1–9.

_____, ed. (1971). *Language Use and Social Change.* Oxford University Press.

_____, ed. (1974). *Language in Kenya.* Oxford University Press.

_____, ed. (1974a). "The Classification and Distribution of Kenya's Languages," in Whiteley, ed. (1974), pp. 13–59.

Wriggins, W. Howard (1961). "Impediments to Unity in New Nations: The Case of Ceylon," *American Political Science Review* 55:313–20.

Wright, Marcia (1965). "Swahili Language Policy 1890–1945," *Swahili* 35/7:40–48.

Index

DATE DUE

MAY 2 0 1993	

DEMCO, INC. 38-2931